Introduction

What exactly is a Catholic heroine? Come to that, what does it actually mean to be English?

The people in this book are a mixture. England is a mixture too, and always has been. Would Etheldreda of Ely have thought of herself as 'English' in the sense that people would do in, say, the reign of Elizabeth I or of Queen Victoria? The England in which Etheldreda lived was still divided up into several different kingdoms. Some centuries later, Lady Margaret Beaufort lived while English kings ruled much of France – and fought among themselves on English soil.

It gets more complicated. Queen Margaret of Scotland was Saxon-born – and included here on that account – but devoted her life to the nation into which she married and is loved and honoured there, and perhaps too little known in the land of her birth. Elizabeth Cellier is an English heroine who was married to a Frenchman at a time when having a foreign 'popish' surname was perhaps not an advantage. Mother Clare Moore was of Irish birth and devoted her life to the poor of London and to the soldiers of the British Army. Caroline Chisholm is definitely really an Australian – and depicted as such for a time on the Australian $5 note – but was born and brought up in Northamptonshire.

And what is a Catholic heroine? Certainly someone who endures torture and death, privations or hardship for the Catholic Faith. We have some stunning examples of these here: Margaret Ward, Margaret Clitherow, Anne Line. But what about those who struggle against odds to try to do what is right, in the face of misunderstandings and misrepresentation? Queen Mary Tudor has been included in order that the facts may be presented about her reign, and the reader recognize the complexities and realities of a tragic era. Does the fact that cruel things were done in her reign – no one can justify burning at the stake – mean that she was wrong in her original aims?

And then there is the more everyday point: is it only persecution, queenship, or living through dramatic events that makes for heroism? We all know that is not so: ordinary life requires heroism too. The nun working in poverty with the poor (Elizabeth Prout), the matron at a busy school (Frances Wootten), can be heroines too.

It proved complicated to tackle adequately the question of Catholic heroines of the twentieth century. Can we put such people into perspective yet? How do we choose the names? How do we evaluate the role that religion plays in someone's life in a more secular age?

It is notable that two of the greatest British heroines of the Second World War – Odette Hallowes and Violette Szabo – were in fact Catholic, both coming from French families. They served in the Special Operations Executive (SOE) – parachuted from Britain into occupied France on different missions to liaise with underground groups in the fight against Nazi Germany. To say that they were heroines is putting things mildly. Both were eventually captured, interrogated, tortured, and sent to concentration camps. Violette was shot in 1945, shortly before the war ended. Odette Hallowes survived, through frail and ill. Both were awarded the George Cross.

We felt that it would be wrong – somehow cheating – to claim them as 'Catholic heroines' simply on the grounds of their religious affiliation, not actually knowing the exact role that religious conviction played in their lives. But no book on English heroines should omit their names, so they merit a special note in this Introduction. We have included

English Catholic
Heroines

English Catholic Heroines

edited by

Joanna Bogle

GRACEWING

First published in 2009

Gracewing
2 Southern Avenue, Leominster
Herefordshire HR6 0QF

ISBN 978 0 85244 185 5

Front cover: Mary Ward embarks for St Omer
from 'The Painted Life', reproduced in
Mary Ward: A World in Contemplation by Henriette Peters

Typesetting by
Action Publishing Technology Ltd, Gloucester, GL1 5SR

Contents

'Therefore *the Church gives thanks for each and every woman*: for mothers, for sisters, for wives; for women consecrated to God in virginity; for women dedicated to the many human beings who await the gratuitous love of another person; for women who watch over the human persons in the family, which is the fundamental sign of the human community; for women who work professionally, and who at times are burdened by a great social responsibility; for *'perfect'* women and for 'weak' women – for all women as they have come forth from the heart of God in all the beauty and richness of their femininity; as they have been embraced by his eternal love; as, together with men, they are pilgrims on this earth, which is the temporal 'homeland' of all people and is transformed sometimes into a 'valley of tears'; as they assume, together with men, *a common responsibility for the destiny of humanity* according to daily necessities and according to that definitive destiny which the human family has in God himself, in the bosom of the ineffable Trinity.

The Church gives thanks *for all the manifestations of the feminine 'genius'* which have appeared in the course of history, in the midst of all peoples and nations; she gives thanks for all the charisms which the Holy Spirit distributes to women in the history of the People of God, for all the victories which she owes to their faith, hope and charity: she gives thanks for all *the fruits* of *feminine holiness*.

Pope John Paul II, Mulieris Dignitatem

another wartime heroine, Sister Mary Richard Hambrough, an English nun who hid Jewish people in her convent during the German occupation of Rome, risking her life in doing so.

Another figure linked with wartime is Sue Ryder, who worked with SOE in Britain, preparing people for missions in occupied Europe, and went on to found a great network of charitable activities, starting in post-war Poland and going on to run an internationally famous series of projects with her husband Leonard Cheshire. Her story is told along with that of Cheshire in the *English Catholic Heroes* book that runs parallel with this one, and although she stands as a great woman in her own right, it is fitting that they are placed together.

We also chose among the twentieth-century figures some women who made a contribution to English Catholic life and were exemplars of the importance of living the faith in everyday things. Since the object of this book is to show the true face of Catholicism in our country, then the place of Catholic women simply living and working in a professional way while holding on to the centrality of the faith is perhaps an important one to emphasize. We have also chosen to emphasize women who were writers and/or involved in education – two crucial areas for the Church in modern times.

Another issue raised by the topic of Catholic heroines is the whole matter of the role of women within the Church. None of the heroines whose stories are told here – covering a great range of time from the Anglo-Saxon era to the present day – showed any sign of believing that women should be ordained as priests, nor did they assume that the Church denigrated the female sex or marginalized women and girls. On the contrary, they assumed – correctly – that Mother Church loves her daughters, takes pride in their achievements, and holds them up often as an example to men. There are more churches dedicated to women than to men, female saints have always been at the forefront of popular enthusiasm and devotion – from the early martyrs Agnes, Cecilia and Lucy through to Elizabeth of Hungary and

Teresa of Avila and Catherine of Sienna and beyond – and the roles of women in public life and in writing, teaching, and in the area of mystical and religious experience has always been central to the Catholic Faith. I thus take issue with the author of the section on Mary Ward when she writes that 'Marginalization of women's experience within the Church, based on the conviction that their access to God was of an entirely different order from that of men, led to a high degree of invisibility and inaudibility in spiritual and ecclesial matters. Women seeking to find a voice and a place in the public forum of the Church were not welcome ...' This denies the centuries of female work and achievement, and the Church's honouring of this and upholding of it as exemplary. Mary Ward was not treated well, but many men have similarly endured injustices through church bureau-cracy – think of John Henry Newman – and it is surely wrong to suggest that women were, or are, singled out for such treatment on the grounds of sex.

Probably most of the readers of this book will be Catholic: if you are not, do enjoy reading and please see this book as an attempt to show the 'Catholic thread' that runs through our country's history. It is a bright thread and it binds us not only to our past but also to things that many people hugely value about Britain today and may not realize have deep Catholic roots: the monarchy and its associated concepts of both service and pageantry, much of our most glorious architecture and music and art and literature, the best of our traditions and values and our sense of duty to one another. The last of these is in danger of fading away along with our Christian faith. Don't let's lose this most precious gift.

Joanna Bogle

Chapter 1

St Hilda and St Etheldreda

Etheldreda Hession, OSB

Consecrated virgins have been known throughout the Church's history. From the time of Philip the evangelist's four daughters in the Acts of the Apostles, women have responded to Christ's call to belong to him alone. Setting aside the human love of a husband and children, they lived in their own homes, small groups, or large communities, and often became the spiritual daughters, friends and counsellors of saintly monks and bishops. Such were Olympias (363–405), deaconess of Constantinople and friend of St John Chrysostom, and Marcellina, the sister of St Ambrose, 'dearer to him than his life and eyes' to whom he wrote many letters and treatises. In sixth-century Gaul Queen Radegund (d. 587), virgin deaconess, founded the monastery of Poitiers on land given her in reparation by her contrite husband Clothair. It was for her that Venantius Fortunatus wrote the famous processionals *Vexilla Regis* and *Pange lingua gloriosi* which became the marching songs of the Crusaders. Partly, no doubt, because of its geographical position, this great Frankish monastery did not have as much influence on Anglo-Saxon England as two others, near Paris: Faremoutiers-en-Brie following the rule of St Columban, and Chelles, refounded by Queen Bathild, formerly an Anglo-Saxon slave.

This study is concerned with two Anglo-Saxon monastic pioneers, both of royal families. Hilda, the older by about twenty years, belonged to Northumbria; Etheldreda, though some eventful years of her life were spent in Northumbria, was from East Anglia. They died within a year of each other – Hilda in 680 at the age of sixty-six, Etheldreda in 679 at the age of about forty-five. Two intensely contrasted threads run through their lives: years in the magnificence and violence of an Anglo-Saxon court followed by years of religious seclusion, though certainly not obscurity. They are striking examples of great saints emerging among people, many of whom were still idol-worshippers at heart.

A cursory reading of Bede's *Ecclesiastical History* suggests an England in the flower of Christianity, an island of saints ruled over by holy kings – an all-too simple picture. Skulduggery and blood feuds abounded; murder, exile and death in battle were the lot of king and common man alike, while Christianity's official position depended on the sway of the political pendulum. Hilda and Etheldreda lived in this world, renounced it, and survived through tenacity and strength of will. Each became a notable example of the influence which could be exercised by women in early Anglo-Saxon society, counterparts of their first-century Germanic forbears of whom Tacitus wrote: 'They believe that women possess an element of holiness and a gift of prophecy; and so they do not scorn to ask their advice, or lightly disregard their replies.'

The two saints knew each other, and their families were related by marriage. This was sufficient to make a strong bond, for Anglo-Saxon family life was close-knit and affectionate, embracing even distant relations. Welfare of tribe or family always took precedence over the individual. Loyalty was a prime virtue. Everyone, from the king's hearth-companion to the common man, received food, gifts and protection from his liege lord, to whom he gave unswerving fealty even to death. The most wretched of fates was to be exiled, cut off from kin, from the warmth and companionship of the mead hall.

'Sundered from my native land, far from noble kinsmen, often sad at heart, I went in wretchedness with wintry care upon me, sought the hall of a treasure-giver who might comfort me.' Hilda's father could well have shared this lament of the Anglo-Saxon poem, called *The Wanderer*, for his exile is one of the few known facts about her early life. A probable course of events is suggested here. The exiled Hereric and his wife Bregosyth took refuge at the Court of King Cerdic of Elmet in Yorkshire, one of the few British kingdoms left in the wake of the advancing Anglo-Saxons, where their two daughters, Hereswith and Hilda, were born. When Hereric was poisoned, Hilda and her mother fled to the protection of King Edwin of Northumbria, Hereric's uncle. Uniting politics with the solemn duty to avenge a kinsman, Edwin conquered Elmet and drove out Cerdic.

Since Hilda probably remained at her great-uncle's court until she was twenty, something must be said about King Edwin. Like other Anglo-Saxon kings, he claimed descent from the gods. Son of that Aella whose name prompted Pope Gregory's pun 'Alleluia should be sung in that land', Edwin had himself spent many years in exile, and at length gained his throne with the aid of King Redwald of East Anglia, Etheldreda's great-uncle. Fickle in his loyalties both political and religious, Redwald sacrificed to Christ and pagan gods on adjacent altars, and was probably the king commemorated with such magnificence by the Sutton Hoo ship burial. In 625 Edwin married Ethelburga, daughter of that king of Kent whom Augustine had first converted. The chaplain who accompanied her to a Northumbria which still worshipped Woden and Thor was Paulinus the Roman, of whom Bede has given us a pen-portrait rare in the literature of the time: 'tall, with a slight stoop, black of hair, lean in face, and having a slender aquiline nose, his features both venerable and majestic'. Hilda must have known that appearance well. There can be no doubt that her great-aunt and Paulinus initiated the Christian training which was to become the guiding force of Hilda's life.

Edwin was the unquestioned overlord not only of Northumbria, but also of the kingdoms south of the Humber. Hilda would have accompanied the Court from one royal estate to another, seeing the glitter and pageantry of a royal progress.

Banners were borne before Edwin as he rode through his dominions accompanied by a guard of hardened warriors, their swords and shields adorned with precious metals. His was a strong hand that crushed lawbreakers, and it was said that a woman with her new-born babe could walk through the island, from sea to sea, unmolested.

Paulinus had been granted freedom to preach the Gospel, and the eyes of the Church turned towards Northumbria, the conversion of which largely depended on one man's will. Pope Boniface IV wrote persuasive letters and sent Ethelburga most unpapal, but truly feminine, gifts of a silver looking glass and a gilded ivory comb. When Edwin and Ethelburga had been married a year, the turning point came. An attempt was made on Edwin's life. One of his thanes thrust himself between king and assassin's knife, dying for his lord in the finest Germanic tradition. That same night the queen gave birth to her first child. As the king thanked his gods, Paulinus praised Christ and ascribed the safe delivery to him. Edwin's adherence to paganism began to waver. He allowed his infant daughter Eanfleda and eleven others from his family to be baptized, the first-fruits of the Church in Northumbria. After the famous Witan had declared in favour of Christianity, the high priest mounted the king's stallion and rode forth, spear in hand, to overthrow the pagan idols. The thirteen-year-old Hilda was an onlooker at these events, but in what followed she eagerly participated. On Easter day, 627, she was among those baptized with Edwin in a wooden church at York. We can imagine her watching her great-uncle and his thanes at the font, then stepping forward in her turn, serious of face, fully aware of the significance of this step. With her characteristic generosity 'she embraced the faith and mysteries of Christ and preserved them un-defiled until she attained to the sight of him in heaven'. The seed of her religious vocation may have been planted during the years which followed. Her great-aunt, later a nun herself, would have learned from her mother, a Parisian princess, about the austere life led at the monasteries of Chelles and Faremoutiers, and passed the stories on.

With Edwin's conversion the Church's future in Northumbria seemed assured. Mass baptisms, at the king's command, took place in the Trent and Swale, and Paulinus gave himself unsparingly to preaching and catechizing. But in 633 all was shattered, and for the second time Hilda's home was destroyed.

Cadwallon, a British king of Gwynedd, North Wales, took bitter vengeance on Edwin, his former foster brother, for the annexation of Anglesey and Man. He invaded Northumbria in alliance with Penda, the future king of Mercia, who dominates the history of the next twenty years. Under this warrior who exemplified the swaggering, gift-bestowing heroes of Germanic saga, Mercia grew from a tribe to a power rivalling Northumbria and Wessex. Undefeated until his last battle, Penda waged a relentless war against Christianity, exploiting for political ends the rivalry between the many gods and the One, at the same time tolerating missionaries within his kingdom. It was as Cadwallon's ally that Penda took the first step in his ascent to power. In a great battle at Hatfield, Edwin was killed. Paulinus took Queen Ethelburga and her young daughter to safety in Kent. As Northumbria lapsed into heathenism, Cadwallon, nominally a Christian but described by Bede as 'a barbarian more savage than any pagan' ravaged the country for a whole year, putting women and children to death with merciless cruelty. It is likely that Hilda was in Northumbria during this terrible year. The slaughter and rapine were only ended by the 'most Christian king' Oswald, who emerged from exile among the Celtic monks of Iona to slay Cadwallon and establish peace, and Christianity, once more.

One of his first acts was to send to Iona for a bishop. The story of how Aidan, Northumbria's second apostle and Hilda's friend, was selected, tells us much about this 'man of outstanding gentleness, holiness and moderation'. The first missionary chosen returned home, declaring to the monastic council that he had been able to do nothing because of the 'barbarous and stubborn disposition' of the Northumbrians. Aidan gently taxed him with having failed to feed his hearers first with milk and not with meat, according the apostle's precept. Predictably, Aidan was forthwith consecrated bishop and sent on the mission. He was given the island of Lindisfarne as his see, and from there he travelled round his diocese on foot, making friends with rich and poor, and drawing everyone to Christ by his gentleness. Like his disciple, Bishop Chad of Lichfield, he was given a fine horse for his episcopal rounds. Chad was commanded by his archbishop to keep his mount, but Aidan promptly gave his away, countering his royal benefactor's protest with a mild rebuke: 'Is that brood of the mare dearer in your sight than that son of God', the poor man to whom the gift was given.

With Aidan's coming, Hilda, baptized and nurtured in her faith by the Roman Paulinus, learned the customs of the northern Celtic church, which had developed in isolation for centuries and retained its own way of life. But Celtic custom never held the monopoly of religious practice in Northumbria. Paulinus' deacon James, a saintly and steadfast man who lived until Bede's time, stayed at his post, continuing to preach, baptize, and teach the Roman manner of chant.

The fact that Hilda and Aidan became friends must mean that she remained in Northumbria after Edwin's death. From this time we know nothing about her until her thirty-third year, except that she remained single and 'spent her life nobly in secular occupations'. In a world where women normally married, this demonstrates a high degree of resolution. With no male relative to protect her, she yet remained in a Northumbria seldom free from the ravages of war and Penda's persistent raiding, though there was a ready refuge with her sister, who had married into the royal house of East Anglia.

Since the reign of the great Redwald, East Anglia had suffered a decline in temporal power, nor had Christianity prospered there until the accession of a king who was baptized while an exile in Gaul. During his reign, East Anglia received from Archbishop Honorius of Canterbury a

Burgundian bishop, Felix, and with him teachers trained in the Canterbury methods. Felix seems to have had a special call to evangelize England in the seventh century, as Dominic Barberi was to have in the nineteenth. Unlike Barberi, however, Felix saw thousands of souls won for Christ during his seventeen-year ministry. He baptized Anna, Etheldreda's father and, when Anna became king, continued to strengthen his faith. Thus, Etheldreda and her three sisters received a Christian upbringing from an early age. All four became religious, all four saints.

The sisters grew up during the unknown period of Hilda's life in Northumbria. Their aunt by marriage Hereswith, Hilda's sister, was deeply religious; possibly it was from her that they imbibed the ideal of a life lived for Christ. After some years of marriage Hereswith's husband, Ethelhere, agreed to his wife leaving him and their two sons to enter the monastery of Chelles. The church authorities granted a permission which today would scarcely be given, and Hereswith crossed to Gaul 'to seek an everlasting crown'. There were at the time no monasteries for women in England. Hilda resolved to follow her sister. Bede's words vividly evoke her wholeheartedness: 'She desired to forsake her country and all that ever she had, and go into France, there to lead a pilgrim's and exile's life for our Lord's sake.' The plan was never carried out. On her way to Gaul Hilda delayed for a whole year in East Anglia. What prevented her crossing to Chelles we do not know, but it is probable that her prolonged stay had a profound influence on her four young relatives. At the very least, her enthusiasm for the religious life would have further inspired hearts set on fire by Hereswith.

Bishop Aidan recalled Hilda to Northumbria, where he gave her a small plot of land on the north bank of the river Wear on which to live the monastic life with a few companions. After a year, he installed her as abbess at Hartlepool where, not long before, he blessed Heiu, said to be the first Northumbrian woman to become a nun. Hilda ruled Hartlepool for eight years, 647–55. She 'began immediately to establish order and regular life under the guidance of learned men. For Bishop Aidan, with other religious men that knew and loved her, frequently visited and instructed her'. Her wisdom became renowned, and at Hartlepool she began to train those in her charge with the remarkable teaching that was to bear even greater fruit at Whitby.

Meanwhile, Etheldreda approached marriageable age in the surroundings of a royal court. As the Sutton Hoo treasure indicates, the East Anglian royal house was immensely rich, a wealth probably equalled, or even exceeded, by that of Northumbria. Shields and swords decorated with garnets set in gold filigree, silver spoons and bowls, jewellery of inestimable value, testify to a court which glittered with splendour. The gathering in the tapestry-hung great hall at night, seen through fumes of smoke and ale, must have been brilliant. As the bards declaimed the heroic deeds of great ancestors or, in Christian times, those of great ascetics, the assembly quaffed ale or mead from silver goblets and took their turn with the harp. The women served the men, neither queen nor princess being exempt. Perhaps Etheldreda, wearing gold armlets and rings and a heavy gold necklace of intertwining circles set with garnets and pearls, took part in scenes similar to that depicted in *Beowulf*:

> Queen Hygd, who loved her people, went round the hall with vessels of mead, and placed goblets in the hands of the fighting men … urging the young men to eat and drink, sometimes presenting a gold ring to one of the warriors before she returned to her seat. Sometimes Hrothgar's daughter, young and adorned with gold, carried goblets of ale to the senior chieftains.

Before the age when women normally married, Etheldreda had, according to Ely tradition, decided to dedicate her virginity to Christ. Her elder sister Sexburga was already married to King Earconbert of Kent, and suitors for Etheldreda's hand came from far and wide, attracted by her beauty and gentle character. The young princess succeeded in refusing all offers until Tonbert, prince of the South Girvii, pressed his suit. King Anna exerted his authority in the face of his daughter's protests, and she was forced by her sense of family and tribal duty to agree to the proposed marriage.

It is at first difficult to imagine why her father, praised by Bede as 'marvellous godly and notable for virtue both of word and deed', should have insisted on her marriage. But Anna was also an Anglo-Saxon king, with his fair share of the ruthlessness needed to maintain that rank, and a duty to protect his people. The South Girvii territory around the Wash made a buffer state between East Anglia and north-east Mercia. Since two of Anna's predecessors had been killed by Penda of Mercia, whose power was still in the ascendant, Anna would be anxious to strengthen friendly ties with these valuable allies. His daughter's resolution weighed little against political expediency. However, there is no need to assume that her marriage was all penance. Probably a Christian, Tonbert respected his young wife's desire, and they lived in continence. This may seem strange to us but it is by no means unfamiliar to Christian asceticism, ancient or modern.

In 654, two years after Etheldreda's departure to live in the fens, Penda again attacked the East Angles. Henry of Huntingdon, a Christian chronicler of the twelfth century, has preserved a vivid account of the battle: 'He marched furiously against the doomed army of King Anna, like a raging wolf he rushed on the sheepfold. On all sides ran streams of blood, nor did he stay till all the kin were destroyed. So King Anna and his army were swallowed up by the sword in one moment.' We may doubt whether Anna and his army were as helpless as sheep, but slaughtered they were, and Anna was succeeded by his brother Ethelhere, Hilda's brother-in-law. Anna's death possibly gave his two younger daughters the chance to enter religion unopposed. Ethelburga entered the double monastery of Faremoutiers and became abbess. Withburga became a recluse first at Holkham, Norfolk, then at Dereham, where she founded a monastery.

Tonbert died after three years of marriage. One would have expected the widow to hasten across the Channel to

Chelles or Faremoutiers. She did not. Perhaps organized religious life did not yet appeal to her, or perhaps she was still uncertain what form her consecration to God should take. Whatever the reason, she retired to the Isle of Ely, a marriage gift from Tonbert. In those days Ely was truly an island, surrounded by miles of reeds and swamps. Unlike the trackless fens, its fertile fields and woods abounded in all kinds of wildlife, and its surrounding waters teemed with fish. The families living on the island had been in Etheldreda's care for the previous three years. Now, leaving the estate in her steward's hands, 'She began to live with herself. Fixing her whole mind on heavenly things, she gave herself up to fasting, vigils and unceasing prayer', as the Book of Ely says.

When, in 642, King Oswald was slain in battle by Penda, his brother Oswy succeeded him. Eager for more power, in 651 Oswy instigated the betrayal and murder of King Oswin, a friend and disciple of Aidan. The murder broke Aidan's heart and he died soon after, in a tent pitched for him outside Bamborough church. Hilda was at Hartlepool when she was deprived of her friend and counsellor. For a time things must have seemed black. Penda was raiding far into Northumbria, destroying all he met with fire and sword. Though Oswy tried to buy him off with great treasure, Penda refused all bribes.

By 655, Oswy was forced to fight for his kingdom against heavy odds, in spite of the fact that his younger son Egfrith was held hostage at the court of Mercia. He 'vowed that if he should be victorious, he would dedicate his daughter to God in holy virginity' and found twelve monasteries. His gamble succeeded, and in the ensuing battle at Winwaed near Leeds Penda was killed. One of Penda's allies at Winwaed was King Ethelhere of East Anglia, who is said to have caused the war, though we are not told how. His death, only a year after that of King Anna, dealt a blow to East Anglia from which, perhaps, that kingdom never fully recovered.

In a complete reversal of fortune, Oswy became overlord of kingdoms both north and south of the Humber. His ten-

year-old son Egfrith returned to him from Mercia. True to his
promise, he entrusted his daughter Elfleda, scarcely a year
old, to Hilda to be trained for the religious life.

Two years after Winwaed, Hilda was given a tract of land,
perhaps one of the twelve Oswy gave in fulfilment of his
vow, at Streaneshalch, known since Viking times as Whitby.
Perched high on ancient cliffs, with the sea dashing against
the rocks below, the site is impressive. Streaneshalch, or
'bay of the lighthouse', is indeed a city set on a hill. Even the
low buildings of Hilda's time must have been visible to fish-
ermen far out to sea, for the ruin of the later, much larger,
monastery church still acts as a beacon through the dangerous rocks. It is unusual for monastic buildings to be situated
in such a commanding position. The choice of this site in
preference to a fold of the moors by a running stream would
seem to indicate that Hilda was a woman of freedom and
breadth of spirit who looked for no shelter from the storms
of life, but opened herself to the mighty power of God.

Whitby was a double monastery, that is a community of
monks and nuns who shared conventual life to an extent
that varied from place to place. This type of foundation
flourished especially in the seventh century. It came to
England by way of Gaul, where the nunneries of Poitiers,
Chelles and Faremoutiers-en-Brie all had associated houses
of monks, who gave the sacraments and preached in the
surrounding villages. During the period when Christianity
was spreading and before parishes were established, these
monasteries provided a centre from which to evangelize a
district. In England the superior was invariably the abbess,
usually a woman of royal blood, born to rule. No accusation
of immorality has ever been made against these monasteries; they owe their disappearance to factors other than
moral laxity. Apart from Gilbert of Sempringham's twelfth-
century revival, and the Bridgettine house of Syon, they have
been few and far between since Anglo-Saxon times. In our
own day there are one or two, including a foundation made
by the Eastern Orthodox Church in Essex.

At Whitby, Hilda found full scope for her talents of

teaching and organization. She taught 'the strict observance of justice, piety, chastity and other virtues, and particularly of peace and charity; so that, after the example of the primitive church, no one was rich and none poor, all property being held in common ... she obliged those who were under her direction to make a thorough study of the scriptures and occupy themselves in good works, so that many were found fitted for Holy Orders and the service of god's altar'. A remarkable statement on the position of women in the Church in those days! This prudence, care for having property in common, and love of scripture, reminds one of the Rule of St Benedict. However, Hilda probably never used this rule. Aidan would have introduced her to the rule and customs of Iona, which followed the teachings of St Columba, and these were probably followed at Whitby. Hilda's training of her monks was so thorough that no fewer than five of them became bishops, a startling achievement when one considers that there were then only about twelve bishoprics in all England.

Modern excavations at Whitby hint at its rich and varied life. Within a two-feet thick stone wall were two churches, one for monks and one for nuns, and a number of other buildings. The discovery of book covers and styli indicate a scriptorium and library, and two roomed cells each with a hearth were grouped in Celtic fashion. Spindles and loom weights tell of weaving wool from the hardy moorland sheep, while a touch which brings these seventh-century monks and nuns close to us is the number of personal items uncovered: buckles, pins, tweezers, needles, all of bronze or bone. 'Guests are never lacking in a monastery,' as St Benedict observed, and Whitby was no exception. Scholars, kings and nobles with their retinues, to say nothing of the poor, called for extensive accommodation. The kitchen with its open fire equipped with spits and large iron cooking pots, must have been kept busy. Folk came from far and near to seek spiritual and temporal relief, finding in Hilda, so Bede tells us, a counsellor of wisdom and prudence with, we may guess, a warm loving heart. 'Mother', as everyone called her, was penetrating in her discernment and fostering of talent. This has already been touched on in the case of her monk-bishops, and Caedmon is another example. Middle-aged and shy, he was one of the laymen who tended the animals on the monastery estates. He avoided taking his turn with the harp at feasts because he could not sing, but in a dream he was bidden to sing about the creation of the world, verse to which he added when he awoke. Only nine lines of this have been preserved by Bede, who is careful to tell us that these are not Caedmon's exact words, but the gist of them:

> Praise now the maker of the heavenly kingdom
> The power and purpose of our Creator,
> The deeds of the Father of glory.
> Let us sing how the eternal God,
>   author of all miracles,
> first created the heavens for the sons of men
>   as a roof to shelter them.
> And how their almighty Preserver gave them
>   The earth to live in.

This has been criticized as clumsy and repetitive, hardly justifying Caedmon's title of the Father of English poetry. However, it should be remembered that his originality lies in using the technique and language of barbaric saga to clothe biblical stories in a form the common man could appreciate. Then, as now, folk listened more eagerly to song than to preaching. Presented with the unexpected gift of a brother taught by God to turn scripture into song, Hilda quickly realized its value for conveying the fundamental beliefs of Christianity to people who could not read. She instructed that Caedmon should be received as a monk and taught the whole series of sacred history, which he reproduced in verse. For ordinary people, the songs reinforced and elaborated such stories as the Exodus and the Acts of the Apostles, depicted on the church walls.

While Hilda busied herself with her community at Whitby, King Oswy was seeking a wife for his second son Egfrith, a boy of fifteen. His choice fell on Etheldreda who, by the year 660, had spent five years as a recluse. On grounds of personal character his choice was excellent, but why choose an anchoress senior by some eight years to the bridegroom? Oswy cannot have been ignorant of Etheldreda's religious life and asceticism, but possibly the union of two dynasties outweighed the disadvantages of such a match. Perhaps his devout wife Eanfleda was behind the choice. She was that daughter of Edwin whose birth thirty-four years before had tipped the scales in favour of Christianity. Inheriting some of her father's strong character, she had forced her husband to found a monastery in memory of the murdered King Oswin; she was quite capable of insistence in the matter of her son's wife also. Etheldreda's uncle, King Ethelwold, had little choice but to consent. It was unthinkable to refuse an overlord, on whose favour the ruined fortunes of his kingdom depended. Once again Etheldreda gave up her own will and, after a splendid marriage ceremony, went to live at York in 660.

Unaccountable as it may seem to us, the couple loved each other, and their early married life was happy, resembling the sketch given by an Anglo-Saxon poet:

> Battle and warfare shall be strong in the man, and the woman shall thrive, beloved by her people, be cheerful of mind, keep counsel, be liberal with horses and treasures. In the hall before the band of comrades she shall present straightway the first goblet to the prince's hand, and be ready with wise counsel when they plan together how to run their household.

The years from 660 to 670 coincide with the rise of Wilfrid, the fiery bishop who bestrides the second half of the seventh century and played a major part in Etheldreda's life. Probably already known to her by reputation, for her sister Sexburga, queen of Kent, had helped the young Wilfrid on his way to Rome, the Abbot of Ripon became Etheldreda's spiritual adviser. Infuriating in his stubbornness, he was extravagant in the corresponding virtue of loyalty to friends and ideals, as Etheldreda was to discover.

There may have been a difference of liturgical custom between Egfrith and Etheldreda, as between the king and queen. Eanfleda, brought up in Kent, adhered to the Roman dating for Easter, to which the Church in Southern Ireland also conformed; Oswy kept the ancient Celtic date still retained by the Irish of Iona and its dependencies. 'As the king broke his fast and celebrated the feast of Easter, the queen and her attendants, still fasting, kept Palm Sunday.'

This diversity was tolerated during Aidan's lifetime, but when his gentle restraining influence was withdrawn, the controversy blazed up with a vehemence which finds its parallel in the differing liturgical opinions of our own day. Even the gentle Bede was roused to indignation. After a list of Aidan's many virtues, he sternly remarks: 'But that he observed not Easter at its proper time, this I neither commend nor allow.'

In 663 a synod was summoned, with protagonists from both sides, under the presidency of King Oswy. That Whitby was chosen for the meeting is a measure of Hilda's achievement. In seven years she had transformed a desolate cliff top into a thriving monastery which could house two kings, several bishops, an abbot and their retinues. Hilda, a supporter of the Iona observance, attended the sessions with some of her nuns; whether Etheldreda was present is uncertain, indeed there is no hint that Hilda and Etheldreda ever met in Northumbria. The chief speaker on the Roman side was abbot Wilfrid, recently ordained priest. Bishop Colman of Lindisfarne vigorously defended the Scottish usage as being derived from John the Apostle, but Wilfrid's eloquence could not be gainsaid. His triumphant conclusion quoting the promises to Peter in Matthew 16 prompted Oswy to declare that he would stand with St Peter; otherwise, the doorkeeper of heaven might shut him out. There the matter ended. Colman and some others, taking some of Aidan's bones with them, retired to Iona. Most of the Irish-trained clergy remained, conforming to the Roman observance, but handing on the spirit of simplicity, poverty and missionary zeal which characterized the Celts. We are not told of Hilda's reaction. Forsaking the custom of her friend Aidan must have been painful, but in her later years Whitby became ever more Roman. A small dependent monastery founded the year before her death was built more on the Roman pattern, while in her successor's time there was at Whitby a cult of that eminent Roman, Gregory the Great, of whom a Whitby monk wrote the earliest life extant.

In the year 670 King Oswy died, a death almost unique among the kings in Bede's history in that it was of sickness, not violence. His widow Eanfleda joined her young daughter at Whitby, which they later ruled jointly. Egfrith's accession to the throne may have brought to a head the growing rift between him and his wife. He began urging the consummation of their marriage. Etheldreda held courageously to her religious vow and pressed in her turn for leave to enter a monastery, a step which must have seemed the best solution to the difficulty. Egfrith persisted, and Wilfrid, now Bishop of York, was called in to arbitrate. 'Egfrith promised much land and money if he could persuade the queen to pay the marriage duty, for he knew she loved no man more than himself.' Wilfrid, heedless of the consequences of crossing the king, encouraged Etheldreda. At last, after many arguments, the queen took off her royal regalia, and entered Coldingham, a double monastery on the Celtic pattern.

These events do not present Etheldreda in an attractive light. We consider her unfeeling, and compare her unfavourably with her sister Sexburga, who bore children and waited for widowhood before entering religion. Yet the woman who built a marriage from such unlikely materials and was so reluctantly allowed to leave it, must have been warm and loving as well as resolute. Her hold over Egfrith is suggested by the legend which tells how he attempted to take her from Coldingham, then pursued her to the borders of her own fens, where he was thwarted by a sudden flood. However, it seems unlikely that the king would make any such attempt after refraining from coercion for several years past. He married again, but had no children, and was killed during a raid against the Picts when he was forty. He was

succeeded by his illegitimate half-brother Aldfrith, a learned
and virtuous man whose encouragement of scholarship
during a long and peaceful reign made possible the great
achievements of Bede.

Coldingham was probably chosen for Etheldreda's entry
into religion because the abbess, the king's aunt Ebba, was
well able to keep her nephew in order. Her memory is kept
alive by the place name of St Abb's Head of Berwick, and to
her also belongs the doubtful honour of ruling the only
monastery in Bede's history which earned criticism.
Although formidable on occasion, Ebba in later life was easy-
going and less than eagle-eyed in the running of her house,
where the religious spent much time in feasting and drink-
ing, and slept instead of attending the Night Office. When an
Irish monk brought this to Ebba's attention she remedied
matters, though after her death discipline again lapsed.
Etheldreda remained at Coldingham for only a year, a period
which suggests the probationary period enjoined in the Rule
of St Benedict, which Wilfrid had recently introduced.
Having made her profession and received the veil at Wilfrid's
hands, she handed over to him the property at Hexham
which had been her marriage gift from Egfrith. There, of
blocks from nearby Roman ruins, he built a house of God 'of
wonderfully polished stones, supported by many pillars and
porticoes, with walls of unbelievable length and height',
which was thought by his biographer Eddius to have no
equal north of the Alps.

In 673 the ex-queen returned to Ely and set up a
monastery for both monks and nuns, where a community
soon gathered round her. She may have used the Rule of St
Benedict exclusively, or at least as one among several. The
site for monastery and church was that of a chapel reputedly
built by Augustine of Canterbury and afterwards destroyed
by Penda. If Etheldreda emulated Wilfrid by building in
stone, the brothers may have brought material by boat from
the Roman ruins at Grantchester, sixteen miles upriver.

Bishop Wilfrid installed and blessed the new abbess.
Perhaps on this occasion the responsories and antiphons

were sung entiphonally 'according to the custom of the early church', on the introduction of which Wilfrid prided himself. The task of the new superior was to establish regular life and to instruct the religious by precept and above all by example. Like Queen Radegunde, she practised austerities without enjoining them on others, and felt so powerful an attraction for prayer that, after the lengthy recitation of the Night Office, she remained in church until dawn.

Five years after Ely's foundation, Wilfrid was expelled from Northumbria and his diocese divided. Before taking ship in order to appeal to Rome, he visited Ely and promised Etheldreda to obtain from the pope a recognition of the rights and liberties of the abbey. Upon his return after a two-year absence in the course of which he had converted many Frisians, he found she had died. Etheldreda is said to have prophesied not only the pestilence from which she died, but also the number of her flock who would succumb to it. She accepted with joy the suffering caused by a great swelling under her jaw, seeing in it a means of atonement for her youthful pleasure in wearing fine jewels: 'for I remember, when I was a little girl, bearing round my neck the useless weight of gold and precious stones'. She died on 23 June 679, and at her own request was buried in a plain wooden coffin in the common cemetery.

Sixteen years later her sister Sexburga, the ruling abbess, decided that the bones should be exhumed and more fittingly interred. In the presence of Wilfrid, exiled once more from his see, and surrounded by the monks and nuns singing appropriate chants, the grave was opened. Sexburga cried, 'Glory to the name of the Lord!', for the body was seen to be 'as free from corruption as if she had died and been buried that very day'. The body was placed behind the high altar in a beautifully decorated Roman sarcophagus from Grantchester. It is noteworthy that the bodies of Etheldreda's two sisters, Withburga the recluse and Ethelburga of Faremoutiers, were also said to have been found incorrupt.

Etheldreda's prominent place in monastic calendars is

evidence of deep interest in her during the Middle Ages. In an eleventh-century Sarum missal she has a proper Mass Preface and is named in the Canon. Incidents from her life are sculpted round Ely's great Lantern Tower, while late medieval paintings of her survive in East Anglian rood screens. Under her Norman name she is remembered to this day in St Audrey's Fair, still held at Ely, where the cheap trinkets sold in her honour gave the English language a new word, 'tawdry'. Her tomb, surrounded by those of her sisters Sexburga and Withburga and her niece Erminilda, the third abbess, survived until the Reformation, but today, the only relic of Anglo-Saxon times in Ely Cathedral is a memorial cross to Owine, Etheldreda's steward.

During most of Etheldreda's short rule, Hilda at Whitby was afflicted with a fever, in spite of which she continued to give instruction to the whole community as well as private counsel in her small two-roomed cell. For six years she suffered, giving thanks to God herself, and instructing others to praise him in all adversity. About cockcrow on her last day, 17 November 780, after receiving Holy Viaticum, she summoned all her nuns. Begging them to keep peace among themselves and with others, she reiterated the peace and charity which was the essence of her rule. As she was still speaking, she passed, with a smile, from death to eternal life.

That same night, a nun at Hackness thought she heard the passing-bell and, looking up, saw a great light in which Hilda's soul, accompanied by angels, was borne up to heaven. A Whitby nun who loved Hilda dearly received a similar vision in the noviciate quarters, which were remote from those of the community. So both the Hackness nuns and the Whitby noviciate were roused in the night to pray for their mother, the news of whose death was received by them at daybreak.

Hilda's influence on the Church of her day was immense, equalled by no other abbess. She not only inspired respect on the human level from men and women alike, but evoked deep love and devotion. It was above all because she was a woman of great spiritual stature who sought God, that she drew men to him. When Hilda was a child, her mother dreamed about a jewelled necklace which illuminated all Britain with its splendour. This dream came to pass in the life of her daughter.

Hilda's cult must have begun almost at once after her death, for her name appears in an early eighth-century calendar of St Willibrord, Northumbrian monk and apostle of Holland and Luxembourg. Though Whitby was completely destroyed by the Vikings about 860, Hilda's supposed relics were translated to Glastonbury about 150 years later. Her cult was always strong in the North, especially after the revival of Whitby as a monastery for monks only in the late eleventh century. Had it not been for Bede, we should know nothing of her; but Bede has kept her memory green, and in the nineteenth and twentieth centuries she has been aptly chosen as patron of churches and colleges.

Hilda and Etheldreda well deserve a place in this book. Although neither of these great saints can strictly be called Benedictine, they paved the way for many centuries of Benedictine monasticism in this country. How perfectly they would have responded to St Benedict's call to take up strong, shining weapons and follow their Lord to glory. Channelling their ancestors' warlike spirit into an energetic love of God, they gave their lives fighting in the service of Christ, their true King.

Bibliography

Bede, *Historia Ecclesiastica Gentis Anglorum*, ed. C. Plummer, Oxford, Oxford University Press, 1956.

Eddius Stephanus, *Life of St Wilfrid*, ed. B. Colgrave, Cambridge, Cambridge University Press, 1927.

The Earliest Life of Gregory the Great, ed. B. Colgrave, Lawrence, Kansas, University of Kansas Press, 1968.

Liber Eliensis, ed. E. O. Blake, *Camden Series*, London, Royal Historical Society, 1962.

Carey, M. S., *Ely Cathedral*, London, Pitkin Pictorials, 1975.

Godfrey, J., 'The Double Monastery in Early English History', *Ampleforth Journal*, lxxix (1974), 19–32.

Hunter Blair, P., *Northumbria in the Days of Bede*, London, Gollancz, 1976.

Kirby, D. P. (ed.), *St Wilfrid at Hexham*, Newcastle, Oriel Press, 1973.

Mayr-Harting, H., *The Coming of Christianity to Anglo-Saxon England,* London, Batsford, 1972.

Stenton, F. M., *Anglo-Saxon England*, 3rd edition, Oxford, Oxford University Press, 1970.

Whitelock, D., *The Beginning of English Society*, Harmondsworth, Penguin Books, 1952.

Chapter 2

St Margaret, Queen of Scotland

Andrea Fraile

St Margaret is such a magnificent figure that it is very difficult to encapsulate her and the profound relevance she still has for us today. Those who, in our own time, wish to champion the cause of the exile, the poor, the arts, nationalism, marriage, motherhood and orthodoxy all have a friend in this woman who died over nine hundred years ago. Her inclusion in a book entitled *English Catholic Heroines* may cause some to fear that the rightful place of their queen has been usurped; others may groan that even their hagiographies are being invaded, but let both positions be silenced: they do injustice to St Margaret, to the Catholicism she so faithfully espoused and to the sheer catholicity of a woman who embraced several cultures and enriched them all.

In truth, she was Saxon. Her mother was Bavarian, her six sons were given Saxon names and she is renowned for reforming the Celtic Church and conforming it to Rome; there is little in these bare facts to endear her to the Scots. Yet if we are to understand why, in fact, she is so loved, then we must understand something of her deep sincerity and holiness – qualities that quite simply made her an outstanding wife, mother, queen, reformer, reconciler, scholar (and embroiderer, even!). It has been written that

> there is, perhaps, no more beautiful character recorded in history than that of Margaret. For purity of motives, for an earnest desire to benefit the people among whom her lot

was cast, for a deep sense of religion and great personal piety, for the unselfish performance of whatever duty lay before her, and for entire self-abnegation, she is unsurpassed and the chroniclers of the time all bear testimony to her exalted character.[1]

St Margaret's life would have remained quite a mystery were it not for the invaluable writings of her biographer, Turgot (d. 31 August 1115). Prior of Durham and Bishop of St Andrews, he wrote her biography for the benefit of St Margaret's daughter, Matilda, who requested a 'life' of her mother who was very quickly venerated after her death – and Turgot was the ideal biographer since, according to his own claims, 'thanks to her great and familiar intercourse with me ... I am acquainted with the most part of her secrets'.[2] Those who feel exasperation at the marked lack of hard facts and intricate detail should bear in mind that Turgot was no historian or chronicler of his day; nor did he ever pretend to be. What he wanted to write was a hagiography and in *this* endeavour he was entirely successful. For although he may have been prey to the odd exaggeration (like the '300' poor people who sat round the royal banqueting table), Turgot concentrated on empirical facts to outline her sanctity and steered clear of the overtly supernatural (in any case, the sheer fact of having *any* poor people round the table of a royal court is startling, then and now). Thus Turgot showed how remarkable this queen was, not by relying on accounts of her miracles, but on accounts of her daily obedience to the will of God. That is why he is trustworthy, and also why we should thank him above all for establishing Margaret so thoroughly into the history and life of Scotland.

The first character in the tale of Margaret's turbulent

1. Skene, W. F., *Celtic Scotland: a History of Ancient Alban*, 5 vols, Edinburgh, David Douglas, 1876–80; vol. ii, *Church and Culture*, p. 344, quoted in Turgot, Bishop of St Andrews, *Life of St Margaret Queen of Scotland*, trans. William Forbes-Leith, SJ, William Paterson, Edinburgh, 1884.
2. Turgot, pp. 19–20.

ancestry is her paternal great-grandfather, Aethelred the Unready. A Saxon through and through, he made a treaty with Duke Richard, a Norman, and sealed it by marrying Richard's sister, Emma – and so the first threat, a Norman thread, wove its way into the Saxon realm. Aethelred's son fared no better: Edmund Ironside married the Danish Ealdgyth in 1015 (a second threat to Saxon Kingship) and was King of England for a short period before dying in battle and leaving the way open for the notorious Danish King Cnut, who now found himself master of Saxon England.

Anxious to secure his reign, Cnut was acutely aware of the threat posed by Edmund Ironside's two sons, Edmund and Edward, the fruit of Edmund's brief marriage and rightful heirs to the Saxon throne. Yet not even he could stoop so low as to kill them on their own soil, so he sent them to his half-brother Olaf that he might do it – and Olaf, having become a Christian, sent them in 1028 to the court of King Stephen of Hungary instead.

Edmund and Edward thus spent much of their youth in Hungary, a country which, under the Arpad Kings, was profoundly Catholic. St Stephen's father had introduced Christianity in a stroke of political manoeuvring and remained pagan all his days but Stephen, along with his wife Queen Gisela, embraced the faith to the full. We know little of the contact the two princes had, if any, with allies back home in England, yet it seems reasonable to expect that St Edward the Confessor, who had in the interim become King of England and who had no progeny, would have sought out his two nephews and natural heirs to the throne to secure the Saxon dynasty that remained so precarious. We do not know what became of Edmund – he appears to have died earlier – but Edward Atheling, Margaret's father, returned to England after nearly thirty years in Hungary, with his wife Agatha of royal descent and three children, Margaret, Christina and Edgar.

When Edward died very shortly after his arrival in England, the Confessor's only hope was invested in his dead nephew's children. They lived at his Court from 1057 until he died in 1066, an environment that would further have built on the Catholic foundations established originally in Hungary. It is quite possible that Margaret met Malcolm Canmore at the Confessor's court: having lived there for fourteen years, he left in 1057 just as Margaret arrived.

The political landscape was to change quite dramatically in 1066, however, with the death of Edward the Confessor and the arrival in England of Duke William of Normandy. (Given his description as feeble in mind and body, very few ever truly considered Edgar Atheling a viable contender to the throne.) Victorious at the battle at Senlac (near Hastings), William was crowned king and the family of the Atheling was dispossessed once more.

Malcolm returned to his homeland to be crowned King of Scotland at Scone in April 1058. William was now Saxon king but the north and west remained to be convinced and they did all in their power to make life difficult for him. The revolt that had long been brewing boiled over at the Humber 1068. Spearheaded by Swein, King of Denmark, and joined by Edgar Atheling with some powerful English lords, the revolt ended in defeat. William proved himself conqueror and many either submitted to him or fled to Scotland.

Margaret and her family were among those who fled, but they intended to return to England after the winter was over. William meanwhile wished to secure the north definitively, and did so, despite Danish intervention – and once these last had fled, William thought it fitting to punish the ordinary people of the North for their allegiance to the rebels and invaders. The slaughter and devastation were incalculable, and the vulnerability of the situation made it easy for King Malcolm to invade. As William left Yorkshire in 1070, so Malcolm appeared: from Teesdale right up to Wearmouth he plundered savagely, and it was at Wearmouth that he encountered the Atheling family, who were now on their way to Hungary when inclement weather swept them in his direction. The chronicler Symeon of Durham writes of that particular meeting that 'when they came to him he spoke to them kindly and granted them with his firmest peace to dwell in his realm so long as they would, with all their followers'.[3]

The Athelings duly sailed up the coast and landed at the Firth of Forth at a place since called St Margaret's Hope. Whether this was the first encounter between Malcolm and Margaret or not, it was the one that was to change forever the shape of their lives, the Church and the country. In late 1070 Malcolm and Margaret were married in a small Romanesque Celtic church in Dunfermline. The twenty-four-year-old laid aside her desire for religious life and embraced her new vocation with generosity and spirit. Malcolm was almost forty. As though to seal the marriage, one of Margaret's first acts as queen was to erect a grand church on the very site of their wedding and she had it dedicated to the Holy Trinity.

The man Margaret married was none other than the son of Macbeth's tragic victim, Duncan. When he killed Macbeth in 1057 he regained the throne and was notorious for his brutality on the battlefield. Yet in every other respect he was no brute. Much of his youth was marked by the beneficence and holiness of his guardian, St Edward the Confessor; and his love for Margaret reveals most clearly a man of sensibility, a man who proved himself entirely susceptible to the ways of virtue. And so, as wife, Margaret influenced her husband enormously: he joined her in prayer and in countless works of charity. Though he could not read (yet he was educated and fluent in a number of languages – was he dyslexic?) he knew which books Margaret favoured particularly and he would take them to himself and kiss them, as though they were relics. Often, too, he would send them to craftsmen to have them encrusted in gold and precious gems.

[3.] The quotation itself is from Simeon of Durham, *Historia Regum* (written, *c*.1129). Vol. II, p. 190 in Stevenson, J. (trans.), *The Historical Works of Simeon of Durham, The Church Historians of England*, vol. III, London, Seeley's, 1855. Quoted in Wilson, Alan J., *St Margaret Queen of Scotland*, Edinburgh, John Donald Publishers Ltd, 1993: 2nd edn, 2001, p. 63.

Her saintly influence also had its effect on the six sons and two daughters of their marriage, all of whom survived to adulthood (which in itself is a miracle). Three sons, Edgar, Alexander and David all became kings, as did David's two grandsons Malcolm IV and William, and William's son and grandson Alexander II and III. Under their reign, Scotland experienced 200 unbroken years of peace. One son, Edmund, fell away from his faith but returned repentant and became a monk at Montacute, a monastery in Somersetshire founded by William the Conqueror. As regards their daughters, the eldest called Edith (born 1080) came to be known as Mathilda or Maud, and it was she who united the Norman and Saxon royal houses by marrying Henry I of England in 1100. Margaret's other daughter Mary married Count Eustace of Bologna and gave birth to Queen Maud of England, the wife of Stephen, grandson of William the Conqueror.

Though we have little record of how these royal children were brought up, their lives speak eloquently of a solid, Catholic upbringing. The love that Margaret had for the Benedictines was shared by her son David especially, who was to continue his mother's legacy and found several monasteries under St Benedict's Rule. The first was founded in 1113 and eventually another seven in Scotland followed.

Margaret was a devout Catholic: what of the Church in Scotland in which St Margaret now found herself? Ireland had never been part of the Roman Empire and did not therefore succumb to the various invasions of Visigoths, Vandals, Huns and others who ravaged Europe after the fall of the Roman Empire. The Roman Church was at the centre of the turmoil and had to reorganize herself while the Celtic Church in Ireland, on the other hand, developed quietly and steadily in her own way, namely that of a local tribal system that knew little of the diocesan structure of hierarchy. The faith was spread through local missions; all the clergy were monks; and each community had a superior (which did not necessarily make him a bishop). This ritual independence from Rome inevitably resulted in conflict since, from the end of the sixth century, two colliding missionary activities were taking place in the British Isles – the Roman mission led by St Augustine of Canterbury and the Celtic missionaries carrying on the legacies of Ss Columba and Aidan. The tensions resulted, for example, in the Council of Whitby in 664.

By the time the Athelings landed on the Firth of Forth, the Church was ministered to by the Culdees, a name which comes from 'cell de' and means 'companions of God'. These many men lived in scattered cells throughout the country, living quiet, ascetic lives. The Queen and her family certainly loved and respected the Culdees, granting land to various Culdean settlements, and there is no question that she admired them for the austerity which characterized so much of her own spirituality. Nevertheless, she could not allow the Culdees to continue ministering to the Church in Scotland: she believed the Church, after five centuries of Columban influence, was tired and her clergy in spiritual decline. It needed reform.

What Margaret longed for was to dissolve all those disparate rules and rituals of the Celtic Church into the living tradition of the universal Church. To this end, she called several councils throughout her lifetime, but the most significant was one held in Edinburgh Castle that lasted for three days in which she called for five areas in particular to be realigned to Rome. She was flanked by a few of her friends, notably three Benedictines sent by Margaret's spiritual father, Lanfranc, Archbishop of Canterbury and former monk of Bec in Normandy; and her devoted husband, familiar with English as well as Gaelic and Latin, acted as faithful interpreter. He must have been extraordinarily proud of his Queen as she presided over such an illustrious assembly composed entirely of men. Quite unruffled, Margaret held forth with great dignity and passion, and with the confidence that comes with great scholarship. In defence of her position, she cited Scripture and the writings of the saints, and the devastating combination of wisdom, diplomacy, persuasive charm and impeccable logic confounded her opponents.

What precisely were these contentious issues? Margaret's first point related to the observance of Lent: the Scottish Church began the season officially on the Monday of the first week, a tradition the Culdees adopted from Rome; yet Rome had gradually developed the practice of starting Lent on Ash Wednesday thus becoming more faithful to Jesus' forty day fast (rather than thirty-six). The Scots had been left behind. She was also concerned by the level of abstention from Holy Communion on Easter Sunday and set about establishing reception of the Sacrament. Of course, such abstention is not necessarily an indication of the Culdees' insularity: in this period of history and for centuries beforehand, penitents in the universal Church were given ferociously severe penances that would have included abstention for several years.

The ritual of Mass was also subject to Roman reform since, in the current dispensation, 'Masses were celebrated according to some sort of barbarous rite'[4] – we do not know precisely the nature of the barbarity but it may have reference to the rite being in Gaelic rather than Latin, or the less-than-angelic singing of the clergy … Further areas of reform included keeping the Sabbath by avoiding servile work (and on Sunday, not Saturday, for St Columba considered Saturday to be the Sabbath) and abolishing marriages of affinity, namely that of a man marrying his stepmother or his brother's widow.

The fundamental thrust of St Margaret's reform however, beyond the particulars, was simply to reconnect Scotland to the rest of the Catholic world. From the late sixth century until the twelfth, the political map of Europe had changed at a phenomenal rate, and the Church, amid all this change, was like an anchor holding fast. It perturbed Margaret that there should be so little contact between her country and Rome (despite King Macbeth's visit there in 1050), that many of the great figures of Catholicism at that time should be unknown to the Scots, that the great issues – like that of

4. Turgot, p. 48.

how papal authority was impacting on relations between Church and State throughout Europe – should be unheeded. The Church in which her faith and scholarship flourished in Hungary and her contact with the saintly Edward the Confessor had provided the foundation for a deep-rooted faith as well as a keen awareness of the Church as an all-embracing Mother under whose mantle we can all seek protection; but it also fuelled in her a zealous desire to spread the truth and majesty of the faith wherever she went, and Scotland, whose queen providence led her to be, was to reap the benefits.

It was therefore extremely important for Margaret that God be glorified through an integrated, coherent practice of the faith. She also believed that the things we *use* in the practice of our faith – the vestments and sacred vessels – should give glory to God, too, through their sheer beauty and craftsmanship. Indeed much of her daily round was spent in what could be called a workshop of sacred art, where 'copes for the cantors, chasubles, stoles, altar-cloths, and other priestly vestments and church ornaments, were always to be seen, either already made, of an admirable beauty, or in course of preparation'.[5] Margaret, along with several other female members of the nobility, spent hours in this employment, their fingers in feverish activity, their hearts in contemplation.

Nor did the Church alone benefit from Margaret's aesthetic appreciation. In her day, merchants from all over the world brought their precious wares to Scots traders who were encouraged by their queen to buy jewellery and exotic clothing in fine colours. It seems that, under her guiding hand, the palace and the Court became more picturesque and more human. In this extraordinary woman, it was these external realities that went hand in hand with a deep interior life of asceticism and self-denial.

The fact that Margaret embraced the unexpected fortune that was allotted her and became a genuine agent for change

5. Turgot, p. 30.

in a country (in a changing Europe) that was ripe for it are already impressive achievements. Yet these facts alone do not give us half the picture: for the greatness of this queen lay in her maternal heart that formed the context of everything else she did. In our own time, we seem to have fallen prey to a very sad dichotomy that so often separates concern about doctrine with concern for social justice – as though our concern for the poor will naturally lead us to pay scant regard to doctrine, while insistence on orthopraxy places ritual above the temporal needs of our brothers and sisters. Far from being mutually exclusive in the life of Jesus (see Mark 6:34), these two areas of concern form the holistic and perfect measure of what is required for human wholeness. The same was true of Margaret. Her desire to bring the wandering Scots sheep to the beating heart of the Catholic Church was all part of her one overarching desire to have them living life in its fullness. Thus she fed and clothed them.

To grasp her love of the poor is to grasp who she was and what motivated her. The truth is, Margaret was a phenomenally pious woman who radiated a profound holiness and it was precisely these qualities which flowed out of her when confronted with the poverty of her people – these, too, are the qualities that render nonsense the charge laid at Margaret's door that she was in reality ambitious and driven by political power. Even the most cursory glance at Turgot's account of her daily rounds would flatly contradict any such hypotheses.

The legacy of King Malcolm's various raids of northern England was still manifest in Scotland in the form of many Saxon slaves who lived there. England had become so destitute after the Conquest that it was not uncommon to find Saxon slaves in many Scottish homes, and these were subject to Queen Margaret's special care. She commissioned secret spies to report on their condition and ensured that they be treated with compassion, sending them help and, wherever possible, paying their ransom. She even visited various prisons throughout the land, not only to visit the prisoners but also to inspect their cells and confirm their suitability for human habitation.

Her compassion towards the poor was renowned. She had only to step out into the street for hordes of people of all ages to flock round her and be assured of some material benefit or at least a word of kindness and comfort. Margaret's generosity was contagious, too, for when she had given everything she had, her circle of attendants would then vie with each other to distribute their own goods and possessions. Even King Malcolm was in on the act: traditionally, he would distribute gold coins on Holy Thursday and at High Mass and it is often related that Margaret availed herself of some of these for the poor while the king turned a blind eye. Sometimes he caught her in the very act, at which he would jokingly threaten to charge her with theft and imprison her.

During Lent and Advent, her charitable regime intensified. After almost the whole night spent praying in church, she returned to her rooms along with the king and washed the feet of six people whom the chamberlain arranged to have waiting for her early every morning. After this she retired to bed and, in the clear light of morning and having prayed the psalms, she ordered that nine tiny orphans be brought to her so that she could mother them, take them on her knee and feed them. Turgot recounts quite precisely that she took them upon her knee, got their pap ready for them and put it into their mouths with the spoon she herself used[6] – far too much detail to be merely a fictitious scene intended to impress us.

Meanwhile, three hundred poor people were escorted into the royal hall in anticipation of the royal couple who would then wait on them as on Christ. For all her almsgiving, there is a very strong sense that she wanted to be with them as much as they did with her: even today, there is a stone in the form of a seat some fourteen miles from Edinburgh, and it has been consistently told that Margaret used to sit there –

6. Turgot, p. 61.

at that time an open field – that the poor might more easily come and converse with her. There could have been no doubt in her mind that the Christ she encountered at Mass was the same she found in the field. It is that clarity of vision that made her, and makes any of us, a saint.

Even today there are two place names that bear witness to Margaret's concern for the poor. North and South Queensferry are the original ports on the shores of the Forth on which Margaret built hostels for all the pilgrims who made their way to Scotland to visit the shrine of St Andrew. Each hostel had attendants to serve the pilgrims, who were also given free passage from Lothian to Fife on specially commissioned ships. Such was their international fame that grants were conferred some years later by Popes Lucius III and Innocent III.

Perhaps the really striking feature of Margaret's generosity to the poor – apart from the magnitude of it – was that it was not hampered by any false notions of equality. It was clear to this humble servant of God that, as children of God, the orphans and widows that reached out to her were truly her brothers and sisters, equal in dignity and sharing the same destiny; but that did not cause her to despise those circumstances of her life that brought her to the throne or the structures that placed her, materially, so far above her subjects. Rather in every possible way, she used what she had been given to enrich the lives of others.

Naturally, the source of all her loving was none other than that source which is available to all of us: prayer and fasting. Margaret prayed constantly. It is told that she would spend most of the night in church, praying silently and intently, often with tears rolling down her cheeks. She would go often and seek advice, solace and intercession from the Culdee hermits, a Celtic version of those 'wise men' Scripture exhorts us to consult (Tobit 4:18). She begged them to avail themselves of her aid and often performed works of mercy at their bidding. Her fasting, too, was so excessive as to weaken her severely and cause her tremendous stomach pains until the day she died.

As she lived, so did she prepare to die. Seeing that her time on this earth was short, she summoned the faithful Turgot to recount the history of her life with many tears of repentance, and then she bid him farewell with a promise that he pray for her and look after her children. She was in Edinburgh at this stage and, for six months, had been ravaged with sickness and pain on account of her fasting and daily exertion, and was confined to bed. Four days before she died, she was unusually stricken with anguish and said, 'Perhaps on this very day such a heavy calamity may befall the realm of Scotland as has not been for many ages past.'[7]

Meanwhile King Malcolm was on the battlefield again. There is no record of Margaret's meddling in Malcolm's business, but every writer confirms that, concerning this final invasion of Northumbria, she did everything in her power to dissuade him from fighting – in vain. Initially the raid was successful but on the return home, William Rufus (William the Conqueror's younger son) made an unexpected and successful attack on the castle of Alnwick in Northumbria. The Scots eventually laid siege to the castle and the surrendering garrison demanded that Malcolm come to receive the keys of the castle in person. As he held out his hand to receive them from a soldier, a spear was thrust in his eye. He had fallen into a trap.

A few days later, severely ill now and with the *viaticum* already taken, she asked the priest to read psalms to her and to have the Black Cross, her Holy Rood, brought to her. She embraced and kissed it. At that point her son Edgar arrived, not only with the news of his father's death but also that of his brother Edward who had died shortly after in trying to avenge Malcolm's death. Wanting to spare his mother's agony, he withheld the bad news but she, already knowing it in her heart, demanded by the Holy Rood that he speak the truth, and he told her everything. Malcolm died on the very day that Margaret had been overcome with anxiety. Even then, she did not complain but rather praised God that this

7. Turgot, p. 73.

suffering and deep sorrow of hers might bring her atonement. She began to recite the prayer usually said by the
priest before receiving Holy Communion and as she said
'Deliver me', so she was delivered at last from the cares of
this world. It was 1093.

The great miracle in Margaret's life was the profound
effect of grace working in a heart that is obedient to God's
will. Nevertheless, there were a couple of specific miracles in
her lifetime that contributed to her canonization in 1250 by
Innocent IV. The first concerns her Gospel Book, a book of
the Gospels that was sumptuously adorned on the outside
with gold, precious stones and a painted image of the four
evangelists; there was brilliant gold lettering on the inside,
too. One of the Queen's attendants was carrying this book
when, unbeknown to him, it fell out of its protective case as
he was crossing a stream. It quickly emerged that the book
was lost and the frantic search ended in its being found a
good while later, at the bottom of the stream. The leaves of
the book were constantly in motion owing to the current,
and the silk leaves designed to protect the gold lettering had
torn away yet, miraculously, the vellum and lettering
remained intact. It is almost certainly the Gospel Book of
Queen Margaret that is to be found in the Bodleian Library
in Oxford today.

The second miracle came to light after her death, when
her body was being translated to its glorious new shrine
under the high altar in the Lady Chapel of Dunfermline
Abbey (most of the shrine was ravaged during the
Reformation). As her mortal remains were being carried past
the place of Malcolm's burial, the coffin quite suddenly
became too heavy. It was impossible to carry it any further,
even when extra bearers came to the rescue. This naturally
precipitated something of a crisis until a voice of divine
inspiration was heard, explaining that Margaret refused to be
buried away from her husband. When Malcolm's remains
were moved, so Margaret's coffin became mobile again and
the two rested under the high altar together.

Because St Margaret's ecclesiastical reforms blew fresh,

life-giving breath into the Church of the north, and because she inspired in her children a deep-seated respect for the forms of religious life and ecclesiastical observance that were found in England and on the Continent, Margaret changed and influenced Scotland and the Church in a way that was enormously significant. Under her reign, she led the Church in Scotland peacefully into a new era in which it was, and remains, fully joined to the rest of the Christian Church in Europe.

Her dedication to her role as wife and mother is even more significant today than it was in her own day – a consoling and inspiring model for all those wives and mothers who strive to live out the greatness of their calling, and a rebuke to those who see motherhood as a type of second-class citizenship. Finally, her appreciation of beauty is a great lesson for us all: she encouraged trade in Scotland, which significantly enhanced the apparel of many a Scot (the traditional kilt stems from her time); she enhanced the beauty of Church and palace to better reflect God's glory; and pre-eminently – and most importantly – she saw a very vivid and Christ-like beauty in the poor of her country, and did everything in her power, through clothing, feeding and teaching them, listening and talking to them, to bring that beauty to fullness. Her name, Margaret, means 'pearl' – anyone who seeks this particular pearl will discover that the years have only made her more relevant and more radiant than ever.

Chapter 3

Julian of Norwich

John Skinner

I first met Julian long ago at the tender age of nineteen. My very first year as a Jesuit novice: we had been plunged only weeks after our arrival into Ignatius's four-week-long Exercises, and I was still reeling. My first glimpse of Julian was a little red book no bigger than the Penny Catechism but square so that it fitted comfortably into the hand. Inside, arranged in three points for meditation were these amazing words: deep sounding echoes of hope, of God's intimacy – above all his overwhelming love – then The Trinity lived out. Could this be for me?

I knocked on the Master of Novices' door: 'Who is this Julian of Norwich?' I asked. Without a word, Father Walkerley crossed over to his bookshelves just inside his cell door and, pulling forward Grace Warrack's translation of *Revelations* blew the dust off its top edge before handing it to me with a silent smile. I bore it away in triumph; this was going to be good reading.

But that was my first mistake ... for Julian is not a book, a good read, she challenges me to a lifelong experience.

We know next to nothing of Julian: we know her gender yet not her name. She is now so-named, beguilingly as a man yet the first woman to write our English tongue, for her long stay in the church of Saint Julian Norwich. Here she was an anchoress for a large part of her life. Yet we certainly know, for this she tells us, the exact date of her revelations or 'Shewings'. These began, 8 May 1373, and lasted a full week as she was struck down by a sudden paralysis that led her and her friends to believe she was dying. She also adds as if to fix the moment firmly in her mind, 'I was thirty and a half years old ... and being still young, I thought it a great sadness to die.'

———◄◦►———

Hermit, solitary, anchorite was an almost common calling in her day; Henry V would consult the hermit of Westminster Abbey at critical moments in his reign. Many towns and cities throughout the land boasted their holy man or woman living as solitaries either within the confines of a religious house or, as in Julian's case, in a small two-roomed attachment to a church. For her days saw the start of an emerging individual voice speaking into agitating groups or living silently within the conformity of a top-down society. The king ruled, lords lorded it, merchants made it and the rest of us fell into step behind. Yet pressure was building to boiling point.

Five years after Julian was born, the Black Death had spread its cancer claws across England. A third and more people in Europe perished relentlessly, painfully and seeming pointlessly over two terrifying years until the tide slowly turned. Faced with this deep-dyed memory of death coming from nowhere, or so it seemed, two movements resulted: a greater faith in God and the Church and a growing resilience of the individual human heart. In Julian's time, the Peasants' Revolt cried one loud shout, raging at established order. Rebellion finally erupted into Norwich led by a bold upstart, Geoffrey Litster. As Watt Tyler was advancing from Kent upon London, Litster raged into Norwich. Some few who stood up to him were slain; then for a week he lorded it in Norwich castle while knights were forced to wait upon him on their knees. His followers dubbed him 'King of the Commons'. Then the warring Bishop of Norwich, Henry le Despenser, himself a former soldier and born into a noble family, took up arms. He rounded upon Litster and his rebels at Mousehold Heath where they had attempted to defend their cause behind barricades of tables and doors. He shrived him before sending him off to be hanged. To celebrate his martial prowess, Despenser commissioned a finely painted Retable, or altar back; it shows the passion of Christ and may still be seen in Norwich Cathedral today.

Against this turbulent civil strife, Julian pursued her prayerful ways in her anchorhold in Norwich. I say we know little about her: we know all. Augustine of Hippo was first to reveal the questing human soul. In his *Confessions*, he opens his heart, and with his gift for language he invites us to share his encounter with the mystery of our making and shaping.

Some few Christian mystics have found similar transparent words to reveal their journey in life. The great Teresa of Avila and her soulmate John of the Cross come to mind who in their writings were able to express for us their lifelong relationship with their Maker – or as Julian has 'our Maker, our Keeper, our Lover'. For Julian is throughout Trinitarian: her greatest insight, her chief experience of God is the loving outward-inward dynamic of her Threefold God.

———◄○►———

Julian's story is dramatic in the extreme. She tells us that as she lay dying, attended by her mother and friends, the priest comes to housel[*] her. A boy bears the crucifix. It is thrust before her face. She is *in extremis*. Then comes her account, her story, and our story too of what Christ's passion, his life, bled into our own lives might mean.

Of her sixteen numbered Showings, five dwell deliberately, lovingly upon her dying Lord. This is partly dictated by the circumstances in which she received them: she was sure that she was dying. But more pertinently, as she herself tells us, the priest came with a crucifix to anoint her.

> My curate was called for to be at my ending, and by the time
> he came I had set my eyes and might no longer speak. He set
> the cross before my face and said: 'I have brought you the

[*]housel: medieval word for Holy Communion

image of your Maker and Saviour: look upon him and find your comfort there.' I thought to myself that I was well, for my eyes were set upward toward heaven where I trusted to come by the mercy of God. But nevertheless, I assented to set my eyes upon the face of the crucifix if I might, and so I did, for it seemed to me that I might manage to look longer straight ahead than upward. After this my sight began to fail and it was all dark about me in the chamber as if it had been night, save in the image of the cross where I beheld a common light, and I knew not how. All beside the cross was ugly to me as if it had been much occupied by fiends.

This dramatic enactment then is the source of Julian's *Revelation* as she herself lies now desperately ill; she sees Christ's painful dying and is invited to share this enactment in order to experience his meaning. And so we are led into her First Showing:

Now at once I saw red blood trickling down from under the garland. Hot and freely it fell, copious and real it was, as if it had just been pressed upon his blessed head, who is truly both God and man, the very same that suffered thus for me. In that moment, I knew clearly that it was he himself who showed me, without any intermediary of any kind.
  Within this same showing, suddenly the Trinity filled my whole heart full of utmost joy. I knew then that heaven will be like this for all who come to it, without end:

> For the Trinity is God,
> and God is the Trinity.
> The Trinity is our Maker and Keeper,
> The Trinity is our everlasting Lover,
> everlasting joy and bliss, by our Lord Jesus Christ.

The startling originality of this vision, comprising the dying Christ with her heavenly vision of the Trinity, is nothing less than an experience of the immanent hidden Face of God linked inextricably with the outward manifestation of his all healing love in the Son of Man who dies upon the Cross. As Julian is shown this oneness of the Trinity's

dynamic, the Inner Mystery of the Godhead feeding outgo-
ing Love, finally his Mother is brought vividly to her mind:

> Next he brought our blessed Lady to my understanding. I saw
> her with my understanding as though she were with me
> physically: a simple maid and meek, so young she seemed
> like a mere child – yet the very same age when she
> conceived. And God showed me then something of the
> wisdom and truth of her soul. In particular, I saw her attitude
> toward God her Maker, how she marvelled with great rever-
> ence when he wished to be born of her, who was a mere and
> simple creature he himself had made. It was this wisdom,
> this truth, seeing how great was her Maker compared to her
> own littleness, that made her say to Gabriel, 'Behold me,
> God's handmaid.'
>
> Then I knew for certain that she was more worthy and
> more full of grace than all the rest of God's creation, with the
> sole exception of the manhood of Christ.

In this very first gift or showing, Julian has sight of a minia-
ture summation of the whole of the Trinity's commerce with
humankind. And she reflects through Mary's heart: 'how she
marvelled with great reverence when he wished to be born of
her, who was a mere and simple creature he himself had
made'. Yet the most searing icon of God's love for us is that of
a naked man dying on a cross: 'If only I am lifted up, I shall
draw you all to myself.' This Julian experiences as she too lies
dying: 'Pray for us sinners, now and at the hour of our death.'
This vision gives way to – as if in complete accord – the heavenly flush of the Trinity as our Maker, Keeper and everlasting
Lover: 'I knew then that heaven will be like this.'

'By our Lord Jesus Christ': the Son of Man is God's sole
instrument in making, keeping whole and saving, loving and
perfecting all his human family. Yet he needs our good will
for this to happen. And the supreme example of human
receptivity of the Divine plan is spoken by Mary: 'Behold me,
God's handmaid'.

———◄०►———

It might be helpful at this point to pause and wonder what precisely is the nature of Julian's showings. They are clearly powerful to the point of becoming overwhelming. And this very power convinces her that they are God-given, a conviction endorsed by the very nature of their content – 'Love is his meaning.' Much later on in her life, Julian receives a visitor to her cell, Margery Kempe, a pious neighbour from Bishop's Lynn. It is the single occasion (apart from two wills that may refer to her) that records our anonymous lady of Norwich. And it is Margery herself who relates this encounter in her dictated autobiography.

Margery is the antithesis of Julian. She too has been touched by God: after bearing fourteen children, running a brewery and falling into an adulterous occasion, she repents and turns to prayer and pilgrimage. She too has had visions and mystical experiences but it is more than she can contain. Hearing of Julian's reputation for wisdom in spiritual ways, she seeks her reassurance. Are these things from God, she wants to know.

Julian was clearly encouraging, for Margery stays several days with her as she pours out her experiences. Here is Margery's witness to Julian of Norwich:

> When she heard about our Lord's wonderful goodness, the anchoress thanked him with all her heart for visiting me like this. Her advice was that I should remain always obedient to God's will, carrying out with all my strength whatever prompting he put into my soul. But I must always be careful that these were not contrary to God's glory or to the benefit of my fellow Christians.
>
> The Holy Spirit can never urge us to do anything against charity; for if he did so, he would be acting against his own self, for he is the sum of all charity.

The two holy, God-seeking women, could not be more opposite. Julian feels the Divine Presence as she is apparently at her end: Margery pursues her maker in a relentless journey of pilgrimage and confrontation. Julian puts down anchor in Norwich in order to seek her soul and its maker:

Margery charges here there and anywhere in search of anyone likely to yield an answer – Canterbury, Compostella, Rome and Jerusalem.

So, it seems wiser to stay with Julian. She tells us that she experienced her Showings in three ways: one, bodily visions, so that she was aware of them with her senses, sight and hearing, sometimes even smell ('of the fiends'). Secondly, 'ghostly visions', she experiences deep spiritual meanings in the form of sayings imparted directly to her soul. And she names a third, intellectual enlightenment, as when she reports 'Next he brought our blessed Lady to my understanding.'

I dwell on these seeming technicalities for a purpose. If I am to receive the full impact of Julian's meaning, her sharing in the love of the Trinity, I too must somehow open my receptive faculties. She speaks of her threefold-enlightenment. For myself, I do not see visions, bodily or even ghostly, but I can listen prayerfully to the Silence within, which sometimes speaks. And if I hear little, I may still continue to attend.

Julian is eloquent on prayer:

> After this our Lord showed me about prayer. And in this showing, according to our Lord's meaning, I saw two conditions for prayer: one is rightfulness, and the other is sure trust.
>
> For many times our trust is not complete; we are not sure whether God hears us, or so it seems, owing to our unworthiness, and we feel quite empty. How often are we barren and dry at prayer, sometimes seeming even more so when they are done. Yet this is only our feelings and caused by our own folly, coming from weakness; I have felt as much myself.
>
> And among all this confusion of thoughts, our Lord suddenly came to mind and showed me these words, saying: 'I am the ground of your beseeking: first it is my will that you have it, and then I make you want it: now since I make you seek and then you do seek, how should it then be that you should not have whom you seek?'

Her teaching here is transparently clear: if we only think of prayer as asking, putting our world to rights in the presence of our Maker, we get it wrong.

Two conditions: Right-full-ness, that is to say God is utterly loving towards us – right full of Love; next, trust – we must simply open our hands and heart. The wonderful word be-seeking: all we are looking for is who we are, our true being. And where alone will we find this – only in him. Julian expresses this in her perfect prayer:

> God, of your goodness, give me yourself;
> for you are enough to me;
> and I may ask nothing that is less that may be full
>   worship to you.
> And if I ask anything that is less,
> I am ever left wanting;
> but only in you I have all.

My purpose in this brief chapter on Julian is to draw you to her words. Her account of her extraordinary experiences portray a person who insists that her lifelong message is merely ordinary. Repeatedly, she tells us that her revelations are not some private, privileged matter, but offered to her for us all. Mary's conception, the birth of her son, is the unique Mystery; yet his coming was an invitation to all to receive his Word within. So Julian echoes that same amazing story.

> God is nearer to us than our own soul; for he is the ground in whom our soul stands, and he is the mean that keeps the substance and sensuality together, so that they shall never part. For our soul sits in God in very rest and our soul stands in God for very strength and our soul is kindly rooted in God in endless love. And therefore if we wish to know our soul and have communing and dalliance therewith, we will need to seek into our Lord God in whom it is enclosed.

As Julian opens her story, she tells us:

> This is a revelation of love that Jesus Christ, our endless bliss,
> made in sixteen showings or revelations particular; of which
> the FIRST is the precious crowning of our Lord with thorns; it
> includes the showing of the Trinity with the Incarnation and
> tells of the unity between God and the soul; with many other
> fair showings of endless wisdom and teaching of love, in
> which all the showings that follow are grounded and oned.

So here speaks Julian, her own words; this first Showing
encapsulates all she has to give us. Impossible, within this
short study, to tell more of her story. I may merely invite my
readers to journey for themselves. One single caveat: beware
of taking Julian into your hands as any normal book. She
should never be read from page one onwards. Far better to
taste and see, dip in where you will and find. She herself –
the first woman to write in our English tongue – lacked that
necessary luxury of all coherent writers, the editor. Julian
was on her own. She scribbled, miraculously, for something
like two decades and more. And we may only remain grateful
for her harvest, dense though it be.

Always circular, her story unfolds in magic wise. By all
means begin at chapter one, and listen. Then perhaps skip a
little, just as one learned to do after the hard throes of one's
first Reading Scheme. Beacon Books is my apprenticeship:
and how I would groan at Henny Penny in her farmyard and
yearn to move on. As for Julian, her words will bounce off
the page and into the heart at will. All is possible, yet all
takes its own time.

I have a friend, ancient she would call herself, who
laments 'Why did I take so long to appreciate her?!' But now
she is given: we may play catch up. As she herself remained
dormant and unknown for centuries. Until now: when most
we need her message – 'Love is his meaning.'

Before leaving you with a pressing invitation into a
journey of amazing bliss and invention, I must detain you
with the most curious and significant section of Julian's
record. Her Parable of the Servant.

To explain: each of her sixteen Showings are digested in a series of circular meditations comprising eighty-six chapters. Fear not, each one is brief, no more than a couple of pages. Save the blockbuster chapter fifty-one which extends to thirteen pages. It is a complete conundrum in that it halts the flow of her exposition even to the point of her spelling out her own uncertainty as she unravels the meaning of this new invention.

I use that word, since this parable alights unexpectedly and at first appears incongruous and out of step with the rest: but I believe it to be the hinge of her work that unlocks her deepest intent. It seems to be apart from her original sixteen Showings since it is not named in her chapter one as she lists her agenda. But now, halfway through, it lands in the most prominent manner, her longest chapter by far. How to understand? We are in the good hands of our Julian, as she teases out her newfound riddle.

My own fancy is that her parable, her story, was a dream. Given like any another, deeply planted in her psyche, welling up with good will when she was most perplexed by all she had received. A kind of key to her kingdom. And so it turns out to be.

She had endlessly asked the core question of mankind:

> In this mortal life, mercy and forgiveness is the path that leads us steadily to grace. And because of the tempest and sorrow that fall across our way, we are often dead, according to humankind's judgement on earth; yet in the sight of God, the soul that shall be saved was never dead nor will it be. Yet I wondered and would ponder with all the diligence in my power, thinking to myself: 'Good Lord, I see that you are very truth, and I well know that we sin grievously every day and are much to be blamed; and I can never avoid this truth, yet on your part, I can see no suggestion of blame. How may this be so?'

And now Julian has quarried back to the coal face of our very existence: look around the world, gaze into your own heart. What do we find, failure all around. No need to detail:

it is the endlessly published pabulum of our newspapers –
which we cannot cease to read.

And so begins Julian's questing, resolving chapter; a
majestic summing up of all God's purposeful love of
mankind he has made, mankind that has failed, mankind
into which he has invested his own self from the beginning.
The Son of Man stands firm upon our side. Here begins her
story:

> And so our courteous Lord answered by showing none too
> clearly a wonderful example of a lord who has a servant; and
> he enlightened my understanding as to them both . . .

Julian now elaborates a simple stage set, almost too plain
at first to attract our attention. She sees a lord who is seated.
Before him stands his servant. Presently, the servant dashes
off to do his lord's will. But at once he falls headlong 'into a
boggy dell and takes very great hurt'. He can no longer see
his lord, every part of his frame is hurting and he is stuck
there it seems for good. The lord feels tenderly towards his
servant and speaks his mind:

> Lo, lo, my beloved servant. What harm and disease he has
> taken in the service he undertook for my love, yes, and with
> such good will! Is it not right that I reward him for his terror
> and fright, his hurt and his wounds and all his woe? And not
> only this, does it not fall to me to give him a gift that would
> be better and more reward to him than ever he had before?
> Or else it seems I give him no thanks at all.

And now Julian begins to dissect and examine in precise
detail each aspect of her picture parable. She looks at the
servant, what he wears, the colour of his clothing, that too of
the lord.

> The place where our lord sat was simple; he sat upon the
> barren earth, in a desert, alone in a wilderness, his clothing
> was wide and flowing, very seemly as befits a lord; the colour
> of his clothing was blue as azure, most solemn and fair. His
> mien was merciful, his face was bronzed, of feature fair; his

eyes were dark and lustrous and showed loving pity: his watchful gaze extended far and wide, seeming to fill the endless heavens. And with this lovely look he watched his servant continually, especially as he saw his falling; I thought to myself it might melt our hearts for love and break them in two for joy ...

The compassion in the pity of the Father was for the falling of Adam, who is his most loved creature ...

In contrast, the servant is poorly clad, 'like a labourer ready for work ...' And Julian, as is her wont, goes into great detail. But what was his purpose, dashing off like that only to fall helpless so that he could no longer even see his lord. She tells us:

I was answered in my understanding: 'It is a meat most desirable that will please the Lord.' For I saw the Lord sitting like a man, and I saw neither meat nor drink that one might serve him; that was one strangeness. Another was that this same solemn Lord had no other servant than the one he had sent out ...

Slowly Julian teases out the tangles of her mystery play. And at last she grasps the intricate and pleasing sense of her tale.

Our good Lord showed his own Son and Adam as but one man. The virtue and goodness we have is of Jesus Christ, the feebleness and blindness is of Adam; both of which were shown in the servant. And so has our good Lord Jesus taken upon himself all our blame; and therefore our Father may assign, neither will he, no more blame to us than to his own Son, dearworthy Christ ...

He set off promptly in answer to his Father's will, and at once he fell down low into the Maiden's womb, regardless of himself or his hard pains.

And Julian continues to play out her story in minute detail until its triumphant and joyful conclusion:

Now the Lord no longer sits upon the earth in a wilderness, but he sits in his most noble throne which he made in heaven most to his liking. Now the Son no longer stands before the Father in awe like a servant, poorly clothed, part naked; but he stands before the Father an equal, richly clad in generous bliss, and with a crown upon his head of precious richness; for it was shown that we are his crown, which is the Father's joy, the Son's glory and a liking to the Holy Spirit, and an endless marvellous bliss to all who are in heaven.

As Julian concludes this lengthy chapter, one can feel her tone changing. She is no long searching after some hidden meaning for all has fallen into place. The last few clues of the crossword puzzle are easy. Her task is almost done: she is now at her most bold as she begins to reach its conclusion.

God, the blissful Trinity, is everlasting Being; as surely as he is endless and without beginning, so surely was it his endless purpose to make humankind. Yet humanity's fair nature was first prepared for his own Son, the second Person: then, when the chosen time came, by full accord of all the Trinity, he made us all at once; and in our making, he knitted us and oned us to himself. And, by the power of this same bond we are kept as clean and as noble as at the time of our making. And, by the power of this same precious bond, we love our Maker and like him, praise him and thank him with a joy in him that has no end. This then is the task which he works continually in every soul that shall be saved all according to this said plan of God.

I am reluctant to describe Julian as a heroine. And I believe she herself would shrink from such a naming. What is undeniable is that the long years spent in her anchorhold in Norwich yielded a unique and universal invitation for 'all my even Christians' to receive all that is on offer. Nothing less than total intimacy with our Maker, Keeper, Lover: for 'Love is his meaning.'

Chapter 4

Lady Margaret Beaufort

Tracey Rowland

Lady Margaret Beaufort, the Countess of Richmond and Derby, was the mother of Henry VII, grandmother of both Henry VIII and Margaret, Queen of Scots, the niece of Jane Beaufort who became the wife of James I of Scotland, and grandniece of Cardinal Henry Beaufort. She was thus one of the most powerful women in late medieval England living between the years 1443 to 1509. A summary snapshot of what we would now call her lifestyle may be found in the following paragraph of E. M. G. Routh:

> Her activities were varied and her recorded benefactions too many to enumerate. She endowed chantries and made frequent gifts to churches and monasteries: she might be found at different times endowing a priory in Lincolnshire and another in Yorkshire; building or restoring a chapel over a 'Holy well' in Flintshire; repairing Corfe Castle in Dorset; draining fenlands and settling a boundary dispute in Lincolnshire; going to Calais on business, granting a deed to incorporate a guild of tanners and shoemakers founded in Barnstaple Church, or becoming a member of the guild of St. Katherine, the objects of which were 'charitable, devotional and convivial'.[1]

---

1. Routh, E. M. G., *Lady Margaret: A Memoir of Lady Margaret Beaufort, Countess of Richmond and Derby, Mother of Henry VII*, Oxford University Press, 1824, chapter VIII.

According to Routh she would often say that if only the Christian princes would organize another crusade she would go along with them and wash the clothes of their troops. In 1476 she contributed to the cost of raising a fleet against the Turks who where then enjoying an expansionist moment under the leadership of Mehmet II (1451–1481), otherwise known as Mehmet the Conqueror. Ottoman incursions were to continue for another century until they were decisively thwarted at the Battle of Lepanto in 1571. Out of the same concern in 1507 Lady Margaret gave money to the monks of St Catherine's Mount to ransom Christians captured by Muslims. She was thus a defender of Christendom at a time when the whole framework was beginning to unravel. Not only was a militant Islamic revival thrusting its way into the very heart of Christian Europe, but there was also the Hundred Years War between the two Christian kingdoms of France and England, the civil war between the Houses of York and Lancaster within England, the rise of retro-pagan elements in the Italian renaissance, and the ascendency of Protestantism in Germany and Bohemia. In *The King's Mother*, the distinguished biography by Jones and Underwood, the authors noted her interest in politics, history and chivalry:

> Her life, like those of her contemporaries was a mixture of rights and duties, of power and obligation, of aggression and compassion. She was no recluse, but a veteran of bruising political battles. A powerful figure in her age, she shared its cultural preoccupations, not only as has often been stressed, in the expression of a strong personal piety and interest in the advancement of learning, but in the fascination of the time with history and chivalry. These were not passive concepts, but part of the dynamic of political life. Like the possession of land and retinues, interest in them helped to define an individual's social importance.[2]

Lady Margaret thus managed to hold the flag for Christendom and its notion of *noblesse oblige*, particularly

---

[2.] Jones, M. K. and Underwood, M. G., *The King's Mother: Lady Margaret Beaufort, the Countess of Richmond and Derby*, Cambridge University Press, p. 171.

the obligations of the nobility to care for the sick and the poor and to place themselves on the front lines in the defence of the faith, at a time when civil wars made public life a very dangerous business. It was not just a matter of finding oneself on the wrong side of a political battle, of enduring the social opprobrium which goes with being politically incorrect, but for those from the noble families of influence, being on the wrong side could often mean imprisonment and execution. The life of her only son was at risk throughout his childhood and early manhood and she was herself for a time under house arrest. This was the era of the famous Princes in the Tower incident when the two prince sons of the Dowager Queen consort, Elizabeth Woodville, went missing and were presumed to have been murdered, while being confined to the Tower of London. In these times when the leaders of ostensibly Christian families killed their potential political rivals before they had a chance to grow to maturity, Lady Margaret was a great survivor. She thought ahead and today would be described as a brilliant strategic planner. Not only did she die in her bed from natural causes, but her son became the king, and the bloody Wars of the Roses were brought to an end by her masterminding of the marriage of her Lancastrian son Henry to Elizabeth of York.

In contemporary Catholic and educational circles Lady Margaret is better known as a friend of the Cambridge University luminary St John Fisher whose various educational projects she financed. The young John Fisher found the intellectual climate in the Oxbridge colleges of his day to be somewhat stagnant. He was abreast of the more dynamic intellectual currents in Europe and a friend of the Christian humanist scholars Erasmus and Sir Thomas More. He believed that too many of the best minds in England had either fallen on the battlefields of France during the Hundred Years War, or under the executioner's axe in the Wars of the Roses.[3] He was opposed to the Protestantism of Martin Luther but open to aspects of the new humanism,

---

[3.]   Routh, E. M. G., op. cit., chapter IX.

especially the revival of interest in classical and biblical languages and the use of the vernacular for evangelical work.

When he met Lady Margaret in 1495 he was a Fellow of Michaelhouse in Cambridge and the Senior Proctor. He became Lady Margaret's confessor, though he claimed that he learned more about virtue from her than he was able to teach himself, and that he was as indebted to Lady Margaret as to his own mother. Together they made a major contribution to the renewal of the intellectual life of Cambridge University in the fifteenth century. Christ's College, Queens' College and St John's College all acknowledge Lady Margaret as one of their most significant benefactors and for St John's and Christ's she is also their foundress. Erasmus was to describe these three colleges as places where 'youth was exercised, not in dialectical wrestling matches, which serve only to chill the heart and unfit men for serious duties, but in true learning and sober arguments, and from whence they went forth to preach the Word of God with earnestness and with an evangelical spirit and to commend it to the minds of men of learning by a weighty eloquence'.[4] They were to produce true scholars who cared about the resolution of the problems of the day, not merely people who enjoyed intellectual disputation as a parlour game.

The discipline closest to the heart of Fisher and Lady Margaret was Divinity. Lady Margaret endowed two readerships in Divinity, one at Oxford and one at Cambridge. These are now the Lady Margaret professorial chairs. The pair were also particularly interested in what today would be called homiletics. Fisher was strongly of the view that popular preaching in the English language needed to be encouraged. To this end the Lady Margaret Preachership was founded in Cambridge in 1504. This required the holder to give a specified number of sermons each year. According to Jones and Underwood, it was the belief of both Fisher and Lady Margaret that the Church's problems lay less with the papacy than with the spiritual and intellectual conditions of

[4.] Ibid., chapter XII.

the lower clergy and laity – 'their hope was to help the spiritual life of the Church through appointing men of good quality and endowing nurseries of good learning'.[5] In particular, Fisher believed that the clergy needed improved intellectual formation. They were often completely out of their depth in the theological and social controversies of their day. As an ancillary educational initiative Lady Margaret also helped William Caxton to establish a printing press in England. This, in turn, assisted the dissemination of devotional texts some of which she translated from the French originals herself.

While in Cambridge the influence of Lady Margaret lives on in the three great colleges of Christ's, Queens' and St John's, in Oxford her memory is evoked by Lady Margaret Hall. It was founded almost four centuries after her death in 1878 as the first college for women in Oxford. A more recent foundation also named in her honour is the Margaret Beaufort Institute of Theology at Cambridge. This is a house of studies for women specializing in theology and leadership for lay ministry. It was founded in 1994 and is affiliated to Cambridge University. It is thus impossible to walk the streets and lanes of the two great university cities without running into some long-lasting memorial to her influence. The Beaufort family's coat of arms with its trade mark spotted yale supporters is to be found over many halls and archways.

Fisher's eulogy for Lady Margaret, known as the mourning remembrance, delivered a month after her death, is a major source of information about her private life in the twilight years of Catholic England. He begins by comparing her to the biblical character Martha. He notes that they share four qualities in common: they are of noble blood, well disciplined in matters pertaining to the body, godly, or one might say, holy, and they are both associated with the gift of hospitality. With respect to the first quality, Lady Margaret's nobility, Fisher further argues that she was noble in four

5. Jones and Underwood, op. cit., p. 192.

different senses of the word. First, her blood line was as blue as the Danube. She was a lineal descendant of Edward III and daughter of John, the Duke of Somerset. By lineage or affinity she had thirty kings or queens within the fourth degree of alliance. Secondly, she had gracious manners. She was gentle, kind and affable, never vengeful, always ready to forgive, merciful to those who had suffered some wrong doing, open to doing God's will, and an obedient daughter of the Church. Thirdly, she was born with a noble nature or disposition. In Fisher's words, she had 'all that is praisable in a woman in both soul and body'. She was wise, she had an excellent memory and good sense of humour. She enjoyed reading books in French and English and translating French devotional works into English. She reproached herself for not having studied Latin in her youth. Fourthly, her nobility was increased by her various marriages.

Lady Margaret was in fact married three or four times (depending on whether one counts the first unconsummated marriage as a marriage). A general principle of canon law is that a marriage is not binding until it is consummated. This first 'marriage' occurred when she was six years old and historians report that she did not really understand what was happening. This childhood 'husband' was the son of the Duke of Suffolk. Margaret was the Duke's ward since her father died when she was only two years old. Soon after the ceremony the Duke of Suffolk was executed and the union was dissolved three years later before she was old enough for it to be consummated. This was in order for her to marry Edmund Tudor, the Earl of Richmond, who was the half-brother of King Henry VI and son of Catherine of France, widow of Henry V. When this wedding took place Margaret was twelve and Edmund Tudor was twenty-six. This time the marriage was consummated and a son Henry, who became Henry VII, was born in 1456. Edmund however did not live to raise his son as he died of the plague some two months before Henry's delivery. Because of his sensitive political position as a senior Lancastrian in a Yorkist regime, Henry was separated from his mother for long periods during his

childhood. In his early years he was for a time in the household of William Herbert, the Earl of Pembroke, an ally of
Edward IV, and then in 1471 when Henry became the most
senior Lancastrian male upon the death of Edward IV, he was
taken off into exile in Brittany for safe keeping by his uncle
Jasper Tudor. His succession was finally secured at the Battle
of Bosworth Field on 22 August 1485, with the defeat of the
Yorkist Richard III by Henry's forces, comprised mostly of
French and Breton mercenaries. The battle brought to an
end the Plantagenet dynasty and began the Tudor era.
Throughout his childhood and early manhood Margaret's
parental decisions all seemed to be focused on the task of
keeping the young Henry and his claim to the succession
alive. If this meant that mother and son had to be separated,
she endured the separation, and the pair communicated by
letter.

With the death of Edmund Tudor from the plague and the
birth of his son, Margaret was a mother and a widow by the
time she was thirteen. Her third marriage occurred three
years later to Henry, Lord Suffolk, the son of the Duke of
Buckingham. This marriage lasted until Lord Suffolk's death
in 1482 following a battle wound he sustained fighting for
the cause of Edward IV. The twenty-three-year marriage did
not produce any children and according to scholarly opinion
the birth of Henry when she was only thirteen had the effect
of destroying the possibility of further issue. Lady Margaret's
final marriage was to Thomas, Lord Stanley. Stanley died in
1504 but some five years before his death Lady Margaret
took a vow of chastity and moved into her own house at
Collyweston in Northamptonshire which she transformed
into her private palace. Lord Stanley enjoyed visiting rights
and had his own suite of rooms. By this time she was the
greatest landowner in England after the king and queen. She
presided over a household of some 230 persons and interested herself in their private affairs, especially their
education. Even children of servants were recipients of her
educational grants. Those who benefited most were the children recruited to sing in the choir of her chapel.

Lady Margaret was, as Fisher testified, a devout Catholic. She not only attended daily Mass and regularly went to confession, she also fasted in the penitential seasons and she had a special devotion to the Holy Name of Jesus. Her favourite saints included St Mary Magdalene, St George, St John the Baptist, St Catherine of Alexandria, a patron of scholars, and St Leonard, a French hermit who was the patron of prisoners and the sick. She was a member of the confraternity of the Reformed Franciscans, known as the Observants, and she was also close to the Carthusians and to the Bridgettines of Syon Abbey.[6]

Margaret died on 29 June in 1509 at the Deanery of Westminster Abbey. She is buried in Westminster Abbey in the chapel of Henry VII between the graves of William and Mary and the tomb of Mary, Queen of Scots. As she lay dying she reportedly cried and told Fisher that she feared that the adolescent Henry VIII would become so puffed up by his power that he would turn away from God. She had drawn up a list of privy councillors for Henry VIII and strongly recommended the counsel of Bishop Fisher to him but by the time of her death it seems that she was not exerting any influence over her grandson. Although she took an active interest in his life during his nursery years, and is recorded as having attended the ceremony in which he was knighted and created Duke of York at the age of three, in the final years of her life she seems to disappear from her hitherto centre stage position.

When Princess Catherine of Aragon became betrothed to Henry's older brother Prince Arthur, Margaret sent her a letter encouraging her to practise her French since the English royal ladies spoke no Spanish. She was concerned that she might turn up in London and find herself in a lonely situation where she could not even communicate with the other members of the royal Court. However when a very homesick teenage Catherine wanted to return to Spain upon Arthur's death, rather than waiting around to be recycled as

6. Ibid., pp. 177–81.

Henry's wife, Margaret did not exercise any decisive influence at these axial moments in English history. The young Catherine was a pawn in a political power game; she was wanted simply to forge an alliance between England and Spain. Her failure to satisfy Henry with the delivery of a healthy son would mean that England and Spain became bitter enemies, the English links to the papacy would be severed, the Spanish Armada would be sunk, a couple of Dutch Protestants would be shipped in to take possession of the English throne and an Act of Settlement passed to prevent an English prince or princess from ever again marrying a Catholic without loss of their place in the order of succession.

Moreover, a mere twenty-six years after Lady Margaret's death her grandson would order the execution of John Fisher and Thomas More because they refused to accept the validity of his divorce from Catherine. Not only were they two of the most learned men in his kingdom, but More had actually been a childhood playmate and then close friend of Henry. Many hundreds of others, including Oxford's Edmund Campion, would later be beheaded or hanged, drawn and quartered because they preferred Catherine's faith to that of the puffed up Henry, or the resolutely Protestant Edward VI and Elizabeth I.

Lady Margaret died when she was sixty-six. In those times this represented a good innings, but it's a pity that she did not live for at least another decade to befriend and mother Queen Catherine and provide Henry with a moral compass. As it was John Fisher claimed that all of England had reason to weep at the news of her death:

> The poor creatures that were wont to receive her alms to whom she was always piteous and merciful; the students of both Universities to whom she was as a mother; all the learned men of England to whom she was a very patroness; all the virtuous and devout persons to whom she was as a loving sister; all the good religious men and women whom she so often was wont to visit and comfort; all good priests and clerks to whom she was a true defendress; all the noble

men and women to whom she was a mirror and example of honour; all the common people of this realm for whom she was in their causes a common mediatrix and took right great displeasure for them, and generally the whole realm hath cause to complain and mourn her death, and all we considering her gracious and charitable mind.[7]

If the definition of a saint is a person of heroic virtue then Fisher was clearly setting Margaret up to be classed within a rather long litany of aristocratic Catholic women who not only defended their integrity in a morally treacherous culture but actually managed to turn the fortunes of Christendom around. They were often good Catholic princesses who for political reasons found themselves married off to some pagan warlord whom they managed to civilize through a mixture of tenderness, heroic patience and shrewd strategic planning. Thus France became the eldest daughter of the Church through the marriage of the Burgundian Princess Clotilde to Clovis, King of the Franks, and the Scots became less interested in sun-worship after the Catholic Margaret of England, daughter of Edward the Exile, married Malcolm III.

If Lady Margaret's cause for beatification is ever successfully taken up she may well become a patron saint of women trying to raise a family in a brutally anti-life culture and of scholars trying to run Christian educational institutions amidst all manner of bureaucratic secularist government regulations.

---

7. St John Fisher, in *The English Works of John Fisher, Bishop of Rochester*, as collected by John E. B. Mayor, Early English Text Society, London, 1876, p. 301. The translation from the medieval English into more contemporary English as used above is that of E. M. G. Routh.

Chapter 5

Blessed Margaret Pole, Countess of Salisbury

Lucy Underwood

At a crossroads near the centre of Cambridge stands an impressive neo-Gothic church dedicated to Our Lady of the Assumption and the English Martyrs. Built a few years after the beatification of fifty Catholic martyrs of the English Reformation,[1] it is a bold celebration of the heritage England's nineteenth-century Catholics laid claim to, preserved and in many ways created. Among the stained-glass windows which decorate the church, there is one – actually two – depicting a certain 'Blessed Margaret Pole'. In the first, helpfully captioned 'Blessed Margaret prays in her cell in the Tower' a woman in Tudor-esque robes kneels at a prie-dieu against a gloomy Tower backdrop complete with three rats eating the lady's neglected dinner. In the second, the same woman stands in front of a block, and over her head a scroll tells us what she says: 'So should traitors, but I am none.'

And that is all the church of Our Lady of the Assumption and the English Martyrs will tell you about Blessed Margaret Pole, leaving a juvenile me to wonder whether she was a colleague of Margaret Clitherow's or a conscientious objector with Thomas More. At any rate, it was a very good line.

[1.] Decree of beatification: Camm, Bede (ed.) *Lives of the English martyrs declared blessed by Pope Leo XIII in 1886 and 1895 / written by fathers of the Oratory, of the secular clergy and of the Society of Jesus; completed and edited by Bede Camm*, London, 1904–5, 2 vols.

Margaret Pole, née Plantagenet, Countess of Salisbury, was the daughter of George, Duke of Clarence, brother of Edward IV, born on 14 August 1473. She was married, aged about fourteen, to Sir Richard Pole; having borne five children, including Reginald, future Cardinal and last Archbishop of Canterbury, she was widowed in 1504. Seven years later, Henry VIII 'restored' her to the lands and title of Countess of Salisbury in her own right, making her a rather rare thing, a female peer. In 1538, she and members of her family were investigated on charges of treason and two executed. In 1539 Margaret was attainted (declared a traitor by Act of Parliament) and in May 1541 she was executed, aged sixty-seven. Opinions still differ as to whether she was killed for her lineage, her faith, her son or her politics.[2]

At her birth, Margaret Plantagenet's position was a promising one, as niece of King Edward IV. Although far down the line of succession (Edward IV had seven children of his own, and Margaret also had a brother born in 1475), she was a member of the royal family and held one of the highest places in the realm. The first shadow to fall across this brilliant prospect was the execution of her father for treason in 1478. George Duke of Clarence had been disloyal to Edward IV once before, returned to his allegiance and been forgiven. By 1477, Edward was again unsure of Clarence's reliability, and this time he was convicted (on rather insubstantial charges) and executed.[3] Clarence's estates and possessions would have been forfeit, leaving Margaret and her brother, the young Earl of Warwick, reliant on the protection of the king. This remained the case until Edward IV's death and during the brief reign of Richard III, who – mindful of their potential claim to the throne – kept the children at Sheriff Hutton castle in Yorkshire under the supervision of John de la Pole, Earl of Lincoln. Warwick was also, however, made nominal head of the Council of the North.[4]

---

[2]. Pierce, Hazel, *Margaret Pole, Countess of Salisbury 1473–1541: Loyalty, Lineage and Leadership*, Cardiff, 2003, is the only modern biography.

[3]. *Oxford Dictionary of National Biography*, George Duke of Clarence.

[4]. Pierce, *Margaret Pole*, pp. 7–10.

The conquest and accession of Henry VII, who defeated Richard III on Bosworth field in 1485 and founded the Tudor dynasty, radically altered Margaret's position and significance. Henry married the eldest daughter of Edward IV, ostensibly uniting the Yorkist and Lancastrian claims to the throne; but the presence of various other Yorkist heirs left him uneasy. The potential threat they posed to the Tudor possession of the Crown had to be neutralized. Thus Edward of Warwick – aged eleven – disappeared into the Tower in 1486, from which he was never to emerge. About the same time, Margaret became the wife of Sir Richard Pole, a half-cousin of Henry VII through his mother Margaret Beaufort and owner of estates in Buckinghamshire. The match was apparently seen by some contemporaries as far beneath the station of a daughter of the house of Plantagenet, an attempt to ensure no powerful husband would press Margaret's claims. What was probably more important to Henry was that Pole was an increasingly-trusted royal servant, loyal to the king and employed in various administrative offices, particularly in Wales.[5]

What fourteen-year-old Margaret thought of the matter is not known, but her biographer suggests that the marriage was reasonably successful.[6] It produced five children, Henry (later Lord Montague, born 1492), Arthur, Ursula, Reginald (born 1500) and Geoffrey (born *c*.1504).[7]

In 1499, Henry VII solved the lingering problem of Edward Plantagenet. Perkin Warbeck, who had claimed to be a surviving son of Edward IV and incited rebellion against Henry, was imprisoned in the Tower in 1498. In 1499, he attempted to escape and Warwick was accused of complicity in the plot and convicted of treason. Warwick's lineage would, perhaps, have killed him sooner or later; but Henry was also at the time negotiating a marriage between his son, Arthur Prince of Wales and Catherine, Princess of Aragon,

---

[5.]   Ibid., pp. 13–17.
[6.]   Ibid., pp. 17–18.
[7.]   Ibid., pp. 22–3.

and Ferdinand of Aragon may have made it a condition that Warwick and the threat he represented should be removed.[8] Edward, Earl of Warwick, having grown to adulthood in the Tower, never married and never taken possession of his inheritance, died under the axe at the age of twenty-four, one of the most innocent of all its victims. Whatever the immediate occasion, there is some evidence that in later years, Catherine would regard herself as the cause of a wrong done to her friend's brother.[9]

Catherine of Aragon and Margaret Pole were to become long-standing friends. Margaret and her husband both held positions in the household of the new Prince and Princess of Wales, and during the difficult years following Arthur's death in 1502 – when the widowed Catherine remained in England, uncertain of her position and dependent on the unreliable generosity of her father-in-law – the two women remained in contact. From 1504, when Sir Richard Pole died, Margaret herself was a widow with five children and limited resources with which to bring them up.[10] The friendship established in these years would be tested again – and proven – during the long persecution Catherine and her daughter endured at the hands of Henry VIII.

Not that this could have been foreseen in 1509, when Henry's accession seemed like a new dawn for both Margaret and Catherine. Shortly after succeeding to the crown, Henry made Catherine his queen; and in 1511, Margaret Pole was by Act of Parliament 'restored in blood', gaining the lands and title of Countess of Salisbury. As Countess, Margaret was engaged in running her estates and household, playing her part in the politics of land, patronage and aristocratic networks. She built Warblington Castle on the Hampshire coast as her chief residence, and entertained the King and Queen. In 1516 she was one of the godparents

---

[8.] *Oxford Dictionary of National Biography*, Edward Earl of Warwick 1475–1499; Pierce, *Margaret Pole*, p. 25.

[9.] Mayer, T. F. *Correspondence of Reginald Pole* (Aldershot, 2002, 4 vols) vol. 1 p. 222.

[10.] Pierce, *Margaret Pole*, pp. 27–31.

at the christening of the future Mary I.[11] Her eldest son, Henry, also trying to establish a courtly career, was Margaret's ally and partner in her activities as a magnate; but although created Baron Montague and repeatedly employed at Henry VIII's Court, he never held important office. This may reflect Henry VIII's lingering unease about the Plantagenet inheritance, and could have been a factor in the alleged disaffection with the Tudors which was to cause the Poles' downfall.[12] Reginald Pole, meanwhile, was promoted and patronized by the king in his career as a scholar and churchman: a debt which Henry was later to call in, with devastating consequences.[13]

The domestic responsibilities of high-ranking women were also a part of aristocratic politics: wealthy families liked to place their daughters in the households of great ladies, for reasons both of education and social advancement. Margaret's household apparently included several such young women.[14] She also gave attention to arranging advantageous marriages for her children, something which involved her in inheritance disputes with in-laws more than once. Margaret's most spectacular success in this field was when she married her daughter, Ursula, to Henry Stafford, heir to the Duke of Buckingham in 1519. Buckingham, like Margaret, could boast a noble lineage going back to before the Tudor accession, and Plantagenet blood; he was also extremely wealthy.[15] This triumph was somewhat marred two years later, when Buckingham was accused of treason; he was executed, and Henry VIII confiscated his lands and titles. Although his son, Lord Stafford, would eventually regain some of his father's lands, the prestige and power of

---

[11.] See Pierce, *Margaret Pole*, chs 2 and 3 for Margaret as a female magnate.

[12.] *Oxford Dictionary of National Biography*, Henry Pole 1492–1539; Pierce, *Margaret Pole*, pp. 161–2.

[13.] Mayer, T. F. *Reginald Pole: Prince and Prophet*, Cambridge, 2000, pp. 46–54.

[14.] Pierce, *Margaret Pole*, pp. 60–1.

[15.] Ibid., pp. 50–5, 67–69, 90–2.

the family was lost, and Margaret was never to be the mother of a duchess.[16]

Probably the greatest mark of royal favour Margaret Pole received was her appointment from 1520 to 1521, and again from 1525 to 1533, as governess to Princess Mary, Henry VIII's daughter and heir apparent. She had responsibility for the young Mary Tudor's education and household, and accompanied the princess to the Welsh Marches when she spent two years there (1525–7). For Margaret, this was a return to the place where she and her husband had been members of the household of Catherine and Arthur.

The education Margaret oversaw combined the accomplishments expected of a great lady, new humanist ideas on education, and the training of a prince. Despite his latent unease with the idea and desire for a son, Henry provisionally accepted Mary as his heir, and this was reflected in her upbringing. It may have been partly to this end that Mary was sent to Wales, where she nominally presided over the Council of the Marches and at least witnessed some of its business. She also became fluent in Latin (the basis for all education at this time) as well as learning French and other subjects such as music. Margaret Pole, herself mistress of large households (in the plural) and extensive estates would have understood the challenges of filling male as well as female roles. The young Mary's main contribution to public life was to be shown off as an attractive potential bride when Henry was considering alliances involving marriage; but just as in widowhood Margaret had become a female magnate, so Mary might one day have also to be head of state.[17]

During the 1530s, the course of English history and the life of Margaret's young charge were irrevocably changed. Henry VIII's quest for a male heir, his repudiation of Catherine of Aragon and determination to marry Anne Boleyn occasioned his rejection of the authority of the pope

---

[16.] Ibid., pp. 85–90.
[17.] See Porter, L., *Mary Tudor: the First Queen*, London, 2007, ch. 2.

and the schism of the English Church. Mary officially ceased
to be princess, and became the Lady Mary, illegitimate
daughter of the King, while Anne Boleyn's daughter
Elizabeth, born in September 1533, replaced her as princess
and as heir apparent. Catherine of Aragon persistently
defended her marriage and her daughter's legitimacy, and
the teenage Mary proved no less stubborn. Henry separated
mother and daughter to prevent them stiffening each
other's resolve: but Mary still had the support of the formidable Countess of Salisbury. In the summer of 1533, when the
King demanded the return of Mary's jewels and plate – a
clear signal that her status as princess was under question –
Lady Salisbury refused to comply, to the exasperation of
Lord Hussey to whom the task had been delegated.[18] Later
that year, Mary's household was disbanded, her servants
including Lady Salisbury dismissed, and she was sent to join
Elizabeth's household: this was quite deliberately humiliating, and intended to pressurize the seventeen-year-old Mary
into conformity. Margaret Pole, unwilling to abandon the
beleaguered princess, apparently offered to accompany
Mary at her own cost, but was unsurprisingly forbidden to
do so.[19] Three years of isolation, humiliation and threats –
including the possibility of being arraigned for treason –
culminated in Mary's signature of a document acknowledging the Royal Supremacy, the invalidity of her mother's
marriage, and her own illegitimacy, five months after
Catherine's death, and one month after Anne Boleyn's
execution on charges of adultery.[20] Mary's capitulation was
complete, and completely insincere. When she signed her
consent to Henry's demands, she also – secretly – signed a
document declaring her consent to be under duress. One of
her biographers has described how, at the King's behest, she
wrote to foreign princes announcing her change of heart
and submission to her father; but at the same time she was

[18.] Pierce, *Margaret Pole*, p. 100.
[19.] Loades, *Mary Tudor: the Tragical History of the first Queen of England*, Richmond, 2006, pp. 36–7.
[20.] Ibid., pp. 48–50.

having the imperial ambassador, Chapuys, inform them that her acquiescence was forced.[21] This, if known, would have been unequivocally treason.

Meanwhile, the King's war with the Church had touched Margaret's own family. In need of scholarly, reputable support for his marital and ecclesiastical proceedings, Henry VIII had solicited Reginald Pole's approval early in the proceedings. Originally prepared to support the King, Pole later grew doubtful,[22] and in 1536 Reginald responded to the king's demand that he declare himself: in a long 'letter', *Reginaldi Poli ad Henricum octavum Britanniae regem, pro ecclesiasticae unitate defensione* (known as *De Unitate*), a lengthy and forthright denunciation of the Royal Supremacy and the divorce.[23] Reginald wrote to his mother at about this time, acknowledging the ' gre[if] it will be to you that I doo not come [back to England]', but maintaining that

> I canno[t] make at this tyme no other annswer but firs[t] to put your Ladyshippe in remembrance of your promys to god touchyng me wiche … from my childyshe yeris … was that evir you had geven me utterly unto G[od] And thoughe you had so done with all yo[ur] children, yet in me you had so given all rig[ht] utterly from you and possession utterly of me that you never took any care to provide f[or] my living, nor otherwise, as you did for other but committed all to God to whome you had giv[en] me. This promys nowe Madame … I require of you … if you will enjoy in me any of that comfort God sendith, the easiest way is putting all care aside of me. Let my maister and me alone … but both touchyng your self and me both commit all to his goodness, as I doubt not your Ladyshippe will and shall be to me the greatest comfort I can have of you. As knoweth almightie God who

---

[21]. Erickson, C., *Bloody Mary: the Life of Mary Tudor*, pp. 166–7; 177–9. Other biographers, such as Loades, have taken a different view, concluding that Mary's submission was genuine, if only temporarily; or at least (as Porter suggests) that she took no contradictory action.

[22]. Mayer, *Reginald Pole*, pp. 56–61.

[23]. Ibid., p. 13.

send you continuall grace in all thing to conforme your
desires and pleasures unto his.[24]

Henry had already executed several people for not repudiating the stance Reginald was now proclaiming so forcefully.
Reginald was in Italy and could not be executed; but his
family, on the less safe side of the English Channel, were not
prepared to identify themselves with his position. In 1535,
Lord Montague had served on the commissions which tried
first the Carthusian martyrs and then Thomas More for
treason; in the summer of 1536, when he and Lady Salisbury
were pressed for a response to Reginald's treason, it was one
of caution and compliance.[25] Lady Salisbury wrote to her son
in July 1536

Sonne Reginald, I send you godes blessing and myne more,
more of my charitie then of your deservyng. For where my
hope and trust was in god to have had comfort of you, this
same by your demeanour is turned to sorowe. Alas that ever
you shuld be the cause that I beryng towarde you so moth-
erly and tender harte as I have done shuld for your folye
receive from my sovereign Lorde suche message as I have
late done by your brother ... Trust me Reginald, there went
never the deth of thy father or of any childe so nygh my harte
as this hathe done ... you write of a promise made of you to
God. Sonne that was to serve God and thy prynce whome if
thou doo not serve with all thy wytt, with all thy power, I
knowe thou cannot please God. And your bounden duetie is
so to doo aboue all other. For who hathe brought you up
and maynttayned you to lernyng but hys hyghnes whom if
you will not with your lernyng serve to the contentation of
his mynde as your bounden duetie is, trust never in me. And
that you maye so serve hys highnes I shall dayly praye to God
to geve you grace to make you hys servant, or else take you
to his mercye.[26]

[24.] Copy in SP 1/139 f.132r-v (State Papers Online). This MS is damaged.
[25.] *Oxford Dictionary of National Biography*, Henry Pole 1492–1538.
[26.] SP 1/105 f.66 (State Papers Online).

Margaret's letter is preserved as a copy in Henry VIII's State Papers: it was clearly meant for the eyes of the King and his ministers. How sincere it is, we can only wonder. Montague wrote to Reginald at the same time, in even more strongly reproachful terms, and would later assert that he had advised his mother to proclaim Reginald a traitor to their servants, disavowing any involvement with him.[27] In a letter of October that year, Pole wrote to a friend that his mother's and brother's letters 'so miserably written' had almost swayed him, and later referred to Henry's attempt at emotional blackmail via his family.[28]

Mary Tudor, probably because it would have been too provocative a request, did not ask for Margaret Pole's inclusion in her re-constituted household. Margaret had lost the royal favour, but retained the Salisbury lands and her seat at Warblington Castle; yet if she hoped her outward conformity would allow her to spend her final years in relatively peaceful retirement, it was not to be. In the autumn of 1538, a series of arrests and interrogations began which culminated in the trial for treason and execution of Margaret's son Lord Montague, his cousin the Marquess of Exeter, and four other men in December 1538. By 1541, the Pole family would have been destroyed.

The storm broke in the summer of 1538, with the arrest of Hugh Holland, a servant of Margaret's youngest son Geoffrey.[29] About this time, Montague and Geoffrey burnt some of their papers, later (not surprisingly) alleged to be treasonable. Perhaps some correspondence with their defiant brother (in which Reginald's mother was also accused of being involved, though she denied this) went up in smoke; perhaps it contained less conformist views of Henry's actions than Montague had expressed to Reginald in 1536. In mid August, Holland's arrest and interrogation were followed by that of Geoffrey himself. It was then that Geoffrey Pole, always the

---

[27.] Pierce, *Margaret Pole*, p. 107.

[28.] Mayer, T. F., *The Correspondence of Reginald Pole*, Aldershot, 2002, 4 vols. Vol.1, pp. 119, 222.

[29.] See Pierce, Margaret Pole, chapter 5 for the events of 1538–9.

least reliable and least sucessful of Margaret's sons, began to bring about the ruin of his family. Repeatedly examined and in fear of torture, he spoke of continued contact with Reginald involving himself and Lord Montague and accused his elder brother of talk expressing disrespect for the King and dislike of his proceedings, and implying that he would have liked a change of regime. In particular, he had hoped for the success of the Pilgrimage of Grace, the great rising in the North of 1536–7 protesting at the break with Rome and the impending Dissolution of the Monasteries. The examinations of Geoffrey and various servants and associates of the Poles also implicated Henry Courtenay, Marquess of Exeter. Inevitably, Montague, Exeter, and also Exeter's wife Gertrude were arrested. Montague, in his examination, put up a far better fight than Geoffrey, refusing to incriminate himself.

In September, Margaret wrote to her eldest son, 'as to the case I ame enformid, that you stand in Myne advise is to enser you to God principally, and upon that ground so to order you both in word and deed to sarve your prince not disobeying Goddys comandments as far as your power and life will serve you'.[30] It is a letter suggestive of a less unconditional loyalty than that she had pressed upon Reginald two years earlier.

By mid November, Margaret herself was implicated. She was interrogated 12–14 November at Warblington, and then moved to house arrest at Cowdray under the charge of Sir William Fitzwilliam. Margaret Pole defended herself and her sons single-mindedly, refusing to admit any treason, insisting 'that if ever it be found and proved in her, that she is culpable in any of those things, that she hath denied, that she is content to be blamed in the rest of all the articles laid against her', and eliciting from her interrogators the comment that 'we have dealid with such a one as men have not dealid with to fore us, Wee may call hyr rather a strong and custaunt [constant] man than a woman ...'.[31] From a

---

[30.] Pierce, *Margaret Pole*, p. 137.

[31.] Ellis, H. (ed.) *Original Letters Illustrative of English History*, London, 1825–46, 11 vols. Series II vol. IV, pp. 111, 114–15; Pierce, *Margaret Pole*, pp. 137–9.

Tudor man, praise for a woman's courage could not be higher. The charges against Lady Salisbury were less serious than those against her sons; she was mainly pressed as to whether she knew about various conversations and intrigues in which they were supposed to have been involved. Informants accused her of colluding with her chaplains to prevent the spread of reformed religious ideas among her dependants and tenants, including the English Bible Henry VIII had authorized. It is difficult to know how seriously to take their allegations. Among other things, Margaret's chaplains were supposed to have been keeping her up-to-date on people's opinions by passing on what was told them in the confessional; this, if true, would have been sacrilege in the highest degree.[32] However, surviving reports of the Countess's examinations do not mention this particular allegation, or any response of hers to it.[33]

On 2 December, Lord Montague was tried and found guilty of treason; the convictions of Lord Exeter, Geoffrey Pole and four others followed. Margaret's eldest son was executed on 9 December, with the Marquess of Exeter. Geoffrey Pole remained a prisoner in the Tower, where it was reported that at Christmas 1538 he attempted suicide.

The Countess of Salisbury was never tried. In May 1539, her name was included in an Act of Attainder which condemned a number of people. The grounds were that she and others had 'trayterously confederate themselfes to and withe the said false and abhominable trayters henrye poole late lorde montacute and Reignold poole', as well as committing 'sundrie other detestable and abhomynable treasons' which the Act declined to specify.[34] Later that year the Countess was moved from house arrest at Cowdray to the Tower of London. Relations with her keeper, Fitzwilliam, were apparently not courteous: during one altercation, Fitzwilliam referred to Reginald Pole as 'that arrant

---

[32.] Ibid., pp. 118–21. Pierce does not appear to notice this aspect of these allegations.

[33.] SP 1/138 f.199r – 202v (State Papers Online).

[34.] Pierce, *Margaret Pole*, p. 171.

whoreson traitor'. Margaret retorted that although he was 'an ill man to behave so to the King who had been so good to him, yet he was no whoreson, for she was both a good woman and true'. By late March Fitzwilliam was begging to be rid of her, since she 'troubleth my mind'; his wife apparently refused to be left in the house as long as Lady Salisbury was in it.[35] But if Fitzwilliam was making a habit of throwing about insults like the above, it is not surprising if Margaret did not go out of her way to make being her gaoler a pleasant assignment.

A year after the executions of Montague and Exeter, Margaret was a prisoner in the Tower, condemned but not executed. Also in the Tower were her grandson Henry, Montague's son, and Edward Courtenay, Exeter's son, both children. Exeter's widow Gertrude, however, was released and given an annuity.[36] It was not until May 1541 that Henry finally made the decision to execute the Countess of Salisbury, by now aged sixty-seven.

The reasons for Henry's attack on the Pole family in 1538 are debatable (and much debated). Historians sympathetic to the Poles have argued firstly that Henry feared their Plantagenet blood, and needed them out of the way for dynastic reasons; secondly that they suffered for Reginald Pole's defection. Henry could not indict and execute the cardinal (though he attempted to have him assassinated),[37] so he wreaked his vengeance on Pole's innocent family, culminating in the savagery of executing a woman of almost seventy.[38] Margaret Pole's modern biographer, Hazel Pierce, takes a more circumspect view of the Poles. She argues that Montague, Geoffrey and their associates were, in fact, disaffected, and if not actually conspiring to overthrow Henry, were coming close to it. They were contacting and aiding

---

35. Ibid., pp. 172–3.
36. Ibid., pp. 173–4.
37. See e.g. Mayer, *Reginald Pole*, p. 67, also *Correspondence of Reginald Pole* 1, pp. 164–5.
38. Pierce, *Margaret Pole*, ch. 6 has a summary of various historians' views as well as her own conclusions.

opponents of Henry's policies who had fled to the Continent, and made themselves the centre of treasonous talk, particularly concerning the Pilgrimage of Grace. Pierce points out that if Henry destroyed the Poles because they were the heirs of the Plantagenets (and thus arguably had a better claim to the throne than Henry himself did) it is strange that it took him a good three decades to do so, and especially that he permitted a marriage alliance between them and the equally dynastically dangerous Duke of Buckingham.[39]

One does not have to agree with Pierce that Henry VIII 'could not have taken any other course of action than the action he took in 1538'[40] to see that neither extreme view will quite do. Cardinal Pole was quite definitely, on any assessment, a traitor – not because he rejected the Royal Supremacy, but because he actively engaged in schemes to overthrow Henry, including support of rebels in England and persuading foreign powers to help.[41] Reginald not only felt obliged to say so, unequivocally, when he concluded that the King's actions were wrong, but believed himself entitled to try to unseat the ruler of England, if it seemed best for England's soul that he should be unseated. Montague and Geoffrey were neither naive nor ignorant, and it would be surprising if they had no opinion on the events which pitted their brother against their king. They may well have been in clandestine contact with Reginald: we will never know what was in the papers they burnt in June 1538. But Pierce's justification of Henry's action rests to a considerable extent on accepting most of Geoffrey Pole's evidence as accurate, which given his circumstances is questionable. Pierce takes the view that Henry Pole's loyalty was a mere 'facade',[42] although such a firmly fixed one that it dictated his letter to his brother in 1536 and his participation in the trials of opponents to the Royal Supremacy. T. F. Mayer,

[39.] Ibid.
[40.] Ibid., p. 170
[41.] Mayer, *Reginald Pole*, ch. 2.
[42.] Pierce, *Margaret Pole*, p. 114.

writing on Lord Montague, certainly considers that the evidence against him is slight, and that he became disaffected, if at all, very late and not very actively.[43] Pierce also acknowledges that Henry's execution of Margaret Pole does look rather like revenge, given that he pardoned the more deeply implicated Gertrude Courtenay.[44]

Henry's position in 1538 was not what it had been in 1509, or 1519. He had his male heir, but he had alienated the Catholic powers of Europe, and did not know whether or when they might start to take the pope's condemnation of him seriously. He had recently faced a major rebellion at home which had used the name of his repudiated daughter Mary, the other major dynastic headache Henry had created for himself. Henry was obviously concerned about the coalescing of these two claims: among the accusations against the Poles was that they had planned the marriage of Reginald Pole to Mary, as joint challengers to Henry VIII. A tunic was produced, alleged (almost certainly falsely) to have been found among Lady Salisbury's possessions, which united the emblems of Mary and of Pole with the arms of England and symbols of the Passion, reminiscent of the 'Five Wounds' banner under which the Pilgrims had marched.[45] The three perceived threats of Mary, the Plantagenet heirs, and religious resistance were literally woven together by the government. A lingering unease in Henry Tudor's attitude to the Duke of Clarence's descendants is indicated by the way that, though not ignored, they were never permitted to be at the centre of politics or power; and by the fact that, though he permitted the family's union with the Buckinghams, he destroyed it along with the Duke of Buckingham two years later. His unease could be pushed into the background in 1509; but by 1538 he had more reason to fear for his throne, and it resurfaced, devastatingly.

Perhaps in the end the Poles were neither traitors nor loyalists. The fact that the Tudors possessed the throne

---

[43.] *Oxford Dictionary of National Biography*, Henry Pole 1492–1539.
[44.] Pierce, *Margaret Pole*, p. 173.
[45.] Ibid., p. 153 and notes.

meant that common sense dictated a practical loyalty to them; but the heirs of the Plantagenets simply did not feel a moral obligation of fealty to Henry Tudor. So when he attacked their family and the Church they believed in, while more or less toeing the line in their actions, the Poles said what they thought behind what they hoped were closed doors.

On 27 May 1541, Margaret of Salisbury was executed in the Tower of London. Why it had not happened two years earlier, and why it happened then, are unclear. It seems to have been done quietly, almost secretively: the two ambassadors' reports which are the only contemporary accounts suggest that relatively few people witnessed it.[46] Margaret reportedly asked those witnessing her death to pray for the King, Queen, Prince Edward and Princess Mary, remembering especially the young woman she had taken care of through such traumatic years. Then 'she was told to make haste and place her neck on the block, which she did'.

There is no mention in these accounts of the colourful story by which Margaret Pole is commemorated in stained glass. It appears in Edward Lord Herbert's 1649 work *Life and Raigne of Henry VIII*:

> The old Lady being brought to the Scaffold (set up in the Tower) was commanded to lay her head on the Block; but she (as a person of great Quality assured mee) refused, saying, So should Traitors do, and I am none: neither did it serve that the Executioner told her it was the fashion; so turning her gray head every way, shee bid him, if he would have her head, to get it as hee could: So that he was constrained to fetch it off slovenly. And thus ended (as our Authors say) the last of the right Line of the Plantagenets.[47]

Historians have adjudged this later version inaccurate. Dom Bede Camm, in his 1904 work on the recently beatified

---

[46.] Spanish and Venetian ambassadors. These accounts are the ones used in Pierce, *Margaret Pole*, pp. 177–8, to which I refer.

[47.] Herbert, E., *The Life and Raigne of King Henry the Eighth*, London 1649, p. 468.

English martyrs, concludes 'I think it will be generally felt that the true story is more in accordance with the calm dignity of the royal martyr than the fictitious one.'[48] The designers of Our Lady and the English Martyrs church clearly disagreed.

Reginald Pole was probably the first person to claim his mother as a martyr: according to his earliest biographer, Beccadelli, he responded to the letter informing him of her death by telling Beccadelli

> Until now I have believed that the lord God has given me the grace to be the son of one of the best and most honoured ladies of England and I have gloried in that and given thanks to his Divine Majesty. But he has wished to honor me more and increase my obligation, for he has also made me the son of a martyr, whom that king, because she was constant in the Catholic faith, has had publicly decapitated, even though she was more than seventy years old and his aunt. Thus he has rewarded the efforts which she took for a long time in raising his daughter. God be praised and thanked.

The cardinal then disappeared into his private oratory for an hour, and came out perfectly composed.[49]

Pole's biographer points out that if the scene occurred, it would have to have been some months after Lady Salisbury's death (since Beccadelli was in Regensburg at the time); letters from the summer of 1539 suggest a more palpably distressed man.[50] But this is Pole's chosen interpretation of the event, and in his speech to Beccadelli it is all there: Margaret's lineage, her son the cardinal, her connection to Mary (one day England's Catholic queen), Henry VIII's tyranny. And yet, apart from her dislike of the English Bible, Margaret's constancy in the Catholic faith does not appear in the charges on which Henry brought about her death. She never refused the Oath of Supremacy or spoke against the

---

48. Camm, *English Martyrs*, vol. 1, p. 53, n. 1.
49. Mayer, *Reginald Pole*, pp. 112–13; (mother and brother saints) letters p. 314.
50. Ibid.

Church of England. Her standing by the young Mary Tudor's side perhaps indicates where her sympathies lay, but she rejected Reginald's defence of such a position when required to do so. She was accorded no trial, so her voice was never heard in court telling us what she did or did not think. The Act of Attainder by which she was condemned to death merely accused her of treason through being in unspecified ways Reginald's 'confederate'; which brings us back again to her son.

That son defended the Catholic faith loudly and controversially; and lived in exile. His mother was never a confessor; and died in England. It is interesting that Reginald Pole (who would one day be an archbishop, but never a martyr) speaks of the 'honour' to him in being the son of a martyr; it is almost as though her 'martyrdom' was vicariously his, while his uncompromising confession was vicariously hers. Reginald might have regarded his mother as a martyr in something like the way that the Holy Innocents qualified as martyrs: not voluntary confessors of the faith, but killed by the enemies of Christ on His account. Bede Camm vehemently concurs with Reginald's view:

> She was to be the victim of his [Henry VIII's] hatred against the Cardinal, and that hatred was a hatred of fidelity to God and his Church. The cause of her death was the vindictive fury of a bad man because his wicked will was thwarted in the working out of its schemes against the Church's faith and unity.[51]

In other words, Margaret's killer was definitely acting out of *odium fidei* ('hatred of the faith'), one of the canonical qualifications for a person to be considered a martyr.

Few of Margaret's relatives were left to survive her. Henry Pole, her grandson, died in the Tower at some point between 1542 and 1553, another child victim of the blood he had inherited. Courtenay survived to be released and given his father's earldom of Devon on Mary I's accession, dying in

---

[51.] Camm, *English Martyrs*, vol. 1, p. 532.

1556.[52] Mary Tudor seems to have remembered her old governess, for a grant she made as queen to Lord Montague's daughters specifically notes Margaret of Salisbury's service to Mary; she was also generous to Margaret's daughter Ursula and her husband Lord Stafford (Buckingham's son).[53] Reginald Pole became Archbishop of Canterbury during Mary I's reign, restoring and reforming the English Catholic Church with considerable success in the short time he was given. He died on 17 November 1558, the same day as the queen. Geoffrey Pole, who had been pardoned and left to support his ten children and wounded conscience as best he could, also died in November 1558.[54] Montague's daughter Catherine died as Countess of Huntingdon in 1576,[55] while two of Geoffrey Pole's sons died in the Tower of London, after nearly a decade's imprisonment on charges of conspiracy against Elizabeth I.[56] So the royal line of the Plantagenets did not quite end in May 1541; rather it faded out of history during the reign of the last Tudor.

Born into the royal house of a nation scarred by civil wars, Margaret Plantagenet died a casualty in the war for England's soul declared by the dynasty which professed itself the healer of old divisions. Her ancestry, for good and ill, shaped her destiny and her character; her son forged his identity out of a rather different conflict. But, ultimately, faith and lineage could not be separated for either of them. However fictitious, there is something vivid and telling about Herbert's story of Margaret's final actions preserved in the stained-glass window. A faithful Catholic was not a traitor to her country, unless both words are first re-defined out of recognition; the last Plantagenet princess need not define herself by any fealty to Henry Tudor.

[52.] Pierce, *Margaret Pole*, p. 181; *Oxford Dictionary of National Biography*, Edward Courtenay 1526–1556.

[53.] Pierce, *Margaret Pole*, pp. 179–80.

[54.] *Oxford Dictionary of National Biography*, Geoffrey Pole, d. 1558.

[55.] Pierce, *Margaret Pole*, pp. 180–1,184 (family tree).

[56.] *Oxford Dictionary of National Biography*, Arthur Pole 1531/2–1570?

Chapter 6

Queen Mary Tudor

Antony Conlon

A recent and very successful film called *Elizabeth* portrayed Mary I as a bitter and twisted woman surrounded by a court of sinister individuals and devoid of compassion or redeeming qualities of any kind. Elizabeth is always portrayed as the heroine whose accession heralded the dawn of a golden age of nearly half a century of prosperity and progress while Mary is the ugly sister whose reign, marked by tyranny and cruelty was mercifully much shorter. Despite so much evidence to the contrary, the myth of the sequence of cruelty combined with the infamous title of 'Bloody Mary' survives. It remains deeply ingrained in the national consciousness. Even apathy and indifference to established religion has not really altered this perception. Repugnance to any deeply held conviction has now replaced the old attitude of righteous outrage as a new reason for reviling her memory and continuing to regard her as a monster of history and inhumanity. Yet this is the Queen of whom the Bishop of Winchester, the Wykehamist scholar John White spoke so movingly at her funeral oration.

> She was never unmindful or uncareful of her promise to her realm. She used singular mercy towards offenders. She used much compassion towards the poor and oppressed. She used clemency among her nobles. She restored more noble houses decayed than ever did prince of this realm, or I pray God ever shall have the like occasion to do hereafter. I verily

believe the poorest creature in all this city feared not God more than she.[1]

For his pains, the Lord Bishop received next day a message from the new Queen that 'for such offences as he committed in his sermon at the funeral of the late queen', he was ordered to keep himself a prisoner in his own house, at the Queen's pleasure.[2] The old order for which the late Queen had stood was never again –apart from a brief period under King James II – to be in favour as it had been during her reign. The direction in which the country was going to be taken would necessarily include the demonizing of her actions and her memory so that in time both her religion and her reign would become synonymous with foreign domination, coercion and repugnant religious excesses. All this would be seen in contrast to the wise and moderate compromise of the Elizabethan settlement that contrived to present a middle way, allegedly drawing upon both the Catholic and the Calvinist traditions and capable of satisfying all but fanatics and traitors. Adherence to Catholicism would be regarded as a crime, in many cases ultimately punishable by death. Whereas the Protestant victims of the religious policy of Mary's government would be remembered as national martyrs, those executed under Elizabeth would be portrayed as unpatriotic traitors.

Seen from the perspective of objective study of the known details, there can be little doubt that Mary's life was tragic. She grew up the only surviving child of her parents, her father's presumed heir and beloved daughter, enjoying all the benefits of a classical renaissance education. At an age when she might have expected to crown her intellectual and physical attributes with marriage to a prince of equal status, she became a pawn in his political intrigues and shifting alliances and then was cruelly degraded of status and expectation by the estrangement of her parents and the advent of

[1.] Strype, J., *Ecclesiastical Memorials*, vol. III, pt. 2, pp. 546ff.
[2.] *Acts of the Privy Council, Philip & Mary*, vol. VI, p. 141.

rivals for his attention, not only to her mother's and her place in the affection of the King, but also of a rival princess. The process by which Henry divested himself first of his wife, and then of the natural claims of fatherly affection for his only daughter is fairly well known. Its political and religious consequences have shaped the history of this nation. Perhaps too, we should be evaluating the immediate personal affect it had on the Princess Mary. In an age that is increasingly familiar with the implications of parental divorce and paternal rejection on vulnerable young teenagers, we can appreciate the psychological effects of the divorce on Mary. It is asking a great deal that a girl brought up in the full awareness and expectation of inheriting the mantle of royalty should adjust easily to the complete reversal of that destiny, when, not only is she no longer heir or even princess, but she has lost even the right to the natural bond that should exist between parent and child. The personal and political uncertainty of this period of her life left its mark upon her. The father she adored turned into a tyrant whose policies and appetites indiscriminately ended the lives and careers of those closest to him and those who sought to serve him. The usurper of Queen Catherine's position was to fall victim herself to his cruel indifference to ties of blood or relationship when once they stood in his way. By the time of her father's death, the scene was well and truly set for a major struggle for power in the land and all that Henry had sought to do to make the throne secure was now in jeopardy with a weak child of nine succeeding and two women to follow, both unmarried, of different religious persuasions and having had their legitimacy questioned and impugned publicly both in England and in Europe generally.

As was both right and legitimate by royal and canonical custom of the age, Mary could, and did, accept happily the position of her younger brother as immediate heir after her father. His accession in 1547 and his reign of six years found her both loving and dutiful towards her brother, save in the one area where she could not follow him, the repudiation of Catholicism. She even pleaded that the laws against that religion enacted in his minority went far beyond what the late King had done or desired and by standards of international law at the time were illegal. His bequest for Masses to be said for his soul would not indicate a repudiation of the Catholic notion of the Mass as the Prayer Book of his son envisaged. Mary's recorded statements show this while her letters indicate the extent to which she believed that Edward was greatly influenced or dominated by his Seymour uncle, Somerset, and the Earl of Warwick (soon created Duke of Northumberland and Lord Protector) in this as in other matters. Her personal audiences with the young King occasionally ended with both of them in tears, she pleading love and respect for him but inability to go against her conscience, and he expressing no desire to harm or obstruct her in any way.

We shall never know how Edward would eventually have altered or improved the situation when old enough to act independently. By 1552 he was already beginning that slow decline that would lead to his death. It would appear that from at least six months into King Edward's final illness, Northumberland laid plans to annul the will of King Henry VIII and alter the succession the moment Edward died. In May of 1553 his fourth son married Lady Jane Grey, granddaughter of Henry VIII's sister Mary by her second marriage to Charles Brandon, Duke of Suffolk. It is known that Edward was willing to exclude both Mary and Elizabeth as illegitimate and likely to marry Catholic husbands, in favour of the assuredly Protestant line of the Suffolk heirs. On 6 July, King Edward died and Northumberland persuaded the Council to sign a document repudiating Mary and acknowledging Lady Jane as rightful Queen.

Jane's reign – if we may call it that – lasted but nine days. It is an extraordinary tribute both to the popularity and courage of Mary that, against all the odds, the rebellion against her ended so soon with hardly a skirmish. Even John Foxe, Mary's bitterest enemy, allows that her popularity was a decisive factor. 'God so turned the hearts of the people to her, and against the Council, that she overcame them without bloodshed, notwithstanding there was made great expedition against her both by sea and land.'[3] Few people supported the traitors and once the remainder of the Council, who had been persuaded by Northumberland to go along with him, saw that defeat was inevitable, they rushed to join Mary as soon as he left the Tower to confront Mary and her troops, now heading towards the capital from Suffolk.

The proclamation of Mary as Queen was rapturously received in the capital. A contemporary writer says, 'Great was the triumph here at London; for my part I never saw the like, and by the report of others, the like was never seen.'[4] On her entry into the City on 3 August, shouts of joy from the thousands assembled to greet her were heard on all sides. One aspect of it however could not have failed to give cause for thought to the beholders. Behind the Queen, in place of honour, rode her half-sister. Elizabeth had stayed inactive during the rebellion, cautiously or cunningly waiting to see which side would emerge victorious. The visual contrast between this elegant, tall, pale-complexioned redhead of twenty and the visibly care-worn face of the thirty-seven-year-old Mary, already prematurely aged by illness, sorrow and anxiety, could not have been more pronounced. For the moment, justice and right had prevailed over treason and treachery and with the exception of the extreme Protestants there was almost universal satisfaction. There was virtually no sympathy for the vanquished conspirators. It should be noted however, in the face of those who claim cruelty and vindictiveness as characteristics of Mary, that she exercised the maximum degree of clemency possible for a sovereign in those circumstances and times. Of the twenty-seven persons listed as prime suspects, she struck out sixteen. These were again reduced to seven. Of these all were found guilty and sentenced to death. The Queen again intervened and only three,

[3.] *Acts and Monuments*, vol. VI, p. 388.
[4.] Quoted from a contemporary source in J. M. Stone, *Mary the First, Queen of England*, London, 1901.

Northumberland, Sir John Gates and Sir Thomas Palmer were executed. She was even disposed to pardon these, but the Emperor Charles V insisted they should be executed. He also urged the Queen to order the execution of Jane Grey but Mary steadfastly refused to do so. If we consider the reprisals following the Pilgrimage of Grace in Henry's reign and those after the Prayer Book Risings in Edward's reign, Mary's clemency is all the more remarkable. It was the opinion of the Emperor and others that she gained little by it and that in fact it paved the way for further outbreaks of rebellion. They were to be proved correct.

For a description of Mary at this time, it is worth considering that of the Venetian Ambassador – an unbiased observer of the reign. He describes her as 'In appearance, very grave and seemly, and never to be loathed for ugliness, even at her present age.'[5] When speaking, her voice commanded attention and could be heard from far off. But her eyes were her most arresting feature. Piercing, they commanded respect and fear in all upon whom she fixed her gaze. Her nearsightedness obliged her to hold close to her face whatever she needed to read. Her well-formed face was marred by wrinkles caused more by anxieties than by age. But whatever her physical shortcomings, her mental endowments were vast. Nothing was too complex for her grasp and her gift of languages was highly praised. The intelligence of her replies in Latin, surprised everyone.[6]

In considering the various factors that influenced the progress and policy of Mary's reign, there are a number that stand out as of overriding importance. She was the first English Queen-Regnant. There were therefore no precedents that could be followed. It was both expected and anticipated of her that she should soon marry and that her husband and not she should reign as well as rule. Her role would then change into that of the mother of an heir. In the important question of political advice, with the exception of

---

5. Calendar of State Papers, vol. VI, pt II, p. 1054.
6. Ibid.

Bishop Stephen Gardiner who was released from the Tower and made Lord Chancellor, her Council had capable individuals from the past but in some cases could hardly be considered loyal. Most of her advisers had been implicated in the rebellion against her. How much could they be trusted in the future? The religious upheavals, first under Henry and then more radically under Edward, had sown both confusion and division throughout the country. Particularly in London and in parts of Essex there were many extreme Protestants, some of them of the Anabaptist persuasion. Lutherans, Calvinists and Catholics regarded these latter as utter heretics and felons worthy only of condemnation and burning.

Mary faced serious financial shortages. Good money was scarce. Revenues were mortgaged for years ahead to repay existing debts and the policies of both Henry and Edward had been financially ruinous. Queen Mary was to discover that her precarious finances would be stretched beyond their limits. Much alienation of Crown and monastic land had diminished the Crown's potential for raising subsidies. In the past a levy on the Church could produce instant cash. This was no longer possible.

Abroad, the hostility of the French King was a constant and serious threat to the stability of Mary's government. His enmity with Spain automatically would include Mary and the plots and intrigues of the French Ambassador would undermine and undo a great deal of any of the good that Mary sought for her people. She looked to the Emperor principally for support. Even in this respect she was betrayed. The Emperor Charles, her cousin, from whom she sought advice above all others, was content to use her as one more sphere of influence in the vast patchwork of European and New World territories over which he reigned. Both he and his son Philip were to involve Mary in a costly and unpopular war out of which she gained nothing and her reputation suffered. She would come to be seen as less of an English Queen than a Spanish one.

Xenophobia – especially against the Spaniards – was rife

among the population in the southeast. The marriage of Henry VIII to Catherine of Aragon had been a most popular event at that time. That had been over forty years earlier and much had changed since then. Finally, the factor that ultimately led to the final demise of Mary's political potential was her infertility, once it became accepted. Her ailing health made it clear that she would not survive for long and would leave no heir to continue what she had begun. This was to be Elizabeth's ultimate ace in the political game that she played throughout the reign. Taking these factors into account, they might have been overcome by cunning and subterfuge but this was not part of Mary's way of ruling. However, former judgements of Mary as ill-equipped to reign or lacking in ability and wisdom are contentious to say the least. Her most recent biographer represents her much more fairly and broadly.[7] Her mother Queen Catherine was the daughter of Isabella of Castille, a ruler in her own right. Both Catherine and Henry – before his fatal entanglement with Anne Boleyn – had educated Mary to the highest level of renaissance learning and that had included classical political theory as well as religious writings. It was not lack of determination and decisiveness but shortness of time and a succession of unfortunate circumstances which robbed Mary of the fruits of many initiatives which she never lived long enough to follow through.

Mary's first priority was the return of her realms to the obedience of the Roman pontiff. By English law, this could only be achieved by Act of Parliament. Early attempts to restore Catholic worship were passed without debate in the Lords but in the Commons there was some dissent. There was disquiet on the part of many that the repealing of the Act that dissolved Henry's first marriage implicitly restored papal jurisdiction and that the repeal of the Act of Supremacy would mean the restitution of seized church property. Scholarly analysis of Mary's parliaments makes it absolutely clear that religious dissent played a very little part

[7.] Richards, Judith, M., *Mary Tudor.*

in opposition to legislation to restore the Catholic religion. It was always concern that church property might have to be restored by its new owners that caused the members to hesitate on religious restoration.[8] Within days Mary went in person and prorogued her first parliament. By way of compromise, two new bills were framed, reversing the divorce but without mentioning the pope. The second bill aimed at re-establishing religion as it had been in the last years of King Henry with no restitution required. Despite the presence of a majority of friends of the reformed religion in the House of Commons the bills were passed after two days' debate and without a division. Mary had achieved a partial restoration.

The most urgent matter before the Queen and the government was her marriage. The idea of a foreign marriage was less than appealing to her subjects – as the Speaker of her first Parliament less than tactfully reminded her – and to many of her advisers. In a true display of Tudor directness she thanked him for his advice but reminded him that 'The English Parliament has not been wont to use such language to its sovereigns, and when private persons on such matters suit their own tastes, sovereigns may reasonably be allowed to choose whom they prefer.'[9]

The Emperor Charles V proposed his twenty-eight-year-old son as a husband for the Queen. The prospect must have pleased Mary. She would marry the son of the one ruler who had stood by her through all the years of her tribulation and was also, the grandson of her mother's sister. But it would be wrong to say that she accepted him without any hesitation. She initially married out of duty because it seemed the proper thing for a Queen Regnant to do. Charles however saw in the marriage an ideal way to link England to his continental string of allied states and territories, while Philip, who idolized his father, wished only to do his bidding at all

[8]. Loach, Jennifer, *Parliament and Crown in the Reign of Mary Tudor*, pp. 74–8.
[9]. Stone, op. cit., p. 262.

costs. The notion that he loved the Queen has never been suggested as a reason for or a consequence of this marriage. He would do his duty and support his father. Mary, on the other hand braved unpopularity and danger in embracing this union. By 31 October Mary had made up her mind. Kneeling in a room before the Blessed Sacrament exposed, she pledged to Renard, the Imperial Ambassador, that she would marry no other person but Philip. It is the almost unanimous opinion of biographers favourable to Mary that this decision cost her the affection and loyalty of her subjects. That said, her decision was not one of a feeble mind or without any justification. First, it shows a determination that in other Tudors is applauded. The Venetian Ambassador – more objective than either his French or Imperial counterparts – described Mary at this time as 'brave and valiant, unlike other timid and spiritless women, but so courageous and resolute that neither in adversity nor peril did she ever display or commit an act of cowardice or pusillanimity ... (She) kept a wonderful grandeur and dignity ... the dignity of a sovereign'.[10]

The negotiations between the Emperor and the English Court regarding the status and position of Philip as the Queen's Consort, were both protracted and precise. Philip and she would use each other's style and title but within her realms his power would be limited. The only advantage to him and his father would be the geographical position of England, near the Low Countries and the hope that the marriage would provide an heir.

Meanwhile as news of the inevitability of the marriage became public, the French Ambassador intrigued with certain malcontents and notably with Edward Courtenay to raise a rebellion against the coming of the Spanish. Evidence shows that Elizabeth was not only informed of this but seems to have played her usual game of tacit support with no direct action. The most incredible and outrageous tales were put about to rouse the people and to stir up as much

---

[10.] Calendar of State Papers, *Venetian,* vol. VI, pt II, p. 1055.

discontent and xenophobia as possible. Wyatt, aided by the
Duke of Suffolk, father of Lady Jane Grey, and supporters of
Courtenay from Devon were jointly to raise the standard of
rebellion as soon as it was known that the Prince of Spain
was coming.

On 26 January, 1554, Wyatt marched on London with an
army of 15,000, mostly Kentishmen. As he marched on
towards the City, he daily increased his following. Mary
stayed at Whitehall from which she had access to
Westminster. On 1 February, with Wyatt's forces fast
approaching, a meeting was held in the Guildhall to discuss
what was to be done. The Queen addressed her Council in
words that showed not only her courage and clarity of mind
but also her ability to evoke loyalty against all odds. The full
text is found in Foxe, *Acts and Monuments*.[11] Reminding
them of her lawful descent and royalty and their duty to her
she repudiated all notion of a marriage designed to enslave
them and declared that she would rather live and die a virgin
than to marry with any other thought or design than their
welfare, and concluded with these words, 'And now good
subjects, pluck up your hearts, and like true men stand fast
against these rebels, both our enemies and yours, and fear
them not, for I assure you I fear them nothing at all.'[12] 'God
save Queen Mary', they cheered, and 20,000 of them
enrolled to defend the City. Meanwhile, Wyatt and his rebels
eventually managed a crossing of the river at Kingston and
by 7 February, were at the City gates. At Ludgate, he
demanded of Lord William Howard, the commander of the
Queen's forces that he be admitted. To which the
Commander replied, 'Avaunt, traitor, thou shalt not come in
here!'[13] By evening of the next day, being Ash Wednesday,
Wyatt was defeated and a prisoner.

Mary was once again victorious, but the extraordinary
clemency she exhibited at the beginning of her reign could
not be repeated if she was to remove the curse of rebellion

[11.] Vol. VI, p. 411.
[12.] Vol. VI, p. 414.
[13.] Stone, op. cit., p. 290.

from her kingdom. She was advised to act within the remit of normal state punishment of traitors and rebels and their associates and did so. About four hundred of those arraigned were pardoned, but both Lady Jane Grey and her husband were to be included among those of the sixty most prominent figures in the rebellion to be executed. Mary has been vilified much on account of the deaths of these two young people. But her contemporaries do not see it in those terms.[14] It was Foxe who began the calumny that would later become the established view on Mary's vindictive cruelty. Lady Jane herself, at her execution, acknowledged her guilt and asked pardon of the Queen. Referring to Mary's known clemency, the Venetian Ambassador wrote of her in 1554; 'for although she has many enemies, and though so many of them were by law condemned to death, yet had the executions depended solely on her Majesty's will, not one of them perhaps would have been enforced; but deferring to her Council in everything, she in this matter likewise complied with the wishes of others, rather than her own'.[15] While in the Tower, Wyatt confessed to the involvement of Elizabeth in the plot. She had already been requested by the Queen to attend at Court and after a fortnight had still delayed in coming. Mary sent again for her, commenting that during her father's reign none would delay in coming. Escorted by several of her officials and at Mary's request treated with courtesy and respect, Elizabeth made as much difficulty as she could. Feigning or actually suffering from illness she and her escort took two weeks to accomplish a journey that would normally have taken no more than two days. She used her entry into London, from Highgate to maximum effect, riding in the Queen's litter, the covers open so that she could be seen in her white dress. She was accommodated in the Palace of Westminster but the Queen declined to see her.

During the April session of Parliament, the Royal Marriage

---

14. Stone, op. cit., pp. 293f.
15. Quoted in Stone, op. cit., p. 319.

Bill was discussed and passed unanimously by both Houses. The Queen dissolved Parliament in person, making a speech that was frequently interrupted by cheers and acclamations. Lords and Commons assured her that the Prince of Spain would be welcomed by a dutiful and affectionate people.[16]

Her Council could not advise what to do with Elizabeth. There was no agreement. Some were secretly on her side while others said she should be given short shrift. Asking each of them in turn if they would undertake her custody and finding none willing to do so, the Queen finally issued a warrant for her committal to the Tower. Needless to say Elizabeth was more than frightened by the prospect that now loomed before her. The story of her entry to the Tower has become one of the great scenes of the Elizabethan legend. Nevertheless her confinement there was as comfortable as was possible under the circumstances. She continued to deny all knowledge of the plot and of the letters written by her. Mary believed she was guilty but refused to see her convicted on the evidence of letters written in cypher that could be forged. Years later, Elizabeth herself did not show such scruples in agreeing to the conviction of her cousin Mary Stuart on letters denied by her. Eventually released, Elizabeth was allowed to travel to Woodstock, under house arrest, to be guarded by Sir Henry Bedingfield.

Now in the strongest possible position following the defeat of Wyatt's uprising, the Queen was able to conclude the final details for her betrothal and the coming of Philip to England. The Prince travelled from Valladolid on 4 May, accompanied by 4,000 picked troops and a concourse of the nobility of Spain together with their wives and attendants. He had been advised by the Imperial Ambassador to travel simply, but Philip was at pains to impress and gain the respect of the English people by the power and wealth of his position. In appearance, the Venetian Ambassador describes him as of medium height, well-proportioned and agile. His hair and complexion was entirely Flemish, being fair but in

16. Lingard, *History of England,* vol. V, p. 218.

manners and outlook he was a Spaniard.[17] He was now
twenty-seven and about to embark on his second marriage.

By 20 July, Philip arrived at Southampton, while Mary,
with her entire Court had travelled to Winchester, staying at
the Bishop's palace. The Prince made a favourable impres-
sion among the English, offending his own suite by insisting
on being served and accompanied by English gentlemen.
Invested with the Garter on behalf of the Queen by the Earl
of Arundel, he made a stately progress towards Winchester,
arriving on 25 July. The cavalcade was magnificent though
spoilt by a demonstration of the peculiarity of an English
summer; it rained incessantly. With due solemnity and pomp
the Prince was conducted to the Queen who – it is recorded
– received him lovingly and joyfully.[18] They talked together
for up to two hours.

The marriage was fixed for 25 July, the Feast of St James,
Patron of Spain. The cathedral, we are told, was entirely
lined with arras and cloth of gold. The royal pair looked
spectacular, Philip in white and gold, ornamented with
pearls and other gems and wearing the collars of the Garter
and the Golden Fleece, Mary also in white and gold, studded
with diamonds. A magnificent banquet followed the ceremony. It seemed that the Court were at least content with
the Prince. The real test would be the entry into London.

This took place on 18 of August. The usual pageants and
triumphal arches were set up but it would seem that the
greeting was less than warm though there were appropriate
cries of 'God save your Graces'. There is a suggestion of
such from a letter of the Imperial Ambassador who noticed
the difference the second time the King visited the City in
September.[19] If the popularity of Philip increased, that of his
Spanish attendants and guards did not. Though they were
few in number, it was claimed that they were everywhere.
Their apparent prosperity was also a source of irritation to

[17.] Stone, op. cit., p. 316f.
[18.] Stone, op. cit., p. 324.
[19.] Stone, op. cit., p. 329.

the Londoners. Throughout Philip's one-year stay, there were constant brawls and incidents that nobody could prevent or control. Even the fact that both he and his retinue paid their own expenses was not enough to assuage the annoyance of the Londoners who charged exorbitant prices for everything.

The Court settled down to the new situation with Philip increasingly being involved in matters of state. It was considered natural that as the King he should be advised and consulted. From the announcement in September that the Queen was pregnant, though she continued her official duties, he took on more. The story of the pregnancy which turned out not to be so but instead the early signs of a critical turn in the health of the Queen, is familiar. During the time of her supposed pregnancy, with the support of Philip, she embarked with Parliament upon that programme of reconciliation with Rome and restoration of Catholicism with which her reign is closely associated. The success or failure of that endeavour is still the subject of study and research. New light leading to a more positive conclusion has been shed by the work of Eamon Duffy in his masterly book *The Stripping of the Altars.* The evidence of parish and diocesan records show a marked desire to restore and to replace what had been destroyed.[20] It would seem that depleted funds and alienation of much property were both major difficulties against which they had to labour. Coupled with the policy of restoration is the vexed question of the burning of heretics. The memory of this enforcement of orthodoxy by penal sanction, more than anything else in her reign, has indelibly blotted her reputation.

The arrival of Cardinal Pole, the Papal Legate, had been delayed deliberately by the Emperor, who feared his opposition to the marriage of Mary and Philip. In November of this year of 1554, Pole finally arrived in England. On 28 November he came before Parliament and explained his commission to reconcile the country with Rome. Two days

[20.] Cfr. op. cit., pp. 524ff.

later, at their request, with both Houses kneeling before him, he pronounced pardon. During December, Parliament repealed the remaining legislation against the papal jurisdiction in England and the pope in return validated and legitimized all the Sacraments given and received during the time of schism. Philip expected a proposal for him to be crowned King but none came. Coupled with the new legislation was a revival of the statutes for the trial and execution of heretics. How this bill was brought into Parliament is unclear but it was seen as a purely procedural change, the death penalty for heresy having been of long standing. The bill was passed unanimously. A nineteenth-century writer, Reeves, in his *History of English Law,* says of the policy that it was, 'the act of the crown, with the authority of Parliament and the assent of the council'.[21] The same author notes that it was opposed by the Emperor, by the Papal Legate and by Philip's confessor and represented a policy of statecraft to which the Queen yielded rather than initiated. That said, burning was considered appropriate in these times as a just punishment for heresy. Luther, Calvin, Knox, Melanchton, Bullinger and Farel, all prominent Reformation leaders, wrote in approval of it and on occasions used it. Cranmer sentenced and handed over a number of people to be burnt at Smithfield. It is worth remembering that death for religious dissent continued to be a feature of the government of these islands until well into the late seventeenth century. It is to Foxe and his *Acts and Monuments*, a work that made a penniless man a fortune, that we owe most of the detail that has been credited ever since regarding details of the burnings of Mary's reign. Later writers have exposed literally hundreds of lies and inaccuracies in his work, making one doubt its veracity in a great many instances.[22] The saying arose in later times that 'Many who were burned in the reign of Queen Mary drank sack in the reign of Queen Elizabeth.'

Many of those who suffered were among the less

[21.] Op. cit., vol. III, p. 560, note.
[22.] Cfr. Stone, op. cit., pp. 365ff.

educated and more confused of the population. These were people who had been exposed to nearly twenty years of religious confusion and argument. It was not to be wondered at that many of them had been led astray. However, the obstinacy and contempt for the law and for the Queen and government was an aspect that gave an altogether more serious character to their crimes. Attempts – seen as browbeating by Foxe – were made over and over again to persuade them out of their heresy. That the views of many of them counted for treason as understood at the time, is clear from their statements and their vitriolic responses to reasoned argument. But it is also true that the bishops who judged them had themselves taught and defended heresy in King Henry's time and their arguments to the dissidents were weakened by this fact.

The reunion with Rome was something of a compromise because it had only been accomplished by the understanding that no seized church property would be restored. But to Mary it represented a major triumph after years of affliction. Her belief that she was pregnant seemed the sign of divine favour and would ensure the continuity of her religious restoration. But there were those among her people and within her own Court who saw things differently. Rumours and libels abounded. Every kind of story was believed, the more outlandish, the better. From the Continent came pamphlets flooding from the pens of those disaffected and fled. The shrillness, sedition and malice of all of these writings, gradually compelled a change in Mary towards their writers. At home, outspoken and treasonable statements were being multiplied among those who rejected the Queen's religion. New libels against Mary were thrown into the streets every few days, stirring up fears and encouraging rebellion. Religious figures of dissent played their part in fomenting the disorder and attacking the Queen's religion. A notable figure in this regard was John Hooper, Bishop of Worcester, who regularly preached on the absurdity of the Real Presence. Finally brought to trial he refused all accommodation and was condemned to be burned. His burning in

February 1555 was conducted in the most appalling manner and took much longer than normal. His sympathizers saw it as a crime against God while most at that time saw it as punishment long overdue. The records contain very little about Mary's attitude to the death of Hooper and others at this time. One statement, written with her own hand, makes it clear that she saw the policy as a temporary measure only, to be carried out judiciously and not vindictively or with hesitation.

> Touching the punishment of heretics, I believe it would be well to inflict punishment at this beginning, without much cruelty or passion, but without however omitting to do such justice on those who choose by their false doctrines to deceive simple persons, that the people may clearly comprehend that they have not been condemned without just cause, whereby others will be brought to know the truth, and will beware of letting themselves be induced to relapse into such new and false opinions.[23]

Those sentenced and executed were seen to be as much traitors as heretics and as such merited the death penalty. The burnings of Bishops Latimer and Ridley in autumn 1555 as well as of Archbishop Cranmer five months later, had been delayed in the hope of some change of heart. None came, though the latter did sign several recantations that he later rejected. High profile burnings of this kind were both remarked and written of to add to the general store of hostile criticism of the government. Of the 272 alleged persons burned for heresy in Queen Mary's reign, most either spoke or behaved in a manner that was treasonable, according to the laws and statutes of that time. Most were of the artisan class and according to Foxe, their deaths constantly evoked the sympathy of those who witnessed them. It is customary to claim that the burnings turned most of her subjects against Mary and finally lost her their affection. This must be considered questionable in the light of

---

[23.] Quoted in, Loades, D., *The Reign of Mary Tudor,* p. 330.

known attitudes to capital punishment at the time and its continued frequent use in England until the eighteenth century. There is a contemporary diary of a London merchant that frequently mentions and chronicles the progress of the Catholic restoration and the burning of heretics.[24] Nowhere does he ever express and regret for the victims but simply records the fact of their executions. On the other hand, he records in great detail and with enthusiasm the revival of Catholic customs.

Before long, except among the poor of the country, it is claimed by historians that Mary's popularity was declining. If true, it may have had as much to do with the disastrous loss of Calais or simply reflect the sense that her life was drawing to a close and people started to look to Elizabeth as the future. There is ample written evidence of Mary's charity and kindness to those in need, but none of this mattered to those for whom her religion and her marriage were odious.[25] A new threat appeared in the form of impostors claiming to be the dead King Edward VI. Measures to deal with this, and the proliferation of heretical texts and scurrilous writings, only increased the fanaticism of the Queen's enemies. Mary's hoped-for child proved to be a cruel delusion. As the nine months of her pregnancy passed and there was still no sign of labour, the truth became known. There would be no birth at this time. Throughout the summer of 1555, one of the worst ever remembered, for cold, rain and lack of sunlight, the Queen bravely struggled on, her hopes of motherhood dashed. By August, Philip was gone, needed by his father to help him conduct a war with the French and incidentally with the new Pope, Paul IV an ally of the French. The latter, aged eighty, displayed the vigour of a man of forty and had two known objectives, the annihilation of heretics and the humiliation of Philip of Spain. Mary was now obliged to see her husband regarded as an enemy by the Sovereign Pontiff. The death of Stephen Gardiner, in November,

---

[24.] *The Diary of Henry Machyn*, Camden Society, 1885.
[25.] Cfr. Stone, op. cit., pp. 352ff.

deprived her of a valued counsellor and she now turned more and more to Cardinal Pole for advice and support in the absence of her husband.

She devoted herself throughout 1556 to the government of the nation while hearing constantly of how her husband, now installed in Brussels, was enjoying himself after the fashion of young princes of the day. His letters to her became more and more businesslike and less personal. She continued to write to him expressing her desire for his return; he continued to delay while at the same time he sought to involve her in his Continental war. He wanted to be crowned King but Mary could not persuade Parliament to agree. Had she been of a more ruthless stamp she might have forced the issue. In the Netherlands, an integral part of Philip's dominions, the religious situation was no less tense than in England. There had been 1,300 executions in a period of eighteen months. The war with France was going badly and Philip was desperate for both money and troops and increasingly he saw that the best way to obtain both was to come in person to England. His father, the Emperor, was now so ill and so weak that he could barely speak or stand upright. He was worn out with ruling a vast area and about to divest himself of every trace of his Imperial and Regal status in order to retire and die in peace. At the same time Philip had changed and become more serious and sombre than ever. The burden of ruling was taking its toll even on him. The summer of 1556 in England, in stark contrast to that of the preceding year, was unbearably hot and crops failed from the drought that gripped the country. For Mary, only her strong faith can have sustained her during these times. There is plenty of evidence that at least on the religious front, Catholicism was not only gaining ground but also repairing the damage of the previous reign. Most of this evidence is to be found in parish records and in diplomatic and state papers. Similarly, recent research on Cardinal Pole has likewise provided positive details of just how much was achieved in religious terms against incredible odds and poor finances.[26]

[26.] Mayer, Thomas F., *Reginald Pole, Prince & Prophet,* pp. 220–330.

By 1557, Mary was trying to raise money for Philip in every way that she could and making preparations for war with France. The reward was to be a visit from her husband. He arrived in March of this year and they rode in through London attended by nobles, the Lord Mayor and Aldermen. The Queen, despite her anxieties and her woes presented her usual spirit of indomitable courage and dignity. But increasingly her childlessness weighed upon her mind. All that she was doing and had done would come to nought unless she could have an heir. Desire for change was in the air and all about her courtiers and those in the know were beginning to look and think ahead. There were the usual plots and this was coupled with lack of funds to meet her expenses. In the background was the still young and attractive Elizabeth, quietly but confidently waiting in the wings to replace her ill and ageing half-sister. Even Philip who arrived with his current mistress in tow did little to comfort the Queen. On 7 June England declared war on France – a decision that was to lead to the loss of Calais, England's last foothold on the Continental mainland. By 6 July, Philip was gone again, this time never to return. Cardinal Pole, now Archbishop of Canterbury, was seen to be himself visibly failing. He could no longer serve in any true sense as a help or adviser to Mary. Even the pope had turned against him and the illness that ultimately caused his death was already upon him. In the autumn, Mary began again to believe that she was pregnant but kept quiet for some time until certain of the fact. It was unfortunately a phantom pregnancy and the swelling was in fact nothing more than the tumour from which she would eventually die. At the time the thought of being pregnant gave her hope and strength for the last time, though she took a decision to write her will.

By the spring of 1558 it was widely know that there would again be no birth. Further worries for Mary came with the publication of Knox's *First Blast of the Trumpet Against the Monstrous Regiment of Women*, a diatribe aimed at the female rulers of the day. As Mary's health declined Philip began to consider the best way forward and to ask Mary to arrange Elizabeth's marriage to a candidate of his choice. Mary was not well enough to consider this but on advice from Philip designated Elizabeth as her heir, an action that must surely have cost her more than anything else she had had to do in her life. On 17 November Mass was said in her bedchamber and she answered the responses throughout. She prayed for forgiveness and mercy and as the Mass ended lapsed into unconsciousness, from which she never emerged. The story of how Elizabeth received the news at Hatfield of Mary's death and her accession as Queen has now passed into legend. She is said to have sunk to her knees, declaring 'This is the Lord's doing and it is marvellous in our eyes.'

Chapter 7

St Margaret Clitherow

Josephine Robinson

The 'golden age' of Queen Elizabeth I was a leaden age for many of her subjects. England was a police state, without a police force. A widespread network of spies rendered individual life a hazard for all who did not obey the requirements of the Crown in many particulars. Catholics suffered, when their long-held and historic beliefs were denied by the Queen and her officers of state so that on one Sunday in 1559, priests said Mass, essentially as it had been said in this country since the arrival of St Augustine in AD 597, and on the following Sunday in 1559, it was proscribed and priests had instead to lead communion services which were a parodic version of the sacrifice of the Mass, in which there was no sacrifice. It was only a memorial of the Last Supper, not a sacramental actuation of the sacrifice of Christ on the Cross. Indeed, in 1563, Masses were described in Article 37 of the Thirty-Nine Articles as 'blasphemous fables'.

Margaret Clitherow was born in York, in the middle fifties of the sixteenth century, a few years before this decree was carried out. Her father Thomas Middleton was a 'wax chandler' and Sheriff of York (1564–5). The family had been prosperous, but as a candlemaker, he had suffered financially from the various religious upheavals during his lifetime. Henry VIII's seminal break with Rome which made the King head of the Church on earth, as well as head of the state, would not initially have affected his business, which involved the use of candles in church, since devotion to the saints, for instance, still flourished. There were, however, voices being raised against these practices, which Henry had hitherto upheld, by 'forward-looking' clerics. The King increasingly looked to the reformer, Cranmer, the future Archbishop of Canterbury, and during his royal progress through Yorkshire in 1541, saw that many of the traditional devotions were still being enthusiastically used, even though they had been discouraged.

Middleton began to lose business as reformist attitudes were imposed. When the young Edward VI succeeded to the throne, his regents as overt Protestants set about the re-ordering of churches, which were deprived of everything that made them sacred and, at the same time, engaging. The restoration of Catholic worship (involving, no doubt, the use of many candles) during the four years of Queen Mary's reign, was followed and again forbidden by the accession of Queen Elizabeth.

Lay people did not take easily to sudden changes in the way their churches looked, or the way they were invited to worship. The church had long been the centre of the community, which had given expression to the beliefs, sorrow and joys of the people. By the time of Margaret's birth, they had suffered repeated changes. No doubt, some people became cynical about Government prescriptions in the field of religion, and some were appalled. It is reported that the elderly and sick Thomas Middleton complained bitterly about the effect of religious changes on his business and it may be that this complaint covered real distress over their effect on the life of the Church he had known since childhood. As his craft was candle making, he had been involved in the Nativity scenes in the Corpus Christi plays. It may be that little Margaret had seen with awe the star of Bethlehem, signified by a great candle proudly provided by her father, before the plays were forbidden by the new authorities. He died in 1567: the plays were forbidden a few years later.

Marriage in sixteenth-century England was a pragmatic affair. Four months later, Margaret's mother, Jane, married again. Her husband was a bright, ambitious younger man and she was a woman of property, owning the house her husband had left her. Henry May, her new husband was described locally as 'a foreigner', 'a southerner', and 'an adventurer'. He was also, he claimed, a 'convinced Protestant'. He was helped by his new wife's position, since she was well established in the town, and he became a churchwarden – one of those volunteers who were central to reporting the way in which services were performed, marking whether the clergy were still harking back to old ways, and also to observing who attended church, as all were bound to do, and who did not. Non-attenders were fined. It was a brilliant touch that the humble figure of the church-warden, respected, but essentially homely, known to all the locals, became the kingpin of government intelligence in the community. It was a voluntary job, but its importance led certainly to eminence and some may well have received rewards on the quiet. This position was a stepping stone to influence in the town and a year or so later, Henry May became a sheriff, with responsibilities over aspects of the administration of criminal law.

When Margaret was in her teens, a marriage was arranged for her to a widower of thirty-one, a farmer who owned his land and raised and butchered his own stock for sale. His first wife had died, leaving two boys, one about three years old and the other still a baby. John Clitherow accepted the new religious dispensation as Margaret did. His brother, however, was a Catholic priest.

Margaret was described as a beautiful girl, with a sharp and ready wit, cheerful, warm and generous. She worked hard without resentment, running the household, which would have included servants and apprentices living with the family and looking after her two stepchildren. The ground floor of the house in the Shambles, in York, which John Clitherow owned, was the shop where the meat was sold and Margaret would have had to run it, when John was away on business trips, or seeing to the flocks he grazed on his estate some miles from the city. All the butchers in York, some sixty around this time, were gathered in the Shambles, where they lived as well as having their shops. It must have created a lively community with much rivalry, but shared interests as well.

Her first child was a boy, called Henry, after Henry May, the baby's godfather and Margaret's stepfather. He was baptized at the Church of the Holy Trinity. Margaret's family life was happy and their prosperity allowed them to take part in the social life of the city and its surrounding countryside, attending dinners and banquets, to which Margaret would sometimes go alone, if her husband was away on business. He trusted her entirely and was happy for her to go to such gatherings even if he could not go.

Her path to conversion was necessarily secret. We do not know exactly how it came about, but the influence of friends is mentioned. There would have been many, because possibly even a majority of the population did not welcome the reformers, who so narrowed the compass of the Christian faith, removed the beautiful objects, like the hanging pyx where the Blessed Sacrament was characteristically kept, the frescoes depicting the saints, the lovingly carved roodscreen (the 'rood' being the word for the cross; it was Margaret's stepfather who took it down in their local church), reducing churches to the 'bare, ruined choirs' that Shakespeare refers to, adorned only by the black letters of the Ten Commandments, which many in the congregation would not, in any case, have been able to read. Worse still, they imposed their views on a largely unwilling population, who were forbidden to believe in the Real Presence of Christ in the sacrament of the altar, in the forgiveness of sin in the sacrament of penance and of the comforting duty of praying for the dead to hasten their journey through purgatory to their heavenly home. Many people attended church, because fines made it costly not to, but went to Mass in secret whenever they could.

One can imagine that there was a deep weariness among people throughout the country. In 1536, while Henry VIII was still on the throne, the Pilgrimage of Grace raised huge numbers to demonstrate against Henry's religious changes, which left the monarch as the final arbiter and head of the Church. They had hoped to persuade the King to remove his advisors, and he had duped them with a pretence of listening to them. The leaders were executed and the effort failed. Many of the clergy were, no doubt, weak, but not all.

In 1572, the leader of an uprising later known as the Northern Rebellion, the Earl of Northumberland, who had escaped after the failed rising in Scotland, was betrayed and brought to York to face judgement. He was to be beheaded. The authorities then realized that if he could be persuaded to accept the established Church in exchange for his life, they would have a signal victory, which would have great influence over local people. However, Thomas Percy, the Earl of Northumberland, refused and his execution took place at the Pavement, not far from Margaret's home in the Shambles. Just before his death, Earl Thomas Percy declared that he was dying in loyalty to the Catholic Church, which has been founded on the teaching of the Apostles, Jesus Christ, himself, being the cornerstone. He asked for forgiveness of everyone present, as he himself 'forgave all from his heart'. His death was recognized by many present as martyrdom and they dipped their handkerchiefs in his blood to keep as relics. We do not know that Margaret witnessed this but she would certainly have heard about it from others who had.

The Catholic faith was strong in York during these years, especially, perhaps, among the butchers, and it is interesting that the women played a large part in keeping it alive in the city. The men had to be busy with their work and they were, no doubt, targeted by informers. The women, 'gossips' in the language of the time, used the customs and opportunities of the day to speak of religious matters, while they assisted each other with the care of the babies, or around a sickbed or at social gatherings. Chats in the street and in the shops often dealt with the religious question. Their gossip served a good purpose. The wife of a well-respected doctor, Thomas Vavasour, set up a sort of maternity unit to assist local women during their pregnancies and in giving birth. She needed helpers and many women could legitimately visit Dorothy Vavasour's house and once there could ask questions and to learn about Catholic teaching. Mrs Vavasour, like her husband, who had been denounced in York Minster and was living away in hiding, was strong in faith and Margaret Clitherow became a close friend of hers.

Visiting priests often used meetings and assemblies to teach the people when they could and were often able to celebrate Mass in private houses. It was likely to have been one of the priests, ordained in the time of Queen Mary, and who had now to conduct an underground ministry, who reconciled Margaret to the Church. There were priests who had a licence to absolve those who returned to the faith, wherever they found them, as parishes were no longer operative.

Fr John Mush, born in Yorkshire, had been a servant (possibly to Dr and Mrs Vavasour) but he had studied for the priesthood at Douai and Rome and he returned to England to minister to Catholics wherever he could. He wrote Margaret Clitherow's biography soon after her terrible martyrdom. He said that she was well prepared to be reconciled with the Catholic Church, revealing 'hearty sorrow and humble repentance for her youth spent out of Christ's Church'. She also expressed 'her vehement desire to convert others that God might be glorified in all his people'. She was also resolved to do nothing, however slight, that she thought offensive to God.

The wholeheartedness of her conversion is very much in line with what we know of her. Having been brought to understand the vastness of the changes to religion which had been inflicted, she embraced with the utmost love and fidelity the Church of Christendom.

As a child, she, like her sisters, had not been taught to read. Since the Dissolution of the Monasteries, the system of education had largely broken down (convents had often given lessons to girls) but, as a married woman, she managed to teach herself to read and subsequently to learn enough Latin to pray the Day Hours of the Office that priests and religious say every day. I wonder if Dorothy Vavasour, as the wife of a doctor, had been able to help her with her studies. Margaret would have had a good excuse to visit her friend, as she gave birth to her daughter Ann, in 1574, probably soon after she was received. She later said that her upbringing had been strict, so that she had not suspected that there was 'any other way to God'.

She now no longer attended the services of the Established Church. This was to put herself in defiance of the new laws which required attendance and thereby to incur fines. There seem to have been a number of women in a similar position. Their fines had to be paid by their husbands and it is a measure of their tacit sympathy and warm affection that many men paid up. Margaret's life was as full as ever with care for her family and the work of the house, as well as the business of the butcher's shop. But her interior life animated her activities and her fervour was lived out in this busy world. Fr Mush describes her faith as 'vehement' in her desire that heretics, schismatics and weak Catholics might 'know God and his truth, be made children of his Catholic Church, serve and love him above all things' and obtain no less grace than she wished for herself. The glory of God became the goal of all her activities.

These did not lessen her love of her husband, which remained strong, though she longed for his conversion, and as a woman of sensitivity she seems to have continued to be on good terms with her neighbours, some of whom were connected to her and not all were practising Catholics. In addition to her visits to Mrs Vavasour's comfortingly Catholic establishment, where her presence may have often been needed to help young women giving birth, she occasionally managed to find a substitute, when she was invited to a social gathering outside the city. According to Fr Mush, she would ride out a distance and then someone else would ride on, leaving her with time for confession or other devotions, while her substitute enjoyed the party. We do not know where she spent such days and it is difficult to see how this subterfuge could have been accomplished, though masked parties did go on. It is possible that the substitute was a relation who was sympathetic and who resembled Margaret – we cannot know.

The 'Housebook of York' for 6 June 1576 records that Margaret was 'detected' for recusancy. 'Recusants' were those who refused to conform to the new religious establishment. Fines were demanded for her non-attendance at the Protestant services and by November, she was 'certified as a recusant to the Council of the North' and imprisoned in the Castle prison.

Prisons were privately run and prisoners had to pay for their food, bedding and anything else necessary for life. As her husband was a prosperous man and a loving husband, he would have provided for her in gaol – though it was three months before he was allowed to visit her – and it is hard to imagine that the gaolers were generous in what they provided for the money they were given. There was a saving grace for Margaret in that a number of her friends and fellow Catholics were imprisoned at the same time. They determined to share everything and to use their captivity to deepen their faith. They made themselves a rule of life, with times of prayer together and talk that helped them to find their spiritual paths. The amount of food available to them collectively was always inadequate, so they decided to fast for four days in the week, thus turning their lack into a means of grace. They ate no meat on those days and only one meal made of whatever else they could get.

For all the cheerfulness that Margaret and her fellow Catholics could display and probably often feel, their time in prison must have been very distressing. They were away from their husbands – except for one couple who were imprisoned together – and their families. The prison was dark, dank and cold. They were encouraged by the fact that when a priest visited York, clandestinely, he was often able to penetrate the prison, and even say Mass. Mass kits and vestment were smuggled in and hidden among the odd corners of the ramshackle building.

We do not know who looked after the children, her two

stepsons, her son and daughter and another child. The year before, a report on those who did not attend the church includes mention of the 'wife of John Clitherow', adding that the reason for this was known as her pregnancy was advanced and, in the custom of the time, she would have been expected to remain at home. Many of the butchers were connected by ties of marriage, so it may be that some neighbouring women of the family stepped in, even if they were not themselves recusants.

In February 1577, Margaret and her four fellow prisoners were all released on bail which their husbands had paid. They were expected to keep to their houses and refrain from meeting (and presumably influencing) others, except for attending the service on Sundays – which none of them was prepared to do. Each service missed incurred a fine of two shillings, a considerable outlay at the time for their husbands.

According to Fr Mush again, she saw the utmost importance of the Mass and the need to protect priests to offer it. By June 1578, she had provided places and 'all things convenient that God might be served in her house,' by which she referred to the Mass. In 1619, an unnamed writer said of her, 'Knowing the persecution to be so great and the eyes of the state watchful over her, she even kept her priest within a chamber in her neighbour's house (which she had hired for that purpose) and had made not only a passage from her own house to the chamber, but also the means for the priest to escape' without coming into her house. He also tells us that all the priests captured and martyred in York had been her confessors. She was at home when a number were captured but she was in prison when two of them were martyred. Within three years of her marriage, her house had become one of the chief Mass centres in York. She also hired a room in another house in the same street, where a priest could hide in an emergency.

Without fuss, Margaret continued her work for God. Priests trained in Douai, across the Channel, in the English College which had been established there, were now arriving in

England anonymously and travelling the length of the country to minister to Catholics. Her husband was always generous to her, and now she used her money to support Catholic priests and people, living simply in what she wore and even what she ate. It says much that the deep differences on religion that existed between them did not cause her husband to withdraw his love from her.

In 1580, after a year in which the then mayor, sympathetic to Catholics, failed to insist on the paying of fines for non-attendance at church, the Council of the North, a higher authority, imprisoned him and ensured that Catholics were frightened into submission, including two of Margaret's neighbours who had become Catholics under her influence, though they never gave her activities away. Margaret was imprisoned again, while she was in the early months of another pregnancy.

Her stepfather, Henry May, was, by this time a man of high influence in the town. He was appointed alderman. He had no sympathy for his stepdaughter's faith or imprisonment. He would no doubt have been pleased by an act stating that all school teachers had to be licensed, on pain of a year's imprisonment, to ensure that Catholic teachers would not be found in schools.

Margaret was allowed home to give birth to her baby and her husband stood bail for her. She would not take her child to the church for christening and her husband was fined forty shillings. The time was particularly bleak for Catholics. Priests were martyred in York in the following year, condemned as traitors, and more recusants were gaoled. Dr Vavasour had long since been imprisoned and at this time his wife was arrested and sent to prison with her daughters, on the grounds that a priest had said Mass in her house. The priest, an old man, was publicly mocked and imprisoned as well.

Once more, in 1584, Margaret found herself inside the prison and at the time when a young, holy and active priest was condemned to death. As he was taken out, she and the other prisoners begged him to pray for them and he replied that he would remember each one by name. Later, a bond, posted by her husband and some friends, allowed her to be released. She determined to send her eldest son, Henry, to France so that he could be educated as a Catholic. It is thought that Fr John Mush was active in getting him to the English College, which had been opened in Rheims. She did not involve her husband in this arrangement, which could have been a danger to him. It was safer if he was ignorant of it. She further decided to open a little school for the sake of her own younger children and children of friends. She appointed John Stapleton as the teacher, someone whom she had met in the castle prison; he too was a recusant. The schoolroom was in the attic, near to the secret room. Margaret was defying the law for a greater good.

Despite all the hostile actions of the city fathers and the deepening crisis for those who still upheld the old faith, the life of the city of York and in particular the Shambles and the network of family, connections by marriage and trade must have gone on in the same way, though with a deepening feeling of oppression. Over the years, hope must have been diminished and no doubt more families conformed. But there were still children and apprentices living in the Clitherow house and other children, whose parents wanted them to have an education, visiting each day. Margaret loved them as she loved her own little ones. Margaret's life, so filled with duties, was, nevertheless also filled with prayer. Her life became increasingly an affair of love with Christ, despite the thickening clouds that she must have foreseen would engulf her. There was no hint of a morbid interest in martyrdom. She sought to continue free, as long as she could. She went to Mass each morning in the secret room of her house, and received Holy Communion on Wednesdays and Sundays. This was very frequent reception for those days, perhaps encouraged by one of the priests, who knew her deep devotion to Our Lord. If it was decided that Mass should be celebrated in the other house, where she rented a room, she did not attend, because her movements would most likely have been noticed and enquiries made.

Fr Rush recounts an anecdote about a social occasion, an evening spent with friends, at which John Clitherow drank too much and started denigrating Catholics, complaining that for all their praying and fasting, they were just as nasty as other people. Margaret, as the only Catholic present, was deeply hurt by this, whereupon he said she was a fool since he had not meant to refer to her as he could wish no better wife. Her only faults were that she fasted too much and would not accompany him to church. She told Fr Mush about this the next day. Her husband had let slip the depths of his antipathy to the faith. She must also have feared that he might use similar unguarded similar words when committed Protestants were present.

1585 saw a new act which made the presence of any priest in the country High Treason and made giving help or a place to live to any priest a felony. A £100 fine was to be exacted from anyone who sent a child abroad to study. It was still illegal to employ an unlicensed teacher and there were always a number of children in Margaret's house coming in for their lessons, as well as young apprentices and maids (who were probably young too, as many families at the time, saw their daughters' work placements as servants in a household as a form of training, which did not cost the parents money they could ill afford).

As life became even harder for recusants, Henry May, Margaret's stepfather, became Mayor of York in 1586. Her mother had recently died and Henry, who had been unfaithful to his wife, arranged to marry one of the two women involved, who came of a family with money. Her money would help him buy his wife's house, in which they had lived and which Margaret now inherited from her mother. It is likely that he was disturbed by her fidelity to the old faith, which could embarrass him, especially in his new position. His own sins were well known, but apparently did not affect his social standing.

It seems as if he decided to frighten her in the hope that she would abandon her religious position. If she did, it would have strengthened his fame and standing with the

Council of the North. In any case, John Clitherow was ordered to appear before the Queen's Council on 9 March 1586. He thought it might be to do with his son's education in France. He was briefly questioned and in his absence the house was raided. Margaret was there, and Fr Mush was in the secret room giving instruction to some people. They all got away. John Stapleton, the teacher got out and the children dispersed, but the men were angry to have missed their quarry and started to search the house in detail. Next, they arrested everyone and threatened the children. There was one child, referred to as the Flemish boy, who was stripped and threatened with a beating. Terrified, he showed them where the Mass book, chalice and paten were kept.

Margaret was imprisoned and interrogated by four city councillors. Her smiling demeanour infuriated them. She knew now, that she would be condemned to death and her faith heartened her. Her husband, servants and the children were all thrown into prisons in the city. The terrified boy who had cracked gave the authorities the names of two priests and the people who attended Mass in the secret room, one of whom, Anne Tesh was a close friend of Margaret. The next day, she was imprisoned with Margaret and they laughed and joked together during the morning. In the afternoon, Margaret was taken to the Common Hall to hear the charges against her.

She was indicted for harbouring two priests, 'Mr. Francis Ingleby and Mr. John Mush'. She was asked by the presiding judge how she would plead and replied that she had done nothing wrong and therefore would not accept that she should be tried at all. No defence lawyer was allowed, but neither priest had been found in the house. Margaret herself thought her execution inevitable and any mercy showed to her would be at the expense of her faith. She may well have thought of the dreadful burden of guilt that would have weighed down the children, if they had had to testify against her. She was then taken to another prison. The following day, she was again pressured to plead and again refused. She was asked if she was with child, in which case she would not have been executed, but she replied honestly that she 'knew not certainly' and 'would not for all the world take it on her conscience either that she was with child or that she was not'. The senior judge then said that because of her refusal to cooperate with the court she should die by *peine forte et dure,* stripped naked with heavy weights placed on her and a sharp stone at her back. It is reported that she said 'God be thanked; I am not worthy of so good a death as this … I confess that death is fearful and flesh is frail, yet I mind by God's assistance to spend my blood in this faith as willingly as ever I put my paps in my children's mouths.' The judge then left the matter with the council, telling them to wait until Friday and then proceed as they thought best, unless he told them otherwise.

In the intervening days, many scurrilous tales were told about Margaret, for instance, that she had slept with the priests, according to the boy who had betrayed her. When she heard them, she said 'God forgive you for these forged tales. If the boy said so, I warrant he will say as much more for a pound of figs.' Her husband was distraught, 'She is the best wife in all England and the best Catholic too,' he cried. Margaret wanted to talk to him, but was told she would have to cooperate possibly by attending a Protestant service. She would not comply. John was then told by the authorities to leave York for five days.

She felt terrible fear and said that her 'own flesh trembleth at these news, although my spirit greatly rejoiceth'. She sewed herself a white shift, short but with sleeves, hoping that she would be allowed to wear it rather than be naked at her death before her executioners. She sent her stockings and shoes to her eldest daughter Anne as a sign that she should follow her mother in the service of God.

The night before she died, she spent mostly in prayer, as the Protestants in her room, in prison for debt, reported. She greeted the sheriffs who came for her with a smile. She was barefoot and wearing her usual clothes, carrying her white garment over her arm, with her hair tied up like a bride.

In the room, the Protestant minister asked her to pray for the Queen. This was a clear propaganda move, and Margaret prayed for the Queen's conversion to the Catholic faith. She was urged to confess her crimes but she replied, 'No, no, I die for the love of my Lord Jesus.' She was told to remove her clothes and the women there helped her put on the shift she had made.

As the weights were piled on her she cried out, 'Jesu! Jesu! Jesu! Have mercy on me.' Then she was silent. It was said that she died after fifteen minutes. It was 25 March, the feast of the Annunciation, 1586. According to Pope Gregory's new calendar, which Protestant England had rejected, it was also Good Friday.

Her body was secretly dumped that night under a rubbish tip. It took Fr Mush and her friends six weeks to find it. They removed the body and buried it, but it is not known where. Her right hand is kept in the Bar Convent in York. She was canonized in 1970. She is called 'The Pearl of York'.

Chapter 8

St Anne Line

Mac McLernon

When I was preparing to take private vows, my spiritual director suggested that I adopt one of the female English martyrs as a patron saint. I wasn't keen on the idea: only three laywomen were canonized by Pope Paul VI in 1970 among the Forty Martyrs of England and Wales, and while I knew about the bravery of the men, especially the priests, who had died for the faith, I had a far sketchier knowledge of the women. I thought that they had been pretty insipid characters, included among the English martyrs only as a sop to political correctness.

However, I'd been given a task, and so I started to look at the lives of the martyred women, and discovered that they were far from insipid. The 'meek and mild' demeanour I had read about, which had led me to scorn them as role models, was an old-fashioned reference to their forbearance and bravery under interrogation rather than a description of their characters.

St Margaret Clitherow, for example, wished to prevent her children and family being forced to testify under oath at her trial. In a climate where the media regularly expose the lies of our politicians, we may forget how seriously a statement made under oath was considered in previous centuries. St Margaret's refusal to plead required tremendous bravery, knowing, as she did, that the penalty was *'peine forte et dure,'* a punishment which involved her being slowly crushed to death.

St Margaret Ward was a young servant girl, working for a family who harboured priests. On hearing about the plight of Fr William Watson, being held in Bridewell prison, she took it upon herself to befriend the gaoler's wife, and then smuggled in a rope with which the priest was able to escape. Once his escape was discovered, it was pretty obvious who was responsible for helping him; St Margaret was arrested. Despite being tortured, she refused to give away the probable whereabouts of Fr Watson, and she refused to conform to the Church of England, despite being offered freedom in return for doing so.

Much less is known of St Anne Line, though her feisty retort to her judges at the trial which condemned her to death, and again on the gallows at Tyburn, was recorded for posterity:

> I am sentenced to die for harbouring a Catholic priest; and so far am I from repenting for having done so that I wish with all my soul that where I have entertained one, I could have entertained a thousand.

It was this show of defiance which first endeared the saint to me, and made me decide to pick her as my patron.

Anne Line was born Anne Heigham, around the year 1567, in Dunmow, Essex. She was the second daughter of William Heigham, a strict Calvinist. Anne became disenchanted with Calvinism, and she and her brother both converted to Catholicism, upon which they were thrown out of the family home and disinherited. This sounds unduly harsh, and our modern sensibilities might condemn Anne's father for his actions. However, under Queen Elizabeth I, the Act of Uniformity (1559) had been passed, which decreed heavy fines for all who refused to attend the Church of England services in their parish church. Later laws imposed numerous penalties and fines on Catholic recusants, effectively barring them from inheriting land, entering the professions or taking up civil or military office. In 1581, a law had been passed which declared conversion to the Catholic faith to be an act of treason so, in merely being disinherited, Anne and her brother were lucky.

When she was about eighteen years old, Anne met and married Roger Line, another convert to the Catholic faith, and they moved to London. Unfortunately, after less than a year, Roger and her brother were arrested at a Mass celebrated by Fr William Thomson in Bishopsgate. Fr Thomson was martyred at Tyburn on 20 April 1586. Roger Line and William Heigham were sentenced to imprisonment and fined 100 marks, but when it was discovered that they were unable to pay the fine, the sentence was changed to one of banishment from the country. Anne's brother, William, went to Spain, where he joined the Society of Jesus, while her husband went to Flanders. There he received a small pension from the King of Spain, and, by sending home what he could, he supported Anne in London. Eight years later, in 1594, Roger unexpectedly collapsed and died, aged only twenty-seven, leaving Anne a penniless widow.

At about this time, Anne made the acquaintance of Fr John Gerard, a priest in the Society of Jesus. Fr Gerard first helped Anne by introducing her to some friends, the Wisemans, who were able to offer her accommodation in their house in Braddox, Essex. When Fr Gerard was imprisoned in a cell in the Clink, he decided that he would need someone to set up and look after a safe house in London, where priests coming from the Continent could stay temporarily, while he arranged suitable clothing, transport and contacts with other Catholic families around the country. The person he chose to put in charge of the house, and act as go-between while he was in prison, was Anne Line. As he wrote in his *Autobiography*:

> I could think of no better person than her to put in charge of it. She was able to manage the finances, do all the housekeeping, look after the guests, and deal with the inquiries of strangers. She was full of kindness, very discreet and possessed her soul in great peace.

All of this was despite her being in chronic ill-health. More than anything, she wished to die for Christ, though she thought that, being a woman, she would be more likely to die in prison than by the hand of the executioner. She did confide to one priest that she had expressed her desire for martyrdom to Fr William Thomson, then her confessor, and he had promised that, should he attain martyrdom, he would pray for her to receive that same favour from God.

When Fr Gerard escaped from prison, she had to give up managing the house, as she was too well known, and it would have been unsafe for the priest to visit any house which she occupied. So she hired apartments in another building, and continued her work of giving shelter to priests. She also found time to teach many children. At about this time, Anne took private vows of poverty, chastity and obedience, to help increase her dedication.

In 1601, on the Feast of the Purification of the Blessed Virgin Mary, also called Candlemas, Anne allowed a large number of Catholics to attend Mass in these apartments, something that, as Fr Gerard noted in his *Autobiography*, she would never have done if she had still been keeping house for him, because she was more aware of the need for his safety than for her own.

Neighbours took note of the large number of people visiting the apartments, and they alerted the pursuivants. When they broke in to the apartments, they found a room full of people, but the priest, Fr Francis Page, had managed to remove his vestments. No one would admit that there was a priest present, but, as the room was prepared and set up for Mass, they admitted that they had been waiting for a priest to arrive and celebrate Mass. The pursuivants were unconvinced, but, while they were trying to get to the bottom of the matter, Fr Page managed to slip out of the room. He knew of the location of a hiding place prepared by Anne Line for such an eventuality, and so he evaded capture, despite the whole house being ransacked.

Anne and the wealthier members of the congregation were arrested and taken to Newgate prison, while others were released on bail. Despite the paucity of the evidence, on 26 February 1601, Anne was charged with harbouring priests, and tried at the Old Bailey. She was so weak that she had to be brought to the court on a chair. Nevertheless, when asked whether she pleaded guilty or not guilty, she replied in a voice which could be heard all round the court-room that she only regretted being unable to help more priests. The evidence against her, namely the presence of an altar in the house set up for Mass, was extremely slender, but the Lord Chief Justice Popham directed the jury to find Anne guilty, and he then condemned her to death.

The next day, Anne was taken to Tyburn, now Marble Arch, the usual place of execution for those convicted of legal treason. The weather was cold and frosty, but a large crowd had gathered; among them were several Catholics, and so eyewitness accounts of her death have been recorded. Anne Line curtly dismissed the preachers who had come to exhort her to abandon her religion and conform to the Church of England, and she declared once more to the assembled crowd that she didn't repent of harbouring a priest, but rather regretted not being able to help even more.

Anne kissed the gallows, said some prayers quietly, and made the sign of the cross. The cart upon which she was standing was then drawn away, and she was hanged. Her death was witnessed by Fr Roger Filcock, of the Society of Jesus, and Dom Mark Barkworth, a Benedictine priest, both of whom had been sentenced to be hanged, drawn and quar-tered at Tyburn. Anne's body, along with the quartered bodies of the two priests, were thrown into a pit beside the road. Their remains were later retrieved by pious Catholics; the Countess of Arundel, Anne Howard, arranged for Anne Line's body to be brought to her own house, where she prepared it for burial.

St Anne Line was beatified on 15 December 1929 by Pope Pius XI, and canonized on 25 October 1970 by Pope Paul VI. She is now venerated as one of the Forty Martyrs of England and Wales.

Little else is known about St Anne. Because of the neces-sary secrecy associated with the various houses kept by Anne during her time in London, the exact address of the house where she was arrested is not known. The site of Tyburn Tree, her place of execution, is now a small traffic island at the junction of Edgware Road, Oxford Street and Bayswater Road; due to extensive railings to protect pedestrians from the fast-moving traffic, it is very difficult to get to it. A small plaque was set into the island, barely visible from the pavement beside the traffic lights, but this has recently been removed; Westminster Council has said that they wish to erect a more accessible monument nearby. All 105 martyrs of Tyburn are honoured by the nuns at Tyburn Convent, Bayswater Road, a few hundred yards from the site of Tyburn Tree.

There are also two churches dedicated to St Anne Line, both in Essex. The first church, Our Lady and St Anne Line, is in Great Dunmow, which was the town of Anne's birth. A large painting of St Anne, probably painted around the time of her beatification, adorns one of the walls of the Catholic Church. The second church, St Anne Line, is in South Woodford. This church boasts a statue of St Anne; at the time of my visit it had been moved to the presbytery garage, to protect it from vandalism, and the parish priest assured me that he intended to move it inside the church as soon as he had found a suitable spot.

St Anne Line is a great example of an English Catholic heroine. She was an intelligent and competent woman, and, although described as gentle, kind and discreet, she was no shrinking violet. She managed a household under very difficult and dangerous circumstances, demonstrating tremendous courage. Despite poor health, she was able to look after visiting priests, as well as teaching young children. Anne was described as having a 'holy envy' of priests, because they were able to give their lives in the service of Christ. She did not have a false view of the priesthood as an exercise of power, but, rather, she saw priests as servants of Christ's faithful people. Finally, and most importantly, in my opinion, she gave her life for love of the Mass. In her generosity, St Anne wanted to allow as many people as possible to attend Mass, and so was less cautious of her own safety than she should have been. Her life and death stand as an example for every Catholic woman to follow.

St Anne Line, friend and helper of priests, pray for us.

Bibliography

Burns, P., *Butler's Lives of the Saints* (New Concise Edition), London, Burns & Oates, 2003, pp. 92–3.

Connelly, R., *The Women of the Catholic Resistance: In England 1540–1680*, Bishop Auckland, Pentland Press, 1997, pp. 107–11.

Gerard, J., *Autobiography of an Elizabethan* (translated by Philip Caraman), London, Longmans Green & Co., 1951.

Holden, M. (ed.) *Saints of the English Calendar*, Oxford, Family Publications, 2004, pp. 82–3.

Chapter 9

St Margaret Ward

Patti Fordyce

On 30 August, the Church in England and Wales celebrates the memorial of three women martyred for the faith in the reign of Queen Elizabeth I. The names of the first two, Margaret Clitherow and Anne Line, are reasonably familiar; the name of the third, Margaret Ward, tends to be forgotten, except, perhaps, by people connected with one of the two schools or the single parish dedicated to her memory. Yet Margaret Ward's courageous example is no less a valuable model of conduct for women of the twenty-first century, when priests, although not locked up and executed for the faith, are no less in need of the support of the lay faithful.

The thirty years between the accession to the throne of Queen Elizabeth I in 1558 and the defeat of the Spanish Armada in 1588 saw a gradual intensification of the persecution of Catholics. The initial objective seems to have been the slow asphyxiation of the Catholic faith by depriving Catholics of the oxygen of the Mass and the sacraments, whilst at the same time compelling their attendance at Protestant services by the imposition of crippling fines.

Elizabeth's policy, in the early years of her reign, was one, as she saw it, of moderation. Although the Act of Supremacy (establishing Elizabeth as the supreme head of the Established Church) and the Act of Uniformity (making attendance at Protestant services compulsory) were enacted by Parliament, and the Elizabethan Prayer Book adopted for use in 1559, Elizabeth was more interested in outward conformity than in inner conviction, having no wish, as she said, 'to make windows into men's souls'. Failure to attend church was punishable by increasingly heavy fines and imprisonment, but Elizabeth, perhaps mindful of Tertullian's maxim ('The blood of martyrs is the seed of the Church'), wished to avoid creating martyrs amongst her subjects.

This moderate policy was harsh enough, however. The penalty for continuing to accept the spiritual or ecclesiastical authority of any bishop other than those appointed by Elizabeth was forfeiture of property or imprisonment for up to two offences; a third offence would result in a charge of high treason.

Priests who had been ordained before Elizabeth's accession to the throne were subject to essentially the same penalties as the laity. Since the imprisonment and exile of the Catholic bishops, no ordinations had been possible; it was presumably intended that the priesthood would eventually die out, and the practice of the Catholic faith with it.

But the faith stubbornly refused to die out. Following the Northern Rising of 1569, and the excommunication of Queen Elizabeth by Pope Pius V in 1570, pressure on Catholics to conform to the established religion increased steadily. Further anti-Catholic legislation in 1571 made it illegal to send children abroad to be educated without a licence from the sovereign; the penalty was a £100 fine. The sending of relief to anyone at a seminary abroad was also proscribed.

By 1574, the products of newly established seminaries in Douai, Rome and Vallodolid were returning to England as ordained priests, prepared to risk their lives to bring the Mass and the sacraments to the suffering faithful. These were followed by Jesuit missionaries from 1580 onwards. The arrival of these priests put an end to the previous government policy of asphyxiation; more drastic measures were enacted.

Reconciliation to the Catholic Church became a treasonable offence in 1581; by 1585 an Act of Parliament was passed 'against Jesuits and seminary priests'. To be a

Catholic priest in England was now in itself high treason, and the laity were also caught up in the provisions of the Act. Provision of any shelter, support or assistance to a priest was now a felony; the penalty for this lesser offence was merely hanging, as opposed to hanging, drawing and quartering. Pardon could only be obtained by swearing the Oath of Supremacy and attending the services of the Established Church.

The refusal of the faith to die out under these conditions is increasingly attributed by historians to the fidelity, resourcefulness and determination of women. Statistical evidence from the period demonstrates that women recusants significantly outnumbered men, and the extent to which Catholic women were able to influence, or at least circumvent, their Protestant or conforming husbands is acknowledged.

Attitudes to women in the Elizabethan period were somewhat complex. Within living memory, King Henry's great matter had arisen out of what was regarded as the absolute disaster of not having a male heir to the throne; this was far from merely an issue of kingly vanity. At least in the early years of her reign, Queen Elizabeth can hardly be said to have sat in total comfort on her throne. Women were regarded as subject to the wishes of their husbands, but they nevertheless had considerable freedom of movement and action, which faithful Catholic women were able to put to the service of the preservation of the faith.

Women were the unquestioned mistresses of their households. They employed the servants, knew which ones to trust, and knew which of their neighbours was likely to gossip. They were responsible for domestic arrangements, and could provide food, clothing and sleeping quarters for an unseen 'guest' without attracting undue attention.

If there were babies to be baptized, marriages to be solemnized, confessions to be heard, conformers to be reconciled, dying to be anointed, it was the women who brought the priest to those who needed him. When a priest was available to say Mass, the women would pass the information to those who could be trusted. In the absence of a priest, the father of the family would lead the prayers of the household, but once again the arrangements were the women's responsibility. Most importantly, women held the primary responsibility for passing on the faith to the children.

It was not uncommon for lone women to come together to live, often under the patronage of the mistress of one of the larger Catholic houses. These women were not religious in the sense of being professed, but they lived in community and they provided a basic education for the Catholic children of the locality. With the establishment on the Continent of schools, seminaries and convents, many of the children sent abroad were the products of these informal 'house' schools. That there was such a flowering of vocations in this period of accelerating persecution is testimony to the quality of formation children received in these schools.

It is conceivable that it was from a domestic situation such as this that Margaret Ward embarked on the course that was to lead to her martyrdom. Born in Congleton, the daughter of a Cheshire gentleman, relatively little is known about who she was, as distinct from what she did. Bishop Challoner, in his *Memoirs of Missionary Priests*, refers to her throughout as Mrs Ward, whilst Pollen and others describe her as a young, unmarried woman. Curiously, the Postulator of the Cause for Canonization of the Forty Martyrs refers to the women martyrs as 'three mothers'. She is described as being 'in service' to one Mrs Whittel, who was known to be 'a great friend of the Douai priests'. As the daughter of a gentleman, Margaret is unlikely to have been an ordinary servant; it is more likely that she would have been Mrs Whittel's companion or, indeed, part of her Catholic household. In any case, she seems to have enjoyed the considerable trust of Mrs Whittel, who was the probable source of Margaret's knowledge about Father William Watson, the priest whose escape from prison she engineered.

William Watson had been sent on the English mission soon after completing his priestly training at Douai. He and four other priests, including Father Richard Leigh, had been captured almost immediately on their arrival in England in 1586 and thrown into the Marshalsea, one of the more lax prisons. He had been offered his freedom on condition he left the country straightaway, but, before he could embark, he was captured by the notorious priesthunter, Richard Topcliffe, and incarcerated at Bridewell. Topcliffe was also responsible for the torments inflicted on Father Watson in prison; these were intolerable and, in a moment of weakness, he agreed to attend a Protestant service in order to gain his liberty.

Almost at once he was filled with remorse; he sought out an imprisoned fellow-priest to make his confession and receive absolution. According to Challoner, he returned to the same Protestant church and, standing in the middle of the congregation, he shouted,

> That he had done very ill in coming lately to church with them and joining in their service, which ... you untruly call the service of God, for it is indeed the service of the devil.[1]

This action immediately resulted in his re-apprehension and return to Bridewell. This time he was confined in a dungeon so low and so narrow that he could neither stand nor lie down full length. He was loaded down with irons, and for a month given only enough bread and water to keep him alive.

At the end of the month, he was moved from the dungeon to a cell at the top of the prison, but he was not left alone as he had been previously. He was subjected by turns to threats and cajoling, designed to induce him once again to attend a Protestant service.

The Catholic community was desperately concerned that

---

[1]. Richard Challoner, *Memoirs of Missionary Priests as well secular as regular and of other Catholics of both sexes that have suffered death in England on religious accounts from the Year of Our Lord 1577 to 1684*, revised and corrected by J. H. Pollen, SJ, London, Burns, Oates & Washbourne, 1924, p. 144.

Father Watson's ordeal might again prove too much for him, and sought some means of providing him with support and comfort. The task was entrusted to Margaret, who took a basket of provisions to the prison, only to be turned away. Undeterred, she set out to make a friend of the gaoler's wife, and eventually the two women persuaded the gaoler to allow periodic visits under very strict supervision. The condition was that Margaret and whatever provisions she brought the prisoner were to be searched, to prevent any letter being brought in or taken out, and a guard was to be posted to listen to her conversation with Father Watson.

A month went by, during which time Margaret came and went, submitting each time to the breaking open of loaves and pies to ensure that nothing was concealed inside them. Eventually, the gaoler became convinced of her sincerely compassionate motives and, no longer regarding her as a threat, relaxed the rigour with which they searched her basket and listened to their conversations.

Sources differ as to whether the escape plan was Margaret's or Watson's. In any case, she brought in a length of rope concealed inside a clean shirt placed in the basket under the usual provisions. The plan was that Watson would lower himself out of the window of his cell; Margaret had secured the services of a boatman to row him away. Having delivered the rope, she went to confirm the arrangement with the boatman, who had by this time got cold feet and refused to have anything to do with the escape.

Margaret was distraught. She had no means of warning Watson that the escape plan had collapsed, and she feared that she had merely given him the means of procuring his own execution. In her distressed state, she encountered a young Irishman of her acquaintance, one John Roche. He enquired what the matter was and whether he might be of service to her. She hesitated to tell him but, realizing that she had nothing to lose, confided the plan to him. He immediately volunteered to take over the boatman's duties.

At the appointed hour, Watson let himself down by the rope. Unfortunately, he had doubled the rope, reducing its length by half. When he got to the end of the rope, he was still a considerable distance from the ground. He had no choice but to jump, leaving the incriminating length of rope *in situ*. He landed on the roof of an adjacent shed, making a terrible noise, waking the gaoler and breaking his own arm and leg into the bargain. Roche immediately came to the rescue, helping Watson to the boat and rowing him away.

Once again, sources differ about what happened next. According to some, they exchanged clothes straightaway, in order to afford Watson some disguise. Others contend that Roche took Watson back to his own lodgings before exchanging clothes, in order to give Watson some opportunity to recover from his injuries. What is agreed, however, is that Watson eventually made good his escape, whilst Roche was captured the next day. Finding him in Watson's clothes, his captors at first assumed that they had re-captured the priest. The gaoler immediately connected the length of rope with Margaret; she must have been the source, since Watson had had no other visitor. Margaret was arrested the next morning, as she was leaving to change her lodgings.

It was the worst possible moment for a woman to be accused of aiding and abetting the escape of a priest. The change in the law enacted in 1585 had made this a felony, punishable by hanging; to make matters worse, a further outpouring of anti-Catholic feeling had been provoked by the attempted invasion of the Spanish Armada, with its purpose of restoring England to the Catholic faith.

Challoner lays the blame for inciting this anti-Catholic sentiment at the door of Robert Dudley, the Earl of Leicester and a great favourite of the Queen, whose avowed aim was 'to see all the streets of London washed with the blood of Papists'. Pollen, on the other hand, accuses Lord Burghley; his sin, in Pollen's eyes, was all the greater, for he knew that there was little support amongst English Catholics for the Armada.

In any case, there was now no question of leniency for a woman on the grounds of her sex. Six new gallows were built in and around London; it is not clear whether the executions for which they were to be used were intended to be seen as examples to those who might be tempted to similar crimes or as a form of public entertainment to fan the public euphoria following the defeat of the Armada. Between 28 August and 1 October, twenty-two executions took place; fifteen of these took place in London.

The attempted escape took place on either 10 or 18 August (Challoner mentions a period of eight days twice, and it is not clear whether he intends this as two periods or one). Challoner records that, for eight days, she was loaded with irons and flogged mercilessly, in an attempt to induce her to betray Watson's whereabouts, which she resolutely refused to do. She was tried at Newgate on 26 August; on being asked whether she were guilty of treachery to Her Majesty by providing the means of escape to a 'traitor of a priest', she cheerfully replied that she never in life had done anything of which she less repented than the delivering that innocent lamb from the hands of those bloody wolves.[2]

When further threats failed to induce Margaret to tell her interrogators where Watson was, the death sentence was pronounced; even then, she was told that, if she were to beg the Queen's pardon and promise to attend the Established Church, mercy would be shown to her. Her reply was forthright:

> That as to the Queen, she had never offended Her Majesty, and that it was not just to confess a fault by asking pardon for it where there was none; that as to what she had done in favouring the priest's escape, she believed the Queen herself, if she had the bowels of a woman, would have done as much, if she had known the ill-treatment he underwent; that as to the going to the church, she had for many years been convinced that it was not lawful for her to do so, and that she found no reason now to change her mind, and would not act against her conscience; and that they might proceed, if they pleased, to the execution of the sentence pronounced against her, for that death for such a cause would be very welcome to her, and that she was willing to lay

2. Challoner, pp. 144–5.

down not one life only, but many, if she had them, rather than betray her conscience or act against her duty to God and His holy religion.[3]

After this, the sentence was duly pronounced, and Margaret was taken to Tyburn for execution with four laymen: John Roche, the boatman who had aided her; Edward Shelley; Richard Flower; Richard Martin; and, in one of history's ironic twists, the priest with whom Father Watson had originally been arrested, Father Richard Leigh. The six joyfully sang hymns throughout the journey from Newgate to Tyburn, where Father Leigh was hanged, drawn and quartered for being a priest, and the others hanged, with the infamous Topcliffe shouting imprecations at them. Challoner notes, however, two bystanders arrested at the execution: a woman who burst through the crowd, exhorting them to be constant in their faith and then, kneeling, imploring their blessing; a man, who on hearing one of the condemned ask for the prayers of any Catholic present, proceeded to kneel and pray aloud for him.

On the day after the execution, Robert Southwell, SJ, himself martyred in 1595, wrote to Father General Claudio Aquaviva:

> She was flogged and hung up by the wrists, the tips of her toes only touching the ground, for so long a time, that she was crippled and paralysed, but these sufferings greatly strengthened the glorious Martyr for her last struggle.

While it is always somewhat speculative to attempt to read the thoughts of historical figures through their actions, Margaret's story shares certain features with other martyrs, not only of that period, but of every age. While there have been martyrs who have actively sought to shed their blood for the faith, for most, martyrdom seems to have been the logical outcome of much earlier decisions about how to live their lives.

[3.] Challoner, p. 145.

There is no evidence that Margaret sought martyrdom. For someone who had chosen the more difficult path of continuing to live as a faithful Catholic in a time of persecution, rather than conforming to the demands of the law, certain obligations logically followed from that choice.

If priests were to risk their lives to bring the Mass and the sacraments to the faithful, it was incumbent on the lay faithful to offer them all manner of support and co-operation, both spiritual and practical. If a priest were imprisoned, he needed to be visited; if there were obstacles, they had to be circumvented. If he needed to be put out of the reach of his torturers, in order that he might not be tried beyond his ability to endure, a means of escape must be found, regardless of the personal risk involved.

Upon being captured, Margaret could not tell her captors the priest's whereabouts, regardless of the provocation; to do so would be a denial of all that had gone before. If the price of freedom were the acceptance of a proposition forbidden by her conscience, then the offer must be rejected. Any other decision at any stage of events would have required a disavowal of what she held to be true.

It would be a satisfying end to Margaret's story if the object of her self-sacrifice, Father Watson, had gone on to a great ministry of service to the 'underground' Church. On contrary, he ended his days also at the end of a noose, in far less noble circumstances.

Having made his escape in John Roche's clothes, Father Watson resurfaced in Liège, where he remained for about two years, before returning to England in the autumn of 1590. He was captured, imprisoned and tortured again by Topcliffe, before once again escaping, only to be recaptured and detained in Wisbech.

Here he became involved in the 'Archpriest controversy', in which the appointment by Cardinal Catejan of George Blackwell as Archpriest of England, in the absence of any Catholic bishops, gave rise to dismay amongst some of the secular clergy because of his allegedly pro-Jesuit views. Father Watson was prominent in this group of priests, known as the 'appellants' because of their appeal to Rome against the appointment; he published some thirty denunciations of the Jesuits, eventually claiming that the Elizabethan persecution of Catholics was only a response to the pro-Spanish intrigues of the Jesuits. He became known as 'the Quodlibet maker', following the publication of his *Decacordon of Ten Quodlibetical Questions Concerning Religion and State.*

This increasingly bitter dispute between the Jesuits and the secular priests caused grave scandal to the faithful and was scarcely conducive to the much-needed unity of Catholics in the face of their increasingly parlous position. Father Watson, however, seems to have been driven by his anti-Jesuit views to seek accommodation with the Protestant establishment. In 1602, when he was imprisoned in the Clink, government agents burst into a clandestine Mass being celebrated by prisoners. It was widely believed that Father Watson had tipped them off; the evidence for this was his removal to the King's Bench, followed by his discharge on the following day.

He entered into negotiations with the Bishop of London, Richard Bancroft (later Archbishop of Canterbury), seeking to devise an oath of allegiance to the Queen that could be taken by moderate Catholics; he evidently believed that if Catholics demonstrated their loyalty to the Crown (which there had never been any concrete reason to doubt), the persecutions would cease.

Father Watson seems increasingly to have seen himself as a man of some influence in secular circles. On the death of Queen Elizabeth in 1603, he rushed to Scotland to declare his loyalty to King James, and came away convinced that he had obtained the King's assurance of the alleviation of the suffering of Catholics. When, contrary to this alleged assurance, the persecutions continued, Father Watson was enraged, and entered into a conspiracy to kidnap the King at Greenwich and hold him until he should make good on his promise. This conspiracy, known as the Bye Plot, was foiled by Jesuits revealing it to the authorities, and Father Watson was duly executed for treason in 1604.

What, then, of Margaret's sacrifice? In the light of Father Watson's subsequent (and, it might be argued, antecedent) frailty, should her martyrdom be regarded as in some sense pointless? To see the evaluation of right conduct as contingent on the worthiness of the beneficiary is perhaps an error of the modern age, which tends to a rather pragmatic view of such questions. Margaret saw her plain duty to assist a priest in trouble as the obligation of any member of the lay faithful to any priest, for the benefit of the Church and the safeguarding of the sacraments. That her 'innocent lamb' turned out to be a rather weak and self-regarding human being is neither here nor there: what counts is her determination to sacrifice herself to save him, which gave him an opportunity of further service to the Church. That he made poor use of that opportunity does not devalue Margaret's heroic action.

Little-known St Margaret Ward can be seen as a powerful example for Catholics, perhaps especially Catholic women, in England and Wales today. While there is no longer any question of Catholics' loyalty to the Crown and their obedience to lawfully constituted authority, there are nevertheless increasingly occasions when Catholics find themselves, and the teachings of the Church, at odds with prevailing attitudes. Proclamation of the Church's teachings has come close to falling foul of anti-discrimination legislation that makes no allowance for conscience, and it may be that it will require increasing courage to speak plainly of what Catholics believe, particularly regarding issues relating to life, marriage and family.

The example of Margaret Ward and countless anonymous women of the period, who risked everything to support their priests in their ministry is also one for the twenty-first century. To be sure, Catholic priests in England and Wales do not risk imprisonment for their priesthood, but at the same time as finding themselves increasingly signs of contradiction in modern, secular society, good priests find themselves condemned for the unacceptable behaviour of others. Just as St Margaret laid down her life, not for a spectacularly good and holy priest, but for a weak and ordinary one, so modern Catholics who value the Mass and the sacraments need to support, pray for, and occasionally thank, all of their priests.

Bibliography

Burton, DD, E. H., and Pollen, SJ, J. H. (eds), *Lives of the English Martyrs*, Second Series, vol.1, London, Longman, Green & Co., 1914.

Challoner, Richard, *Memoirs of Missionary Priests as well secular as regular and of other Catholics that have suffered death in England on religious accounts from the Year of Our Lord 1577 to 1684*, revised and corrected by J. H. Pollen, SJ, London, Burns, Oates & Washbourne, 1924.

Connelly, Roland, *The Women of the Catholic Resistance: in England 1540–1680*, Edinburgh, Pentland Press, 1997.

Crawford, Patricia, *Women and Religion in England, 1500–1720*, London, Routledge, 1993.

Molinari, SJ, Paolo, 'Canonization of 40 English and Welsh Martyrs' in *L'Osservatore Romano*, Weekly Edition in English, 29 October 1970.

Tigar, SJ, Clement, *Forty Martyrs of England and Wales*, London, Office of the Vice-Postulation, 1970.

Walsh, James, *Forty Martyrs of England and Wales*, London, Catholic Truth Society, 1970.

Chapter 10

Elizabeth Cellier

Fiorella Nash

Elizabeth Cellier has claims to being one of the most extraordinary women of her age.

Midwife, Catholic convert, whistleblower, pamphleteer and visionary, the major events of her incredible life took place against the backdrop of the Titus Oates plot and the renewed persecution of the Catholic minority. Her fearless work to expose the horrific treatment that was being meted out to Oates's victims in prison aroused strong emotions from both sides of the religious divide and caused her to be labelled both a dauntless heroine and a lying papist.

The English Civil War made a huge impact on Elizabeth's life and faith. Her family were Protestants who remained loyal to King Charles I and were persecuted when the Royalists were finally defeated, labelled 'Papists and Idolaters' by the Puritan establishment. By her own account, Elizabeth was so disgusted by the atrocities carried out in the aftermath of the Civil War that she seems to have almost rebelled into Catholicism. She became curious about the Catholic faith precisely because of the hatred her enemies showed for it and in her written description of her conversion, one gets the sense of her thinking; 'If these appalling people hate Catholics so much, there has to be something good about them.'

Upon further enquiry, she discovered that the terrible accusations made against Catholics – particularly the accusation that Catholics were traitors – were fabrications. She wrote:

> Let Calumny say what it will, I never heard from any Papist as they call them, Priest nor lay-Man but that they and I and all true Catholicks, owe our lives to the defence of our Lawful King, which our Present Soveraign Charles the Second is, whom God long and happily preserve so.

She appears to have been particularly impressed by the courage and loyalty of the Catholics who saved Charles II's life after his defeat by Cromwell's army at the Battle of Worcester, 'whom though poor, no Temptation could invite to betray him to those, who, by a pretended Protestant principle, fought his Innocent blood'. This particular comment comes from Elizabeth's famous tract *Malice Defeated,* published in 1680 before the Titus Oates plot was exposed as a sham. It would have served as a timely reminder to England's Protestant majority of the proven loyalty of Catholics to Charles II, at a time when the Popish Plot had generated a new wave of violence and hysteria against Catholics.

Titus Oates is a man so loathed in memory that in 2006, he was selected by the BBC History Magazine as the seventeenth century's worst Briton and the third worst Briton in the past thousand years. At Cambridge, where he attained the dubious honour of being ejected from two colleges before becoming a clergyman, he was described as 'the most illiterate dunce, incapable of improvement' and was described by a twenty-first-century Cambridge don as 'in a league of his own in the depths of his vileness'.

Besides failing miserably at Cambridge, this self-proclaimed saviour of the nation occupied much of his early adult life getting himself various criminal convictions. These included being imprisoned for perjury after falsely accusing a schoolmaster of sodomy, committing buggery whilst serving as a naval chaplain. (Buggery was a capital offence at the time and his life was spared only because he was in holy orders.) He persuaded an extraordinarily naive priest to receive him into the Catholic Church, whilst at the same time agreeing to write anti-Catholic propaganda. He was thrown out of not one but two seminaries by wise rectors who saw him for precisely the man he was.

It has been suggested that Oates' confederate, fanatical Protestant Israel Tonge, suggested to him the idea of a Catholic plot to assassinate the King and may even have played a significant part in concocting the whole story. This is plausible, not so much because Oates was a better person than Tonge but because he was almost certainly less intelligent. Whoever came up with the original idea, the two of them put together an elaborate story that the Catholic Church was plotting to assassinate Charles II and various others, and that the treason was to be carried out by a team of scheming Jesuits. When questioned by the King's Council, Oates made accusations against hundreds of Catholics, including over five hundred Jesuits. When the Protestant magistrate to whom Oates had given evidence – Sir Edmund Berry Godfrey – was found murdered, the death was blamed on Catholics though there was no reason whatsoever why Catholics would have killed a man who was known to have treated them sympathetically. One of the rumours was that Oates and Tonge killed him themselves to lend credibility to their allegations but no substantive evidence has ever been found to link them to the crime.

The Titus Oates plot is a graphic example of how easily a population, fed on a regular diet of propaganda against a religious or racial minority, can be convinced that they are capable of almost anything. There never was and has never been a shred of evidence to support Oates's accusations, but the emergence of the Popish Plot was seized upon by the authorities to tighten the screw on an already persecuted Catholic minority. The penal laws that were on the way out were reintroduced and a wave of mass hysteria was generated that saw Catholics exiled from London, Catholics being attacked in the street, the prisons overflowing with Catholics and very soon, the execution of Catholics for crimes that they had not committed and that had never happened. Titus

Oates's perjured evidence was responsible for the executions of fifteen innocent Catholics – including St Oliver Plunkett – and a further eight in the persecution that followed. The death toll does not include those Catholics who died in prison or at the hands of hysterical members of the public.

Charles II had never taken Oates's allegations seriously – his own wife was a Catholic – and when he questioned Oates himself he found his story to be inconsistent on several major points. However, he was unable to stop Parliament from taking up the affair and using it to harm the Catholic population.

Oates initially did very well out of his lies. He became a national hero and was given apartments in Whitehall and an annual pension that allowed him to live very comfortably indeed. Gradually, however, the tide of public opinion began to turn against him. Men charged with treason on his evidence began to be acquitted, Oates's honesty was called into question and finally he was fined and imprisoned on a charge of sedition. During the reign of James II, Oates was sentenced to life imprisonment and to be pilloried annually. He began his sentence by spending two days in the pillory, then being stripped, tied to a cart and whipped from Aldgate to Newgate. Judge Jeffreys said of him: 'He has deserved more punishment than the laws of the land can inflict.'

Protestant William and Mary did not seem to share this sentiment. During their reign he received a royal pardon and an annual pension, having served only three years' imprisonment. For those who had suffered as a result of this man's crimes and seen their loved ones butchered, it must have been the most appalling insult and a reminder of how vulnerable the Catholic minority remained to persecution and injustice at the hands of the state.

Elizabeth Cellier was already relatively well known at this time as a midwife in London, where she lived with her French husband. (The very fact that she was married to a Frenchman would count against her later on.) Hence her nickname, 'the popish midwife'. As part of her charitable work, she regarded it as her sacred duty to visit and offer help to 'poor Imprison'd Catholicks, who in great numbers were lock'd up in Gaoles, starving for want of bread'.

As a result of her profession, she was known to a number of wealthy Catholic ladies who were able to use her as a channel for their charitable endeavours. She became almoner to the Countess of Powis, who gathered funds which Elizabeth distributed during the course of her almost daily visits to prison, though she admitted in her narrative that she also contributed to the fund herself. Her constant contact with prisoners, both Catholic and non-Catholic, opened her eyes to the terrible conditions faced by those deprived of their liberty.

Besides the daily torment of hunger, she became aware that many were being subjected to torture. Her pamphlet describes the many incidences of torture, extortion and mistreatment she came across and it reads very much like a twenty-first-century human rights report. One particular incident is described in considerable detail, including a transcript of the conversation she had with the jailer.

> I came down into the Lodge with five Women, of which three were Protestants, and we all heard Terrible grones and Squeaks which came out of the Dungeon, called the Condemn'd hole. I asked Harris the Turnkey, what Dole-full cry it was, he said, it was a woman in Labour. I bid him put us into the Room to her and we would help her, but he drove us away very rudely, both out of the Lodge and from the door; we went behind the Gate, and there Lissened, and soon found that it was the voice of a strong Man in Torture, and heard as we thought, between his grones, the winding up of some Engine: these Cries stop'd the passengers under the Gate, and we six went to the Turners shop without the Gate, and stood there amazed with the Horror and dread of what we heard, when one of the officers of the Prison came out in great hast, seeming to run from the Noise.
>
> One of us catcht hold of him, saying Oh! What are they doing in the Prison.

Officer: I dare not tell you.
Mistris: It's a Man upon the Rack, Ile lay my life on't.
Officer: It is something like it.
Cellier: Who is it Prance?
Officer: Pray Madam do not Ask me, for I dare not tel lye, but
it is that I am not able to heare any Longer. Pray let me go.
With that he Run away toward Holborn as fast as he could.

The narrative goes on to describe the tortured man being
heard screaming for another three hours and then repeatedly, each time for several hours, over the days that
followed.

She gained the trust of prisoners and former prisoners,
who had their own terrifying stories to tell. Francis Corral, a
coachman falsely accused of murder, described to her how
he was kept in heavy chains for over thirteen weeks which
made it impossible to stand. He showed her where the metal
shackles had chafed the flesh away from his legs and
described being 'squeez'd and hasped into a thing like a
Trough, in a dungeon under ground', which caused him
such agony that he fainted. He also related being beaten and
repeatedly threatened at the point of a sword, all under the
watchful eye of a religious minister, having his hands
chained behind his back for days at a time, being dehydrated
to the point of trying to drink his own urine and being
forced to watch his wife beaten by a gaoler for trying to bring
him food.

Another prisoner, one Captain Clarke, incarcerated for
debt, was locked up for two days and nights with the rotting
remains of two men who had been hanged, drawn and quartered 'the extream stench of which, had perhaps kill'd him,
had he not took the miserable relief of holding a foul
Chamber-Pot to his Nose'.

The list of abuses goes on and on: starvation, the use of
massively heavy chains to restrain prisoners in painful positions for hours and even days at a time, isolation and the
indiscriminate use of torture that had the capacity to leave a
person maimed for life. One can almost feel, reading
Elizabeth Cellier's account of these abuses, her sense of

outrage at the cruelty that was going on out of public view, towards innocent men and women, even pregnant women who were not spared the savagery of England's penal system.

Elizabeth's account includes descriptions of a heavily pregnant woman who was subjected to seven weeks in close confinement:

> Not only burthen'd with excessive Irons on both Leggs, but for two days together, kept from any Victuals or other sustenance; and after this, was by the Jaylors order, removed to a Room call'd the Condemn'd Room, and there for six weeks kept with the Irons on her Legs and though big with Child to the Gaolers certain knowledge, yet did he cause her to be put in the Bilboes,[1] and boulted her hands down to the ground with Staples of great bigness, by which inhumane and immoderate torments she was so afflicted that her Child died soon after it was born.

It was whilst doing her charitable work that she fell foul of Thomas Dangerfield, an imposter and conman not unlike Titus Oates in his way of operating. An Essex man by birth, he robbed his father, ran away from home and made his living forging money. Like Oates, he fabricated evidence of plots, most famously the so-called 'Mealtub Plot'. He put together an elaborate lie that Elizabeth Cellier and her patron Lady Powis had aided his release from prison on condition that he take part in a Catholic plot to kill Charles II and others. He claimed that a mealtub in Elizabeth Cellier's house contained incriminating documents accusing notable Protestants of treason. One of these was Sir Thomas Waller, the official in charge of searching Elizabeth Cellier's house.

The planted documents were found as planned and she was arrested. The betrayal makes particularly horrible reading because Elizabeth had befriended Thomas Dangerfield and attempted to help him before realizing the

---

[1.]   A contraption similar to the stocks made of a metal bar with two metal loops, through which a prisoner's legs were restrained.

sort of man she was dealing with. He met a particularly sticky end. When Elizabeth was eventually vindicated and he attempted to tell his side of the story by publishing *Dangerfield's Narrative,* he was convicted of libel. The sentence was to be pilloried for two days, then to be stripped to the waist, tied to the back of a cart and whipped from Aldgate to Newgate, then after a break of two days so that he could recover, from Newgate to Tyburn. Shortly after concluding this punishment, he was hit in the eye by Robert Francis, a barrister, and died of the injury.

When Elizabeth was put on trial she was brought before Sir William Scroggs, a man who has been described as 'perhaps the worst of the judges who disgraced the English bench at a period when it had sunk to the lowest degradation'. In his capacity as Lord Chief Justice, Scroggs presided during the trials generated by the Titus Oates plot. Either he was immensely stupid and sincerely believed Oates and his confederates to be telling the truth, or he chose to accept their evidence because he was vindictively anti-Catholic and – like so many others who chose to believe Oates – believed that it was politically expedient to do so. He treated the Catholics who came before him as brutally as possible, subjecting them to anti-Catholic tirades, obscene verbal abuse and mockery, and taunting them as he sentenced them to death.

However, in the case of Elizabeth, he dismissed Dangerfield's evidence and had him imprisoned, acquitting Elizabeth when he could quite easily have done as he had in the past and condemned an innocent person to death on spurious evidence.

After Elizabeth's acquittal there was a flood of pamphlets for and against her, including her own remarkable account *Malice Defeated,* which led to a trumped-up charge of libel because of her account of two witnesses in the Edmund Berry Godfrey case being subjected to torture. She was fined £1000 and forced to stand three times in the pillory. It is worth pointing out at this point that being sentenced to be pilloried was a good deal more frightening than it may initially appear. It was a harsher punishment than the stocks, as the person's head and hands were secured, forcing them to stand in an extremely uncomfortable position with their neck pushed forward. They were also unable in this position to protect themselves from attack by passers-by, who were positively encouraged to throw eggs, stones and other missiles in the prisoner's direction. It was also (though not in Elizabeth Cellier's case) routinely used to carry out other punishments such as branding, flogging and maiming such as the cutting off of ears.

According to Roger North, the celebrated biographer, lawyer and man of letters, the libel case was simply a ruse to stop Elizabeth Cellier giving evidence to help other imprisoned Catholics. Like her court case, the publication of *Malice Defeated* and the subsequent libel charge caused a pamphlet war between her friends and enemies. Pamphlets published included such gloriously evocative titles as: *A whip for impudence, or, A lashing repartee to the snarling midwifes Matchless rogue: being an answer to that rayling libel. Devil pursued, or, The right saddle laid upon the right mare: a satyr upon Madam Celliers standing in the pillory; Midwife unmask'd, or, The Popish design of Mrs Cellier's meal-tub plainly made known.* This was the age of the pamphleteer. If she had lived today, in what is arguably the Internet age, she would no doubt be courageously defended on *The Hermeneutic of Continuity* or *St Mary Magdalen Brighton*, complete with hyperlinks to the relevant Government department, and sneered at on one of the *Guardian*'s blogs.

In the relative – and temporary – peace of James II's reign, Elizabeth Cellier devoted her energies to developing midwifery, proposing the foundation of a corporation of midwives and a system by which midwives fees could be used to establish parish houses where poor women could give birth. Historically, complications during childbirth have been one of the biggest killers of women and this continues to be the case in many parts of the developing world. In the absence of modern obstetric care, antibiotics, blood transfusion, analgesia and safe Caesarean section, around one in four women who were admitted to maternity hospitals in labour died shortly after birth, usually of sepsis because doctors did not wash their hands between deliveries. The majority of women at the time of Elizabeth Cellier did not give birth in hospital and access to what little medical care was available was severely limited.

Elizabeth Cellier's writings on maternal mortality read like a contemporary briefing from an international aid agency. She clearly had extensive knowledge of her field and believed passionately in giving women the best possible medical care available in order to reduce the high number of unnecessary deaths. She quotes the available statistics to press her case – 'six thousand women have died in child bed in twenty years', 'more than thirteen thousand children have been born abortive' (miscarried or stillborn) and 'above five thousand chrysome infants have been buried, within the weekly bills of mortality'. However, in the course of her work she would have been exposed time and time again to the people behind these figures, the young lives cut short and the families left without the care of a mother.

Her submission to James II, *A Scheme for the Foundation of a Royal Hospital*, lays out a proposal for the training of midwives and the founding of a hospital to care for abandoned children. She touches upon contentious subjects, such as abortion and infanticide 'by their wicked and cruel mothers, for want of fit ways to conceal their shame' and sets out a practical and humane vision for the care of women and foundlings. Her submission includes the precise number of necessary midwives, the costs involved, details involving ways in which funds could be raised such as poor boxes in churches, the precise management of such an institution and the need for the physical, educational and spiritual welfare of children to be catered for.

She expresses a particular interest in ensuring that children in such a disadvantaged social position should be given every opportunity to rise in society in an age where lineage and name was of paramount importance. She writes:

> By your majesty's royal authority, the children exposed and educated as aforesaid, may be privileged to take themselves sirnames, from the several arts or mysteries they shall be excellent in, or from the remarkable days they were exposed on, or from their complexions, shapes etc and be made capable, by such names, of any honour or employment, without being liable to reproach, for their innocent misfortune.

Children were to be educated and taught skills and trades that would help them through life, with emphasis placed on giving them the chance to excel 'according to their geniusses, strengths, and several capacities'.

Elizabeth Cellier is buried in Great Missenden Church, Buckinghamshire. She was clearly a highly intelligent, articulate and courageous woman, devoted to her faith, her husband and her profession. As far as I am aware, her cause for beatification has never been promoted and I sincerely hope it will be considered at some time in the not so distant future. We live at a time in which conspiracy theories and paranoia about the Catholic Church are once again gaining ground and attacks upon the Church such as the desecration of the Eucharist and the disruption of Mass are becoming more widespread. At such a time, she is a compelling role model for Catholic laywomen and a source of inspiration for all who seek to do good and proclaim the Truth in the world.

Chapter 11

Mary Ward

Gemma Simmonds, CJ

In 1951, during the first World Congress of the Lay
Apostolate, Pope Pius XII paid tribute to Mary Ward, calling
her 'that incomparable woman, given to the Church by
Catholic England in her darkest and bloodiest hour'. His
words are in startling contrast to those spoken by his prede-
cessor Urban VIII in his Bull *Pastoralis Romani Pontificis* of
1631. Nailed to the doors of St Peter's and the Lateran
Basilica it spoke of 'the disgust of all good people' caused by
the outrageous attempt by Mary and her companions to
'employ themselves at [...] works which are most unsuited
to maidenly reserve [...] to the grave disadvantage of their
own souls'. It went on to insist that these 'poisonous
growths in the Church of God must be torn up from the
roots lest they spread themselves further'.[1]

The story of Mary Ward and her attempt in the seventeenth century to found an Order of women based on the
Jesuit model is one chapter in the long history of women's
struggle to fulfil their God-given potential in society and to
find and live their vocation within the Christian community.
In society as a whole, women have historically battled with
male prejudice against unconventional social roles. Within
the Church this was expressed in Mary Ward's time as hierarchical resistance to women working outside monastic

---

[1.] Margaret Mary Littlehales, *Mary Ward: Pilgrim and Mystic*, Burns &
Oates, London, 1988, pp. 253–7.

enclosure and without control by male authorities. Honoured all over the world today as a heroine in women's history and England's foremost pioneer of female education, Mary laid the foundations for the unenclosed, self-governing religious life for women that is familiar in hundreds of manifestations to modern-day Catholics. Hers was a particularly testing vocation, to be given a vision centuries before its time of how women could serve God in a church that would only reject that same vision in God's name. She was denied the title of founder of her own congregation for the best part of three hundred years.

Mary was born into an English recusant family in Yorkshire. Hers was one of many families which suffered severe persecution for refusing to accept State-sponsored religion and attend the Anglican church. She was one year old when the York butcher's wife, Margaret Clitherow, was publicly crushed to death for sheltering priests.[2] Margaret belonged, as did Mary and the women of her family, to an extended network of Catholic women who took inspiration from the example of the English martyrs and the zeal of English priests trained abroad, who ministered in secret to the Catholic underground movement. From this inspiration came a passionate commitment to their faith.[3] There were no religious houses left in Britain, but many of these recusant families lived according to an almost monastic regime within their homes, and became familiar with Ignatian spirituality through the ministry of itinerant Jesuits. Mary's grandmother, aunt and cousin spent years in prison for their faith. In the absence of established Catholic clergy or hierarchy many such women assumed positions of religious leadership at home or within prison, following a life of common prayer and religious instruction. Outside the

[2.] Francis Ingleby, one of the priests whom she sheltered, and who was martyred in York in the same year, was Mary Ward's cousin.

[3.] Margaret and Mary shared the same spiritual director, Father John Mush. See James Walsh, 'Introduction' in Gillian Orchard ed., *Till God Will: Mary Ward Through Her Writings*, London, Darton, Longman and Todd, 1985, pp. xi–xvii.

prisons it was often less risky for Jesuits and other priests to seek the collaboration of women than of men, and a generation of women emerged who, at great risk to themselves, lived at the service of the Church while not being professed religious.[4]

In 1298 Pope Boniface VIII had issued *Periculoso*, a papal decree which imposed strict enclosure on all nuns in the Western Church, making it impossible for female religious to undertake works of charity outside the monastic enclosure, with the limited exception of the education of girls. It was also forbidden for women religious to organize themselves under a general superior or in a province of several houses. The common opinion on women's options in society ran *aut maritus aut murus* – either a husband or a cloister – one or the other providing the necessary enclosure required by the weakness of women's minds and bodies. Angela Merici's Ursulines, founded in 1535, avoided these restrictions by living as tertiaries under simple vows, and were followed by other groups of women, especially in Northern Europe. The Council of Trent later reinforced the restrictions of *Periculoso* and obliged tertiaries to take solemn vows and observe pontifical enclosure. Inspired by a maidservant who told stories of a religious life now lost to England, the young Mary determined to become a nun. Convinced that 'women did not know how to do good except to themselves', she fled to Flanders, seeking the strictest monastery she could find, entering the order of Poor Clares. To her dismay she came to understand that God was calling her to 'some other thing', to a way of life as yet unimagined, and after a period of discernment she left the monastery.[5] In 1606 she returned to London, having made a vow of chastity, doing apostolic work within the Catholic underground networks, at great danger to herself. One morning she experienced a

4. Ibid., pp. xiv–xvi. See also Philip Caraman, ed., *The Other Face: Catholic Life Under Elizabeth I*, London, Longmans, 1960, pp. 135, 198–203 and Jennifer Cameron, *A Dangerous Innovator: Mary Ward (1585–1645)*, Strathfield, NSW, St Paul's, 2000, pp. 14–18, 75–6.
5. Orchard, *Till God Will*, pp. 24–5.

powerful mystical insight, known as the 'Glory Vision', received not during formal prayer, but in the ordinary context of doing her hair.[6] This insight convinced her that the 'assured good thing' to which God was drawing her would be greatly to God's glory.

Mary had lost three uncles in the Gunpowder Plot, and gathered a group of companions, many of whom were related to Gunpowder Plotters. While the men of their families planned an act of religiously-inspired terrorism, the women determined to do something more positive for the sake of the Catholic faith, and set sail together for St Omer in 1609, in order to live as religious. Their inability to clarify what sort of religious life they were to embark upon led to acute difficulty,

> Great insistence was made by divers spiritual and learned men that we would take upon us some Rule already confirmed, several Rules were procured by our friends, both from Italy and France, and [we were] earnestly urged to make choice of some of them. But they seemed not that which God would have done, and the refusal of them all caused much persecution, and the more because I denied all and could not say in what particular I desired or found myself called unto.[7]

But clarity was not long in coming. In 1611 Mary received another major insight, this time an intellectual understanding that she and her companions were to '[...] "Take the same of the Society", so understood as that we were to take the same both in matter and in manner, that only excepted which God, by diversity of sex, hath prohibited.'[8]

Mary and her companions understood that they were to form an autonomous female branch of the recently founded Society of Jesus, taking the Jesuit Constitutions for their own, and living a religious life as closely resembling that of

---

6. See   http://www.loretonh.nsw.edu.au/faith/ourheritage/paintedlife .html, 21.
7. Orchard, *Till God Will*, p. 52.
8. Ibid., pp. 27–9, 60–1.

the Jesuits as was possible for women and non-clerics. Not only was this in direct contradiction to the Council of Trent, but it also contravened the ban which St Ignatius Loyola himself had placed on there ever being a female branch of his Order. Ignatius's reluctance to involve himself with female aspirants to the Jesuit life stemmed from two unhappy episodes in his own lifetime involving influential women. Isabel Roser, a wealthy benefactress from Barcelona, had fallen under the spell of the charismatic founder and his new Order, resolving to make profession of vows in the Society of Jesus. She successfully petitioned the Pope to oblige Ignatius to accept her wish, but difficulties soon arose, culminating in her accusing Ignatius of misappropriating her goods.[9] After a court hearing resolved the case in favour of Ignatius, he successfully appealed to have Isabel's vows commuted to vows of obedience to the diocesan bishop, and to free the Jesuits in perpetuity from the spiritual direction of any women living together in community and wishing to place themselves under obedience to his Society. An even more difficult situation arose when Juana of Austria, sister to Philip II of Spain, determined to live as a Jesuit. Ignatius had no option but to admit her to the Order, though in strictest secrecy, and under the code name of 'Mateo Sánchez'. Juana was the only female in history to have become a member of the Society of Jesus under permanent vows, though this remains a unique case.[10]

In the light of this unfortunate history Mary Ward's Jesuit contemporaries reacted with predictable horror. Some were dismayed at the thought of unenclosed female religious on the loose, others objected because they interpreted her inspiration as an attempt to live under Jesuit jurisdiction in the manner forbidden by St Ignatius.[11] Mary's decision to

[9.] See William W. Meissner, *Ignatius of Loyola: the Psychology of a Saint*, Yale University Press, 1992, pp. 260–70.

[10.] See Hugo Rahner, ed., *Saint Ignatius Loyola: Letters to Women*, Edinburgh and London, Nelson, 1960, pp. 52–67.

[11.] Immolata Wetter, *Mary Ward: Under the Shadow of the Inquisition*, Oxford, Way Books, 2006, pp. 20–2.

use the name Society of Jesus, as female Carmelites or Benedictines used the name of their male counterparts, gave rise to further objections.

> My confessor resisted, all the Society opposed, various plans were drawn up by several persons [...] These were [...] pressed upon us; there was no remedy but to refuse them. This caused infinite troubles. Then they would needs that at least we should take the name of some Order confirmed, or some new one, or any we could think of, but not that of Jesus. This the fathers of the Society urged exceedingly, and still do so every day, telling us that though they recognise that we will not be satisfied unless we take their Constitutions at least in substance, nevertheless they are unwilling that we use the same name or the same written form for our Rule.[12]

In 1615, in what is nowadays called the 'Just Soul Vision', Mary received further spiritual confirmation. She saw a soul returned to its original state of innocence, in which mind, heart, will and senses were all oriented towards the will of God at work in the world through the power of the Holy Spirit. She understood from this that women as well as men were called to the apostolic life, capable of responding to God in a 'singular freedom [...] entire application and apt disposition to all good works'.[13] By 1616 her companions had multiplied across Europe, and her understanding of a call to the apostolic life had made her insist on freedom from enclosure and from monastic practices and dress. The apostolic aims had spread from the education of girls to 'the salvation of our neighbour [...] by any other means that are congruous to the times'. She presented her plan to the Pope, stressing the Ignatian characteristics of freedom from episcopal authority and the role of the General Superior.

The Jesuits themselves showed a marked ambivalence towards Mary Ward's 'English Ladies', to whom many

---

[12.] Orchard, *Till God Will,* p. 33.
[13.] Ibid., pp. 39–40, 43–6.

referred as 'Jesuitesses'. Some who had experience of women's apostolic potential from the English mission supported them. From others there was immovable opposition.[14] The General Superior, Mutius Vitelleschi, often showed personal kindness and support for the work of Mary and her companions, as long as it remained that of a pious association. Any mention of an Order of Jesuitesses, however, drew his unswerving opposition.[15] This was not only because of Ignatius's ban, but also because the English Ladies became weapons in a bitter campaign waged against the Jesuits by secular clergy and Benedictines on the English mission. The secular clergy's instinctive mistrust of Jesuit innovations was only exacerbated by the unprecedented freedoms claimed by these women who gained the nickname 'Galloping Girls'. Some of the clergy did not hesitate to accuse the Sisters of immorality, financial irregularity and usurping priestly functions in reports based on lurid imagination and vicious rumour.[16] Mary Ward was undeterred, however, and proceeded to open houses in cities including Perugia, Prague, Vienna and Brastislava. In London she and her companions worked in hiding, using many disguises. This drew from George Abbot, Archbishop of Canterbury, the criticism that she 'did more hurt than six or seven Jesuits'. The comment provoked her into visiting Lambeth

---

14. Gerard is attributed with having lent Mary his copy of the Jesuit *Constitutions* from which she drew her third, final and most Ignatian plan, while providing for independent governance in respect for Ignatius's wishes. Something of a loose cannon, his lack of prudence was to cause Mary Ward's Sisters considerable trouble. Gerard's support did not survive the suppression of the Institute. See Philip Caraman, ed., *John Gerard: the Autobiography of an Elizabethan*, London, Longmans, 1951; Henriette Peters, *Mary Ward: a World in Contemplation*, trans. by Helen Butterworth, Leominster, Gracewing, 1994, pp. 218–21 and Wetter, pp. 23–5 and 35–6.

15. Cameron, pp. 123–4 and Peters, pp. 326, 408, 485, 522.

16. Orchard, pp. 48–50, 69, Cameron, pp. 118–23. Mary Ward, described as *'vergine d'animo virile'* was accused of behaving like a priest, driving round Europe in a carriage and pretending to be a duchess *incognita*. See Peters, pp. 468–9.

Palace and, on finding the archbishop from home, leaving her signature carved with a diamond on a window pane.[17]

Some Catholic bishops welcomed Mary Ward's foundations in their dioceses, while others objected either on canonical or juridical grounds when secular rulers supported the Jesuitesses on their territory.[18] Years of apostolic experience not only convinced Mary of the aptness of women for the Jesuit way of life, but of the fundamental equality of women and men before God, a theological insight not universally upheld at the time. One Jesuit expressed his conviction that women were not able to comprehend God as men are. Mary refuted this assumption in a speech made to her sisters in 1617,

> There was a father that lately came into England whom I heard say, that he would not for a 10,000 of worlds be a woman, because he thought a woman could not apprehend God: I answered nothing but only smiled, although I could have answered him by the experience I have of the contrary: I could have been sorry for his want of judgment, I mean not want of judgment, not to condemn his judgment, for he is a man of a very good judgment; his want is in experience.[19]

This marginalization of women's experience within the Church, based on the conviction that their access to God was of an entirely different order from that of men, led to a degree of invisibility and inaudibility in spiritual and ecclesial matters. Women seeking to find a voice and a place in the public forum of the Church were not welcome. Despite this, women of differing nationalities joined Mary Ward's congregation in increasing numbers and their works opened and flourished across Europe.

Without papal approval, they could not access dowry funds and had little or nothing to live on.[20] Deciding to

17. Peters roundly disputes this tale in her *Mary Ward,* p.162.
18. Cardinal Keisl of Vienna illustrates this. See Wetter, p. 31.
19. Ursula Dirmeier, *Mary Ward und ihre Gründung: die Quellentexte bis 1645,* Münster, Aschendorf, 2007, p. 359 (spelling modernized).
20. Cameron, pp. 101–10, 125–36.

plead her cause to the Pope in person, Mary set out in 1621 with a few companions on foot across the Alps, braving the outbreak of war and plague and treacherous conditions. There were initial signs of approval for the companions and their work among girls and women. So successful was their ministry among the poor girls of Rome that it was feared they would put the city's brothels out of business. Despite this it became clear that canonical approval for an Order of female Jesuits would not easily be forthcoming.[21]

In 1622 Mary wrote a two-page memorandum entitled 'Reasons Why We May Not Change', which outlined her conviction that the Jesuit way of life, approved by the Church, was suitable for women and had been successfully tested over time by the virtuous lives and effective apostolates of her sisters. Appealing to social changes and their own experience she argued the need for a new form of religious life for women.[22] The appeals and arguments fell on deaf ears. Convinced that this was God's will, and deceived by Urban VIII's practised diplomatic shifts, Mary continued to hope that papal approval would come, but while encouraging her to her face, the Pope was preparing the suppression of Mary Ward's Jesuitesses and he set about ordering the closure of the houses and dispersal of the Sisters.

Still convinced of papal support, on 6 April 1630 Mary wrote a letter to her Sisters urging them to resist an attempt by enemies to bypass the Pope and suppress their communities.[23] This and the determination of her loyal but impetuous vicar, Winefrid Wigmore, to prevent the closure of the institute, were to prove fatal.[24] Both women appeared to be urging disloyalty to the Church and to be placing Mary's authority as General Superior above that of the Pope and his representatives. Some Sisters submitted to the order of

---

[21.] Orchard, pp. 71–7.

[22.] Peters, p. 332.

[23.] To women brought up in a country without bishops the finer points of hierarchical authority were not always clear. See Wetter, p. 33–5.

[24.] Ibid., pp. 39–41.

suppression; others, including senior figures, had abandoned the Jesuitesses when the storm broke. Winefrid and those remaining were interrogated in a manner calculated to confuse women uneducated in theology and canon law.[25] Mary Ward made one final attempt to explain to Urban VIII the dream that women could live according to the Jesuit Constitutions. She appealed for justice, but when she received no answer, wrote ordering all Sisters, in the event of suppression, to obey without question.[26] Both she and Winefrid were arrested and imprisoned on a charge of heresy, schism and rebellion against the Church.[27]

Mary Ward's imprisonment and the suppression of her congregation had a catastrophic impact on the lives of her Sisters and reverberated far beyond their group. Women of various nationalities were rendered homeless and left without dowries to enable them to return home and marry or enter other Orders.[28] The church authorities were unable to distinguish between Mary Ward's Jesuitesses and other groups and pious institutes who were living in legitimate communities and teaching girls. All were caught in the backlash of the storm that broke over the English Ladies.[29] The Bull of suppression, Pastoralis Romani Pontificis, destroyed any hope of establishing an Order of unenclosed women religious in imitation of the Jesuits. The extreme violence of its language exhibits a deep-seated hostility to any attempt by women to transcend social and theological boundaries imposed on them by the Church.[30] Among other places, the Bull of Suppression was posted up near the Campo dei Fiori in Rome. This is where, within quite recent memory, Giordano Bruno had been burned as a heretic. In her letters, written from prison, Mary makes a chilling reference to the

[25.] Ibid., pp. 42–58.
[26.] Ibid., pp. 68–72. Peters remarks that it was this submission to the Pope that proved her a true Jesuitess. See Peters, p. 565.
[27.] Peters, p. 569; Wetter, p. 74.
[28.] Peters, p. 515.
[29.] Ibid., pp. 474–80, Wetter, pp. 147–57.
[30.] Ibid., pp. 129–140, 213–18 and Peters, p. 566.

question of a quiet judicial execution, which shows that she considered it a real possibility for herself.[31] Once released from prison, she and her Sisters fell under the surveillance of the Inquisition. Homeless and destitute, they were forbidden to seek safety in residing together. In time they gathered into houses in Munich, Rome and York, where Mary died during the English Civil War in 1645, the dream of a female branch of the Jesuits apparently destroyed forever.[32]

The 'poisonous growths in the church of God' had been torn up by the roots, as the Bull demanded, but their extinction 'lest they spread themselves further' was not achieved. The handful of survivors in time became a network of apostolic women inspired by the Jesuit charism, dedicated to female education and devoted to the disgraced foundress.[33] Communities spread across Europe and eventually beyond, but recognition came only slowly. In 1749 Benedict XIV's Apostolic Constitution, *Quamvis Justo*, confirmed the office of General Superior for all similar women's congregations of the future, but Mary Ward's Sisters were made to deny that she was the founder of this permitted 'new' institute.[34] Fearing to share her disgrace, the Sisters attempted to gain legitimacy by destroying her memory, burning precious documents and hiding the *Painted Life*, a series of paintings depicting Mary's spiritual odyssey. But among some her memory and founding dream remained strong. Frances Bedingfield, from another famous recusant family, founded the Bar Convent in York in 1686. In the early nineteenth century Frances Teresa Ball made her noviciate there and returned to her native Ireland to found a second branch of the Order, known as the Institute of the Blessed Virgin Mary, or Loreto Sisters, which spread across continents and into a

---

31. Orchard, p. 107.
32. Wetter, pp. 164–73. Orchard, pp. 115-19.
33. Cameron, pp. 157–61.
34. Cameron, pp. 203–5. Mary Wright, *Mary Ward's Institute: the Struggle for Identity*, Sydney, Crossing, 1997, pp. 43–86, 70–7, 196–213. See also Wetter, pp. 196–8.

third, North American branch.[35] It was from the Loreto
Sisters in India that Mother Teresa of Calcutta made her own
foundation of the Missionaries of Charity. Mary Ward's final
rehabilitation by the Church and the confirmation of her
Order came about in 1909 by a coalition of support from
Jesuits and other clergy in collaboration with Sisters of all
three branches.[36]

In 1979 and 1983 respectively, the oldest two branches of
the IBVM adopted edited forms of the Jesuit Constitutions.[37]
Changes in canon law encouraged the first branch to adopt
the fullest possible text, including the Jesuit fourth vow of
universal mission, in 2004.[38] With this came a change of
name. Its precarious formal status meant that Mary Ward's
Institute had no stable name until the late nineteenth
century.[39] She herself had styled her group 'Mothers of the
Society of Jesus', and had always believed that God wished
the name of Jesus to be included in their title.[40] In a compromise which both honoured this wish and the autonomy of
the Jesuits, the name of the first branch changed to
Congregation of Jesus. Nearly four hundred years after the
first foundation in St Omer, Mary's dream was achieved in
full.

The fate of Mary Ward in her attempt to found an Order of
'women Jesuits' has been seen by a number of commenta-
tors as the tragic outcome of a prophetic vision that
emerged too long before its time or as the mistake of a
woman who could not accept the Church of her time as it
was. Her conviction that God intended women to live and

35. Ibid., pp. 199–203. The North American and Irish branches amalgamated in 2002.
36. Ibid., pp. 203–11.
37. Cameron, pp.161–2.
38. A remarkable concession, given that not all Jesuits are permitted to
take it.
39. Cameron, pp. 99–100.
40. See Peters, pp. 488. Cf. John W. Padberg, ed., *The Constitutions of the
Society of Jesus and their Complementary Norms*, St Louis, Institute of
Jesuit Sources, 1996, p. 3 #1.

work in the Church after the manner of the Society of Jesus admitted of little hope in her lifetime. Future generations would struggle and compromise in order to survive, waiting four centuries before the founding vision became a possibility in its fullness.

At around the same time of Mary's arrest, Galileo was also arrested for insisting, in the name of science, that the world had to look at itself from a different angle. In her own way Mary Ward was doing the same thing, claiming a place for women in society and the Church which had never before been imagined or permitted. Since then, Galileo has received a formal apology by the Church, but Mary Ward's story remains largely ignored. Where did she get the inspiration for such a pioneering vision, and what has become of it? There are two axes on which her vision was founded: the Ignatian *Spiritual Exercises* and the lived experience of women within her family and social networks.

The persecuted women of the recusant networks came to rely on their experience as a trustworthy source for spiritual discernment. They also became inventive, in the absence of church structures by which to organize their spiritual and sacramental lives, in developing their capacities for apostolic service. Mary Ward took as the model of life for herself and her Sisters the female companions of Jesus in the New Testament, who followed and supported his ministry and collaborated in spreading the good news of the kingdom. She heard that a Jesuit had commented that she and her Sisters were doing admirably, 'but fervour will decay, and when all is done, they are but women'. Indignantly, she commented,

'Fervour is a will to do well [...] which women may have as well as men.' And again,

It is true that fervour doth many times grow cold, but what is the cause? Is it because we are women? No, but because we are imperfect women [...] and love not verity but seek after lies [...] If we fail, it is for want of this verity, and not because we are women [...] There is no such difference between men and women [...] And I hope in God it will be seen that women in time will do much.[41]

It has not always been easy for Mary Ward's Sisters to think and act with the same freedom. Under the weight of ecclesial disapproval they, like many women's religious Orders founded with a vision of apostolic freedom, adopted monastic characteristics and became far more enclosed than originally intended. It would not be until the Second Vatican Council that the authentic founding vision of Mary Ward would once more emerge and seem a real possibility.

The then Cardinal Ratzinger, himself a former pupil of the Mary Ward Sisters, preached a homily at the Mass commemorating the fourth centenary of Mary Ward's birth in St Mary Major's Basilica on 23 January 1985, in which he said,

> Even when she saw her work destroyed by the authority of the Church she [...] remained, in a rebellious age, firmly anchored in the Catholic Church [...] The Church caused Mary Ward great suffering, but at the same time, the Church was for her, her surest consolation and peace, the ground of all ages, the guarantee of the truth of the promise: one sows and another reaps.

As Pope Benedict XVI he sent a message of greeting for the Mass celebrated in York Minster in January 2009 in honour of the four hundredth anniversary of the founding of the Order,

> For four hundred years, religious women have drawn inspiration from Mary Ward's determination and courage, and following her example, they have dedicated themselves to carrying out God's will through an active apostolic service. Generations of students have cause to be grateful to the sisters for the Christian education they have received, and many more have benefited from the spiritual guidance and the formation of discipleship offered by the 'English Ladies'. His Holiness prays that, through the inspiration of their

41. Orchard, pp. 56–7.

foundress, the members of the two Congregations will continue to be 'fountains of living water in the midst of a thirsting world'.   *Deus Caritas Est*, 42

Today Mary Ward Sisters live in every continent of the world. There are Sisters of whose nationality she had never dreamed: Koreans, Australians, Nepalese, Africans and South Americans. While historically the congregation has largely undertaken the running of schools, the congregation is no more a 'teaching order' than the Jesuits are. Most of the schools are now under lay management, while Sisters work in formal education but also in any other way that will further the kingdom of God. Mary Ward's original conviction that 'there is no such difference between men and women, that women may not do great things' has become a reality in some societies, but is far from being realized in others. With their lay collaborators, Sisters remain convinced that when the situation of girls and women in society improves, the whole of that society benefits. All over the world, from Albania to Zimbabwe, from Mongolia to East Timor, from Cuba to Israel, Mary Ward's Sisters continue, through educational, social, pastoral and spiritual ministries to live as contemplatives in action, in the spirit of Ignatius of Loyola. It would seem that Mary Ward's time has come at last.

Chapter 12

Maria Fitzherbert

Mark Elvins

Not far from where the Shrophire border is intersected by
the M54 lies the village of Tong. The church, with its octago-
nal tower, contains a feast of medieval monuments with
knights of the de Pembrugge, Vernon, Brereton and Stanley
families, immortalized in alabaster, lying with their dames on
an assortment of altar tombs. Where the motorway cuts
across the old glebe land, on the west side of the church,
once stood Tong Castle; here on 26 July 1756 was born Mary
Ann, the eldest child of Walter Smythe. A Catholic baronet-
ical family of Acton Burnel in the county of Shropshire.
Walter was the second son of the third baronet and being
barred from the universities of Oxford and Cambridge and
from holding a commission in the armed services, by virtue
of his Catholicism, his father purchased him a commission in
the cavalry of the Austrian imperial army. After a brief military career of six years he resigned his commission in 1751,
possibly as a consequence of an inheritance. His cousin
Clare Smythe had died unmarried and had left him the
equivalent of £700,000 in modern currency. His marriage to
Mary Ann Errington of Walton Hall, Lancashire in 1755 also
brought him financial dividends. In 1763 another well-
heeled cousin died and left Walter his estate of Brambridge
in the county of Hampshire.

Walter Smythe now had the status of a country squire and
Mary Ann, the oldest of his eight children, left her uncle's
home of Acton Burnel, at the age of six, to enjoy the plea-

sures of Brambridge. As an English recusant family the Smythes, although not unduly pious, kept a domestic chaplain and allowed their tenants and neighbours to come to hear Mass on Sundays and holy days. Later Walter Smythe set up a chapel in the village of which some traces still remain as part of a converted nurseryman's house. No doubt Mary Ann had a tutor or governess but her education was completed by a spell in a French convent in the town of Dunkirk. Her parents escorted her on her journey and on one such occasion took her to Paris, where she witnessed King Louis XV dining in state at his palace of Versailles. She was so tickled by Louis's ferocious dismembering of a chicken that she burst into laughter and was rewarded by the King with a dish of sugar plums.

Thus from an early age she seemed to be at ease with royalty. Her education by modern standards was probably more consistent with a finishing school than an academic institution, but the acquisition of French, certain self-assurance and easeful good manners were to serve their purpose in her future life. In the mid 1770s Mary Ann had returned to England and was no doubt considering a husband. The Catholic squirearchy was a tight-knit element in landed society and Mary Ann was related to the Erringtons (through her mother), the Blounts (through her paternal grandmother) and her maternal grandmother was also mother to Charles Molyneux 1st Earl of Sefton. Given the marriage market of the time, much conditioned by landed family alliances, Edward Weld of Lulworth Castle, Dorset was considered an appropriate consort.

Edward Weld was about forty and Mary Ann twenty-five when they married in 1775; he owned 12,000 acres in Dorset, Oxfordshire, Lancashire, Staffordshire and Derbyshire, and in modern currency received an annual income of £444,000. Edward had been educated abroad at the Jesuit college of St Omer, the forerunner of Stonyhurst, and had been taught the harpsichord and the skills of fencing, as befitted a gentleman of his standing. As was the custom he travelled the grand tour, but in 1761 his father died and he became master of Lulworth at the age of twenty. He did not return to England until 1762 as a refined young man with an ear for music. He married the Hon. Juliana Petre the daughter of the ninth Lord Petre, who brought a dowry of £10,000. Juliana died childless in 1772. As an eighteenth-century gentleman he had the unusual hobby of sailing to the Continent, but when at home followed the conventual pastimes of riding to hounds and shooting hares and pheasants. When in London he would go to the theatre and frequent the gambling houses, his other social adventures included dining with the Stourtons, the Arundells, the Giffards and the Earl of Shrewsbury, not excluding at least four dinner parties with the Smythes.

Mary Ann's marriage is recorded in the register of the recusant chapel at Brambridge on 13 July 1775. However the law obliged Catholics at that time to be married in a Protestant church, and so the ceremony at Brambridge had probably followed some time later. It is interesting to note that Sir Bernard Burke, Ulster King of Arms, wrote in his 'Reminiscenses' at this time that the Catholic gentry were the most noted for the antiquity of their descent and the size of their land holdings. In the secluded fastnesses of Lulworth Mary Anne found herself part of a celebrated Catholic colony that looked to the Welds for protection. The Welds like the Smythes had built a recusant chapel but employed the services of the Jesuits as chaplains, unlike the Smythes who employed Benedictines.

Lulworth Castle had in fact been built by Thomas Howard, Lord Bindon between 1608 and 1610 and was purchased by Sir Humphrey Weld from Lord Bindon's kinsman the Earl of Suffolk. Humprey became a Catholic on marriage and was appointed Queen Henrieta Maria's Cup Bearer and Governor of the various Isles and Castles of Portland and Sandsfoot. The Civil War saw Lulworth Castle lost to the Parliamentarians and slighted against any further military intentions. Come the Restoration Sir Humphrey was knighted, made MP for Christchurch and set about restoring his ancestral pile. Poor Sir Humphrey became implicated in the Popish Plot and his privations forced him to mortgage his estate. He died a debtor in 1684 and was succeeded by another Humphrey, who suffered the consequences of the Jacobite risings. He in turn was succeeded by an Edward Weld, the father of Mary Ann's husband.

It was Mary Ann's husband who put the finishing touches on the restoration of Lulworth Castle, but in less than three months of his nuptials he suffered a riding accident in his park and died. Mary Ann became 'the widow Weld' and after a discreet period of mourning re-entered fashionable society in about 1776. Presentations at Court are recorded from 1785 but Hester Thrale, Samuel Johnson's biographer, some time after the event wrote that 'pretty Mrs Weld a widow', was presented. Mary Ann moved in the company of English landed recusants in London where her youth and prettiness would soon attract the attention of another suitor. Thomas Fitzherbert, heir to a fortune and head of an old Catholic family, became smitten by the young widow. He was tall and well made but perhaps with a tendency towards corpulence. No doubt the first meeting was at one of the numerous musical soirées with which fashionable London abounded. It is uncertain as to whether he was the same Thomas Fitzherbert who was godfather to Mary Ann's youngest sister. Notwithstanding they were married on 24 June 1778 at St George's Hanover Square.

Public attitudes towards Catholics were changing and Thomas was in the forefront of supporting Catholic emancipation. Even George III supported the campaign which resulted in a private member's bill to repeal the bigoted 1699 Act of William III, and on 27 May 1778 the Catholic Relief Bill received Royal Assent. This meant that it was no longer a crime to be a Catholic priest or religious and Catholic bishops and schoolmasters had legal standing. For the Fitzherberts and other Catholic landowners there was no longer any restriction on inheriting land and Protestant kinsmen could not, as before, claim the inheritance. Thus, in good time, on 3 October Thomas succeeded his father as Lord of the Manor of Swynnerton.

Mary Ann was mistress of yet another great house; Swynnerton like Lulworth and Brambridge was at the heart of a small Catholic community dependant on the local landowner for a livelihood. The Fitzherberts lived a full social life and Mary Ann would have had the pleasure of two of her brothers among the house guests: Walter the oldest and Jack. Her younger brothers Charles and Henry may well have also joined the house party. It was during this time at Swynnerton that Mary Ann's's younger sister Frances met the young Carnaby Haggerston, whom she later married. He was from an old Northumberland recusant family and heir to a baronetcy. Another of the charmed circle was the Lady Anne Lindsay, the eldest child of the fifth Earl of Balcarres. She was a witty, intelligent, cultured and garrulous woman with a gift for writing, indeed her writings have provided much of the information on Mary Ann, for they became life-long friends and correspondents.

It was at this time that Mary Ann followed the eighteenth-century fashion of Latinizing her name to Maria, which remains the name by which she is known to posterity. This fashionable world of the English landed recusant families was shattered in the year 1780, when the Catholic Relief Act met with a Protestant backlash. A young Scottish Member of Parliament, Lord George Gordon stirred up an anti-Catholic mob in London, which burnt the Catholic embassy chapels of Bavaria and Sardinia, torched Newgate Prison, pillaged several private dwellings and even tried to attack the royal residence (later known as Buckingham Palace). The riot was eventually quelled by the local militia, with considerable number of casualties: about four hundred and fifty being killed or wounded. The crazed Lord George Gordon was arrested and accused of high treason but was acquitted on account of his cousin's evidence. Despite being undaunted he was later to be excommunicated by the Archbishop of Canterbury, and convicted of defaming the Queen of France and the French Ambassador. A change of heart subsequently compelled him to make his escape to the Netherlands, but he was forced to leave even that country. Upon his return to

England he was promptly arrested and was sentenced to five years in Newgate under harsh conditions.

Thomas Weld was so concerned at the rampaging of the Protestant mob that he feared Lulworth might be stormed. He contemplated sending Maria, who was pregnant, to a place of safety, but King George III himself intervened, and largely due to his timely action the riot was quelled. The stress and fatigue that Thomas suffered, with concern for his wife and his property, found him imprudently taking a cold bath. Although this was not in itself a great danger to his health his tubercular condition would seem to have become subsequently exacerbated. He travelled to Nice, a popular resort for consumptive Englishmen, but to no avail; he died on 7 May 1781 and was buried in the Dominican Priory Chapel at Nice.

Poor Maria had now been twice widowed and was to lose her second child as well as her first. Some friends from England (Fermors) wrote in sympathy, and in her reply she expresses her feelings:

> It gives me some comfort to find I have a few friends left for such real friends as you have ever been to me are rare indeed to be found & at this Crisis the few I have are the only comfort I have in life & they are more necessary to me at this moment than I can describe the thoughts of which help to support the many severe trials with which I am overpower'd & without whom I should never be abler to support myself but sink entirely under the heavy load of afflictions that oppress me.

The lack of punctuation was typical of the time and Maria continues the letter in expressing the dereliction of her loss. She had suffered a fever, and moreover took a year to recover her composure and return to England. She had the house in Park Lane, bestowed on her by her loving husband and an annual income of £1,800, nearer £102,000 in modern currency. She was still a follower of fashion and in keeping with the times she took a apartments in Brighton which had become the most popular watering hole for the London set.

Apart from lodging at her Brighton, Richmond and Mayfair properties she would also tour the fashionable spa towns where she would meet old friends and make new ones.

Maria had spied the Prince of Wales out riding in the London Parks but her first encounter with him was when leaving the opera in 1784. Her uncle Henry Errington had persuaded her to join Lord Sefton's party and after the performance was spotted by the Prince making her departure with her uncle. 'Who the Devil is that pretty girl you have on your arm, Henry?' demanded the Prince. He was promptly introduced to Mrs Fitzherbert. This was the start of a prolonged infatuation with the Prince showering Maria with gifts and even commissioning Gainsborough to paint her portrait. Suddenly she became the focus of public attention and later even a ballad was written to express a now popular admiration – 'The Lass of Richmond Hill', where she had in fact recently taken up residence. Whether she was the lady of the ballad is uncertain, but she became so in the public mind.

Notwithstanding the Prince's ardour the Act of Succession and the Royal Marriage Act were major obstacles to any thought of his marrying a Catholic. Maria, who at first was amused and flattered by all the attention she was receiving, gradually warmed to the Prince's charms and began to find him both attractive and lovable. A marriage between a Catholic and a member of the Royal Family was not only forbidden but was also a bar to succession and the Catholic Stuarts, the rightful heirs to the throne, had thus been superseded by the House of Hanover. Moreover the Royal Marriage Act of 1772 made any marriage without the Sovereign's approval null and void.

Despite these difficulties the Prince was becoming delirious with frustration and Maria was told that unless she came to him he would do himself harm. The rumour was that he had stabbed himself. When she finally visited him at Carlton House she found him bandaged, lying in bed pale and bloodstained. The Prince seized the opportunity and declared that the only thing that would induce him to live was her promise of matrimony. Maria must have been sufficiently overcome by the experience to submit and the Prince, suddenly regaining his strength, popped a ring on her finger. Subsequently Maria regarded her consent as insubstantial as it was extorted under duress and she hastened abroad, no doubt hoping that upon her return the whole thing would have subsided.

Both the Prince and Maria were demonstrative people who could be convinced by their own rhetoric; both loved the social life of London and whereas the Prince was somewhat reckless in his behaviour she seemed to err on the side of caution. During her Continental sojourn the Prince would pursue her with letters delivered by couriers. When she finally returned it seems Maria had succumbed to the Prince's blandishments, not that she was swept off her feet but rather as a sensible woman who desired to shine in fashionable society as the wife and not the mistress of the Prince of Wales. She was sharp enough to realize that any marriage would be unlawful, but nevertheless it was the Prince who insisted upon it.

What ensued was one of the country's great love affairs ending with a rather public secret marriage at the hands of a Protestant clergyman, the Revd Robert Burt, in the drawing room of Maria's house in Park Street, Mayfair. To indicate Maria's arrival in the upper echelons of society she acquired a box at the opera, then housed at the Theatre Royal in the Haymarket. The opera at that time, as in most of the European capitals, was an opportunity for the ruling classes to see and be seen. At this time there was much talk of Maria's supposed pregnancy and there were later several improbable candidates claiming to be offsprings of the union. When Maria was asked to declare that there was no issue from her marriage she declined on the grounds of delicacy. Although apparently childless, she was not averse to children for she adopted two girls in later life.

At this time (1787) the Prince was estranged from his father George III who gave him no responsibilities as the heir to the throne. The Prince's extravagances had also ensured that his father kept a tight hand on his allowance and his debts were mounting. The King refused any help until he was presented with a list of debts and the names of the debtors, and moreover insisted that the Prince promise to reform his life. However the Prince's young circle boasted a number of Members of Parliament, including Richard Brinsley Sheridan, the playwright. These decided to raise the matter of the Prince's income in the Commons to force the King to act in the Prince's favour. In the event William Pitt, the Prime Minister, declared that it was not his position to raise such matters without the King's express permission. On a subsequent occasion however a Mr Newnham brought forward a motion in the Commons touching the Prince's income, without being very specific as to its ramifications. This exposed Pitt to the jibes of the opposition and Fox spoke of the novelty of the Prince's position hinting at his irregular marriage. This was tantamount to cajoling the House into granting the Prince his allowance to avoid the embarrassment of delving into his marital adventures. Pitt stalled but Newnham promised to prosecute the cause.

It became 'open season' as a flurry of pamphlets issued from the presses proclaiming to all and sundry the irregular nature of the Prince's alliance to Maria Fitzherbert. On 27 April that same year Newnham returned to his proposed motion suggesting a more delicate approach to the King on the Prince's behalf, in the form of a humble address. Pitt by thus time had yielded to pressure to avoid embarrassing the King. Sheridan alluded to the Prince's questionable nuptials but Pitt, full of respect for the Crown, did not wish the matter to be debated. The Prince, although convinced that he was secretly married, publicly denied it with Maria's compliance. As it was the Commons was duped by the good offices of Fox, who genuinely believed there had been no marriage, and thus saved the Crown from embarrassment and the Prince from legal prosecution.

However Maria became incandescent in the knowledge that Fox had gone to such lengths to deny her marriage to the Commons; this would make her the Prince's mistress which she had strenuously sought to avoid. Fox on the other hand found he had been lied to by the Prince. Newnham still awaited the introduction of his motion which threatened to bring the truth of the marriage into the public forum. However the King, as if by preternatural knowledge, decided to settle his son's debts and increase his income with the forlorn proviso that he would avoid debt in the future. Newnham withdrew his motion and the Prince celebrated a piece of arch deception.

In October of 1788 rumours began to circulate as to the King's health: his physician informed the Prime Minister that His Majesty's behaviour was bordering on delusion. By November the London coffee houses were agog and Dr Warren, one of the King's physicians and also physician to Maria, declared the Sovereign 'Rex noster insanit'. Pitt was exercised by the need to set up a Regency Government and once again Maria found herself the focus of public speculation. After twenty-eight years the King's reign was drawing to a close, but Maria's Catholicism became the but of ridicule particularly as the so called Protestant 'Glorious Revolution' of William III was reaching its centenary.

On 16 December the Commons finally accepted that the Prince would be Regent but there were grave misgivings as to the constitution if the Prince had taken a Catholic wife. The pamphleteers again seized their opportunity and one Horne Took proclaimed that the Prince could not be legally Regent or King for that matter as long as he was married to a papist. With scant regard for the truth the pamphleteers and newspaper journalists heaped opprobrium on poor Maria and with rumours of the King's recovery the Regency Bill was inevitably delayed. Meanwhile despite the times in 1791 the Second Reform Act was passed allowing Catholics to build churches and schools and to qualify as barristers, solicitor, clerks and notaries and the crime of recusancy was abolished for those prepared to take an accommodating oath.

Maria had by this time become impatient of the Prince's many caprices, as he seemed incapable of any degree of faithfulness, toying with the affections of a bevy of haughty sirens. Lady Jersey, six years Maria's senior and a married woman, determined to supplant Maria, who may even have been relieved at her success. Certainly political circles buzzed with the talk of a treaty of separation. The Prince, mindful of his father's desire to see his debts settled, was enticed by the pecuniary advantages of seeking an official wife who would secure him an extra allowance and satisfy the requirements of state. Thus negotiations were opened in 1794 to secure the hand of his cousin the Princess Caroline of Brunswick.

The Prince's annual allowance was made up to £138,000 with £325,000 to defray the cost of the nuptials. Meanwhile Maria, who had returned the Prince's recent letters unopened had sold her house in St James's Square. Subsequent to his nuptials the Prince had however developed a distinct aversion to his new wife and was narrowly prevented from taking his carriage to find consolation with Maria, who for her part began to cope unenthusiastically with the 'quiet life'. In the eyes of the Catholic Church her marriage was probably considered valid, but in the face of the Act of Succession and the Royal Marriage Act would have been civilly unlawful. It was labelled a 'morganatic' marriage, despite the fact that such conditions did not apply to England, unlike the Continent where a man of higher rank marrying a woman of lower rank would cause the disinheritance of the children. The only similarity would have been that any* children born to Maria of this union would have been debarred by the various pieces of legislation.

The Prince's affections, as inconstant as ever, now turned back to Maria, who despite having had a genuine *amour* must have become exasperated by the fickleness of the royal mood. Nevertheless in 1799 she consulted her confessor, Fr John Nassau, from the Bavarian Embassy Chapel in Warwick

---

* An American researcher, Bruce Shattuck, has alleged that Maria bore the Prince a son who was named James Henry Adolph Fitzherbert. He claims that William IV in 1832 paid for him to seek exile in America. Further evidence would be required to treat this with any seriousness.

Street, as to her marital standing. In consideration of the delicacy of the matter Fr Nassau set out on a clandestine visit to Rome. He had an audience with Pope Pius VII to whom he presented his case in writing. After several days, on 8 August, the Pope's counsellors found in Maria's favour, that in the eyes of the Church she was indeed married to Prince George. However because of the turbulent nature of the times no record survives in the Vatican, but we do know that Maria was allowed to return to her husband if she so wished, however there may have been the proviso that they live as brother and sister. Even Maria's intolerance of the Prince's petulance seemed assuaged, and the Prince for his part seemed to have grown out of his petty jealousies. Maria in writing to her friend Lady Anne actually commented, 'We live like brother and sister.' The reconciliation was on Maria's terms and she agreed to be neither wife nor mistress. In all the Prince's philanderings Maria seems to have upheld a high moral probity, for she refused to share his bed, taking this brother-sister relationship quite literally.

Maria was by now a matron of forty-four years but may well have been acting on the advice of her confessor, for despite the maelstrom of scandal that had swirled about her since she first took up with the Prince, her Catholic faith always took precedent. In her reminiscences Maria recalls the next eight years as being among the happiest she had known with the Prince; she had taken control and he had matured immensely. Maria took up again with her lavish entertaining and the Prince increased her allowance. Something must have changed the public consciousness for on their first drive along the Steine at Brighton they were publicly cheered.

As in the past the Princes's attempts at reformed behaviour were never to last and his indelible weakness of character would inevitably become manifest. It had been Maria's lot to try and coax him into some kind of moral consistency, but as a Catholic of high integrity she was besieged by a society of simmering moral corruption which outweighed any influence she might have had on the wayward Prince. The death of the King's favourite daughter, Princess Amelia, in 1810, was to push him into the utter oblivion of madness, which allowed the Prince to obtain at last his longed-for Regency – not that this seemed to impart any measure of gravitas to his behaviour.

The final parting of the ways came in the same year when, with typical caprice, the Prince even neglected to place Maria at his table at a Carlton House fête. She recalled in later life that this was the last time she saw the Prince. By the 1820s Brighton had become her principal home where she lived with two adopted daughters, Minney Seymour and Marianne who took the name of Smythe. During these later years she devoted more time to her religion and was noted for her generosity to the poor and to the local Catholic school. In many ways, after she had parted company with the profligate Prince, she seemed to come into her own living a life of exemplary kindness and generosity. She donated £1,000 towards the cost of a new Catholic church at Kemp Town in Brighton, having coaxed the Marquis of Bristol to give the land.

In 1820 George III died and the Prince succeeded as George IV; his daughter by Caroline of Brunswick, Priness Charlotte, had died in 1817 and Caroline herself died in 1821. George IV himself was to die in 1830 still with a locket containing Maria's portrait around his neck; even at the end he protested that she was the only woman he ever loved. The succeeding monarch, William IV, offered to make Maria a duchess, mindful of all the difficulties she had suffered at the hands of his brother George IV. Maria replied that 'she had borne through life the name of Mrs Fitzherbert; that she had never disgraced it, and did not wish to change it'.

Despite the gradual improvement of the lot of Catholics in England, with the passing of the Second Relief Act of 1791, Maria lived in the face of constant public hostility and was often the butt of fanatical bigots. The society she inhabited was consumed with decadence and moral turpitude and although she enjoyed socializing among the ruling classes, her own character remained unsullied. Moreover her dignity and refinement projected a better royal image than any other member of the House of Hanover. In fact at the height of her influence all would rise at her entrance and address her with deference as if she did indeed possess royal status. The Church was undergoing some calamitous experiences at the time with the Gallicanism of France and the Febronianism of Austria in which the various sovereigns sought to subject the Church to the State. Moreover Napoleon had arrested Pope Pius VII, thrown him into prison and tried to force him to capitulate.

Despite all these threats to her religion Maria retained a dignified commitment and continued to support the new parish of St John the Baptist at Kemp Town, Brighton. The rather exotic nature of the company she kept in fact enhanced her own moral integrity and as an isolated Catholic in a sea of indifferentism she probably did much to enhance the perception of Catholicism. She had refused to become the mistress of the Prince of Wales, whom she had genuinely loved, and moreover brought some order to his life of restless, flamboyant egocentricity. She was indeed married in the eyes of the Church which flouted all the absurd anti-Catholic legislation. Her story is that of the love of a heroic and kind-hearted woman for a fickle and pampered prince of the House of Hanover.

Maria died on 27 March 1837 aged eighty and was buried in her parish church of St John the Baptist, Kemp Town, Brighton, where her *prie-dieu* may still be seen as witness to her regular devotions.

Chapter 13

M. Margaret Hallahan, OP

Judith Champ

When, on 11 May 1868, Margaret Hallahan died after a long and agonizing illness, one of the leading figures in the Catholic Church in England mourned her as a beloved sister. William Bernard Ullathorne, first Bishop of Birmingham, and by 1868 the most senior and respected figure among the English bishops, described his long friendship with Margaret Hallahan as 'the greatest privilege of my life'. He chose the church of St Dominic, which she built at Stone in north Staffordshire, as the last resting place for his own mother, and also for himself, ensuring that his story, and therefore that of the Victorian Catholic revival, cannot be told without reference to her. Margaret Hallahan was one of a generation of remarkable women in nineteenth-century Britain who established a new style and form of female religious life, which would play a vital and influential part in the emergence of modern Catholic life over the ensuing century. Their stories have many similarities in the dedication, selflessness and determination which women like Catherine McAuley, Elizabeth Prout, Frances Taylor, Genevieve Dupuis, Margaret Hallahan and others showed in the face of hostility both within and beyond Catholic circles. What was it about Margaret Hallahan which won her the high regard and affection of an unsentimental and often rebarbative man like Ullathorne, and the deep respect and admiration of Newman, Manning and other Victorian clerics?

The story of Margaret Hallahan fits, to some extent, into a familiar pattern identified by the growing number of historians exploring the phenomenon of female religious life and experience in Victorian Britain. Despite some attempts to explain this phenomenon simply in terms of social and economic change, the spiritual call to God's service experienced by women has also been recognized, as in Carmen Mangion's recent book, *Contested Identities: Catholic women religious in nineteenth Century England and Wales*.[1] Mangion sets out lucidly how the spiritual call or vocation of women might be experienced.

The desire for a relationship with God was revealed in three ways: first, through a yearning for communion with God, second, through the desire to remedy spiritual or physical poverty, and, third, through a wish to lead an industrious life not restricted by cloister walls. The relationship with God was often interwoven into a relationship with the poor. This trio of objectives merged into a vocation for active religious life.[2]

This 'trio of objectives' was certainly present from a very early stage in Margaret Hallahan's life, but as with so many remarkable lives, it was the chance of circumstance and the providence of encounters with strangers which gave her life its particular direction. She was the only child of London Irish Catholic parents, and was brought up in the 'Irish ghetto' of St Giles in the first years of the nineteenth century. Poverty and sickness were endemic in the city slums and Irish Catholics were often at the bottom of the social and economic scale. The practice of Catholicism was severely limited by lack of resources and personnel, as well as by continued anti-Catholic and anti-Irish sentiment fuelled by the Irish Rebellion and the Napoleonic wars. Although there were Catholic mission schools in St Giles, Margaret was educated in Somers Town in a school established by a French émigré priest, Abbé Carron.

[1.] Mangion, Carmen, *Contested Identities: Catholic women religious in nineteenth-century England and Wales*, Manchester, Manchester University Press, 2008.

[2.] Mangion, p. 61.

The death of both her parents from consumption, within months of each other in 1813, left her destitute and orphaned at the age of nine. She was, through the intervention of the Abbé, placed in service, spending several years with the French émigré family of Madame Caulier. Although Madame Caulier was fond of Margaret and even contemplated adopting her, she treated the child with a severity which induced timidity, and even provoked her to run away on one occasion. Margaret, however, stayed under Madame Caulier's protection on and off until the age of twenty, when she was placed in the service of an elderly doctor for whom she cared until his death. His married daughter, Mrs Thompson, kept Margaret on as a companion and children's nanny for twenty years, fifteen of which she spent living with this family in Belgium. This perilous and uncertain life of patronage by wealthy families, which could be withdrawn at any time, was often the fate of orphaned girls in Victorian society, the alternative all too often being complete destitution. It was an experience of life which could not only inculcate a deep empathy for the poor, but, in those with a spark of religious faith, a profound sense of utter dependence on God. Both of these would characterize Margaret Hallahan's life and work, with her constant motto in adulthood being, 'God alone'.

While staying with the Thompson family in Kent, Margaret met Mary Louisa Amherst who was the daughter of relatives holidaying nearby. It was also around this time that she began to feel the first stirrings of a vocation to serve God in some direct way. Margaret's instincts and Catholic piety had been nurtured by life in a Catholic household, and were greatly enhanced by the decision of the Thompsons to move to Bruges in 1829. Margaret was then twenty-three, but, with little education or financial prospects, she had little option but to accept the invitation to accompany the family. She was fearful of life abroad, yet it was life in Bruges which would shape her future direction and purpose. The environment of Catholic Bruges encouraged her timid aspirations to religious life and she entered the English Convent of

Augustinians in the city, but soon found that it was not for her. She returned to the Thompsons swiftly, to her life of hidden service and to a life of increasing domestic responsibility as the family was forced by straightened circumstances to reduce the size of their household staff. In addition to her domestic role, Margaret gained a considerable reputation around Bruges for her private acts of charity to the poor. The atmosphere of Bruges and the contacts she made there certainly influenced her, and inspired her with a vision of Catholic life and practice as an everyday reality, unlike the constrained experience of English Catholicism.

Through the local priest, Abbé Capron, and Abbé Bruno Versavel, who became her spiritual director, Margaret was introduced to the writings and spirit of St Dominic and in particular to St Catherine of Siena. Like Margaret, Catherine was a laywoman drawn to the charism of St Dominic at an early age, who dedicated her life to the service of God and of the poor. She would become Margaret's patron and model. Born in the mid fourteenth century, Catherine lived in a Europe devastated by the Black Death and a Church riven by faction and division. The most famous achievement of her short and intense life was to persuade Gregory XI to return the papacy from Avignon to Rome. It was not, however, Catherine's public career which appealed to Margaret, but in her reading of Catherine's letters and mystical dialogues she found an extraordinary combination of an intense contemplative inner life with an active apostolate among the poor and needy of her own society, which was an expression of love. In her dialogues, Catherine reveals many of the conversations between herself and the Father and the theme is always one of love. 'Take your tears and your sweat', God told her, 'drawn from the fountain of my divine love, and with them wash the face of my spouse, the Church.'

This devotion to the Dominican Order, and to St Catherine in particular, shaped Margaret's spiritual life and in 1835 she was professed as a Dominican Tertiary, becoming a member of the religious family of St Dominic without entering a religious community, although Margaret chose to make a personal solemn vow of lifelong chastity. Tertiaries, then as now, lived under the charism and influence of the Dominican Order, but continued to live in their own homes and pursue their normal activities in life. This time in Bruges, under the fierce guidance of Abbé Versavel, and the gentler influence of St Catherine of Siena, was her time of real spiritual formation and pastoral development, although a serious illness came close to taking her life prematurely and left her weak and unable to return to work for a time. Indirectly, this led to her return to England. Attempts to form a small residential community of Tertiaries in Bruges met with difficulties, and influential clergy, including her own confessor, put a damper on the project. Abbé Versavel placed her under obedience to accept an invitation to return to England, and the insecurity of her position in life left her little option.

St Dominic's Order of Preachers had taken root swiftly in England in the thirteenth century, beginning in Oxford and founding some sixty houses by the end of the century. Female convents had been an integral part of the Dominican way of life from the beginning, but the Reformation had swept the friars and nuns from English soil. In the middle of the seventeenth century, Philip Howard, later Cardinal, had begun the restoration of the English Dominican friars, but even by the early nineteenth century they were few and far between. Only one female house existed, at Atherstone in Warwickshire, and the Dominican Tertiaries, to which Margaret had committed herself, were unknown in England. The charism of the Tertiaries reflected that of St Catherine, which was so close to Margaret Hallahan's heart, in combining the contemplative life with an active apostolate. This charism shaped Margaret Hallahan's life and her determination to serve God within the Dominican family, rather than to establish any new Order. In this respect, she differed strongly from other foundresses of her generation, who started from scratch in establishing their own characteristic way of life, perhaps borrowing from other traditions. Margaret was determined that, whatever she did, it would be

Dominican, and that it would, as Catherine put it, walk on the 'two feet' of contemplation and action.

Mary Louisa Amherst, the daughter of a Catholic squire, Francis Fortescue Turville of Bosworth Hall, was linked to the Thompson family by marriage, and both families were part of a close-knit Catholic Anglo-Indian network. She was the mother of Francis Kerril Amherst, who eventually became Bishop of Northampton in 1858. Initially he had no plans for ordination and after leaving school, he trained as an engineer, partly in Bruges, where, between 1839 and 1841, he lodged with the Thompsons. Mrs Amherst had heard from her son of 'Peggy' and her role in the Thompson household and in the local community, and urged Margaret Hallahan to return to England, where there was so much work to be done. This coincided with Margaret's failure to establish a house of Dominican Tertiaries in Bruges and Abbé Versavel's insistence that her future lay in England. The Amherst family home was in Kenilworth, Warwickshire, and Mrs Amherst took a close interest in the Catholic mission in nearby industrial Coventry. Her husband, who died in 1835, was buried in Coventry and later reinterred in the new church of St Osburg for which Margaret did much of the fundraising. Eventually, husband and wife were reunited in a tomb in the church built by their own efforts in Kenilworth.

Coventry, an industrial city producing ribbons and silks for the fashionable clothing trade and surrounded by coal mines, contained a great deal of hardship and poverty. It did not have a strong Catholic presence, despite its medieval past as one of the great centres of monastic and popular religious practice. The small and somewhat dispirited Catholic congregation had been cared for by a Benedictine mission, manned by monks from Downside Abbey since 1803, and in 1842 it was placed under the care of William Bernard Ullathorne, newly returned from a punishing twelve years in Australia. Mrs Amherst, the main local benefactor, approached Ullathorne with the proposal that Margaret Hallahan would be an asset in building up the spirit of

Catholics in Coventry and could do much good, particularly
among the large number of women employed in the ribbon
factories. Convinced by Mrs Amherst's warm recommendation, Ullathorne agreed to Margaret's appointment to
Coventry. He assured Mrs Amherst that her arrival would be
providential, and that she would be, 'an instrument destined
to do much in this town'.

On 30 April 1842, Margaret landed in England, and made
her way to Mrs Amherst's home in Kenilworth and thence to
Coventry. There she met Ullathorne for the first time. Her
first impressions are not recorded, but his are quoted in her
biography:

> I shall never forget my first meeting with her, in the little
> house I then occupied at Coventry. She was then in her
> vigour, well-proportioned, very erect, and having an impres-
> sion of dignity and simplicity combined, yet with a spiritual
> softness pervading features that indicated her remarkable
> powers of mind and heart. It seized me with a sense of
> surprise as well as gratification. I at once felt that Mrs
> Amherst's promise that I should find her a valuable co-
> operator in my mission was far more than realised.[3]

Margaret moved into the cramped, damp and crumbling
house, sharing the kitchen with a bad-tempered housekeeper, and within a fortnight found herself alone in her
new post. Ullathorne had been asked to return to Australia
as Bishop of Adelaide and was determined to go to Rome
and plead his cause against the appointment. He was,
inevitably, away for some months, so Margaret simply got on
with the tasks she identified as necessary, in the same way as
she had done in Bruges. On his return, Ullathorne was
amazed and impressed to find that Margaret had already
gathered a hundred local girls into a school, made contact
with all the sick and impoverished people in the area, and
had begun to gather around her a group of co-workers.

[3.] Drane, Sr Francis Raphael, *Life of Mother Margaret Mary Hallahan*,
London, Longmans Green and Co., 1869, pp. 53–4.

Providentially, there were few better priests in England with whom Margaret could have found herself placed at this point. The Catholic clergy in the British Isles were hardly familiar with the forms of religious life available to women. After the Reformation, any women wishing to pursue the life of the cloister had been forced to go abroad, and convents of English nuns sprang up in European towns and cities. Throughout Flanders and France in the seventeenth and eighteenth centuries, there were convents of English women living under Franciscan, Benedictine, Augustinian, Carmelite, Bridgettine and Ursuline rules. Douai, Brussels, Louvain, St Omer, Liege, Paris and Cambrai were as important as refuges for Recusant women as they were for men training for the priesthood. At the end of the eighteenth century, as the French Revolution destroyed refugee Catholic institutions across Europe, the nuns fled to England, often with only what they could carry. They were taken into the houses of gentry Catholics and given bases from which to re-establish themselves. Their own severe financial situation and the increasing demand for female educational provision among Catholics ensured that several of the contemplative houses continued to run schools on their return to England. Slowly and painfully, female religious life re-established itself on English soil in the early years of the nineteenth century. Yet there was still scarcely any thought of an active, uncloistered apostolate being available for women.

Ullathorne's experience had, however, brought him into contact with women religious outside the contemplative or monastic model, and in taking a group of Irish Sisters of Charity to Australia in the 1830s, he had been responsible for establishing the first convents on that continent. His experience of working with the Sisters of Charity in Parramatta, New South Wales, had convinced him of the integrity and value of religious women who were not bound by the cloister, and he learnt to encourage and to value female endeavours which were authentically of God and of the Church. He had witnessed in Australia the value of the

Sisters of Charity in reaching areas of society in which priests could not do much, and, in his own life, owed his psychological survival to the support and affection of the Parramatta convent. Coventry, however, was very different from Parramatta, and the work in which Margaret was engaged was not under the formal authority of a religious Order. Margaret was a Dominican Tertiary, but not a vowed religious, and had no religious community around her. She continued to work and live under the rule of life of the Dominican Tertiaries, although, with Dominican permission, Ullathorne became her spiritual director. The ill-natured housekeeper was dismissed on Ullathorne's return from Rome, and oversight of the household placed in Margaret's hands, with a maidservant to assist her. She now had the confidence, with Ullathorne's support, to embark on her life's work.

Margaret was strongly committed to the Dominican Order, but wanted to introduce to the English mission the concept she had encountered in Belgium of unenclosed Third Order Dominican women actively involved in pastoral work. The European style of life of Dominican Tertiaries had been interpreted in a number of ways, but was unknown in England. The precedents were not good: Mary Ward in the seventeenth century had found herself scoffed at, opposed, and finally subjected to papal imprisonment for such a notion. Her Institute had still not, by the nineteenth century, received any ecclesiastical recognition, and all the English communities of religious women who had returned to native soil after the French Revolution were monastic and enclosed. Bishop Walsh, Vicar Apostolic of the Central District, tried to get Margaret Hallahan to join the Sisters of Mercy, who, in 1841, had established a house in nearby Birmingham. Walsh failed to fully appreciate the fact that she had already taken vows as a Dominican, and was, therefore, not free to enter another religious order, even had she chosen to do so.

Margaret worked alongside Ullathorne in the mission, running a girls' school and establishing contacts among the female factory workers of Coventry. Although not a professed religious in the accepted sense, it was said that even the Protestants of Coventry seem to have understood that the plainly dressed priest's housekeeper had 'something of the nun about her'. She began to gather around her a group of women prepared to devote themselves to the work of the Church in Coventry, joining her in collecting funds to build a new church and helping with the gatherings of young factory women or visiting the poor. By the end of 1843, Ullathorne was convinced of the benefit of establishing a Third Order Dominican convent under the direction of Sister Margaret (as she was universally known). He wrote to the Provincial Superior of the Dominicans and was ready to help her to begin as soon as he had his concurrence.

> I am ready to commence with four excellent persons, all thorough workers, with good sound sense and solid devotion. Sr Margaret is invaluable. The quantity of good works and of charities that pass through her hands is almost inexplicable; the manner [in which] she is spiritualizing this congregation is admirable; and all this amidst a good deal of personal suffering.

On a fundraising visit to her friends in Belgium in February 1844, Margaret collected as much supporting evidence and material about the practice of Dominican Tertiaries as she could. Even before she had chance to place this before the Provincial Superior of the English Dominican Friars, Fr Henry Whiteside, he took the view that his authority, together with that of Ullathorne's superior (the Prior of Downside) and that of Bishop Walsh, the Vicar Apostolic of the Central District, was sufficient for the tiny Dominican Institute to be founded by Margaret. It was, somewhat surprisingly, placed under Ullathorne's direct oversight. Once established in Coventry, with the permission of the Superior of the Dominican Order in England, Margaret placed herself and her Institute under Ullathorne's personal direction. This was an unusual arrangement, given that he was, at this point, simply the local missionary priest and a monk of an entirely different religious Order from the Dominicans, subject to his own monastic discipline as a Benedictine. All that he knew of Dominican life was learned from Margaret Hallahan. The great spiritual partnership and friendship of both their lives had taken root. Ullathorne and Margaret shared a common purpose during the years in Coventry, but their friendship deepened and lasted until Margaret's death in 1868. All accounts of her speak of her great warmth of personality, amongst the conventional compliments paid to her piety, devotion, hard work and dedication. Ullathorne quickly noticed the influence she exercised among young women in the town, and pondered on the source of it. He came to the conclusion that 'it lay not only in that great, warm, loving soul of hers, that was always going to God, but also in her faith in other souls, in what they are, in what they have latent in them, and in what they are capable of'. Ullathorne had seen for himself what women could achieve in pastoral outreach, particularly to other women, and had no reason to doubt their powers of organization and strength of purpose, as well as their faith and sense of vocation. He shared Margaret's conviction that, even in the most depraved human soul, there was the possibility of good.

The promising start made at Coventry was to be tested quickly, when, in 1846, Ullathorne was pressed to accept an episcopal appointment, this time in England, as Vicar Apostolic in the Western District. So fragile were the early foundations of Margaret's institute, and so uncertain was she that even the Dominican friars fully understood the enterprise, that she determined to go with her greatest supporter and friend and uproot from Coventry to Bristol. When, after only two years, Ullathorne was moved again, this time to return to the Midlands as Vicar Apostolic in the Central District and ultimately Bishop of Birmingham, Margaret was torn. Again, the tiny community with its unusual origins and way of life was left without support, although it was clear that the work the Sisters were doing in Bristol was valued and appreciated by those around them. Margaret's ambition settled on establishing a house with a noviciate within the jurisdiction of the Central District. What gradually became known as the English Third Order of the Dominicans was taking shape under the influence of a Benedictine bishop and Margaret's own interpretation of the life of Dominican Tertiaries, strongly influenced by St Catherine of Siena.

Margaret had no desire or will to found a new religious Order, but to establish a way of life for women within the Dominican family, rooted in contemplation but without the limitations of the cloister. This led to early difficulties, as there were those to whom the idea of Dominican Tertiaries living in community was so novel that they did not regard them as vowed religious in the full sense. Yet it was the very strong sense of Dominican identity which inspired Margaret, and with the support of the English friars at Leicester and that of Ullathorne, she was able to continue to insist on the validity of her enterprise. Ullathorne was a stout defender, insisting that the Sisters were part of the ancient order of St Dominic, not some 'fly by night' organization. In introducing herself to Mother Mary Clare Knight, the superior of the Benedictine monastery at Colwich, who would become her greatest friend outside her own Order, Margaret described her enterprise in this way:

> We are of the ancient Order of St Dominic, and called the Daughters of Penance of his Third Rule, and follow exactly the employments for which he instituted it: we instruct the poor and middle classes, visit the sick and prisons, and endeavour to convert abandoned sinners, but above all, to propagate devotion to the Mother of God.[4]

Various foundations were attempted and finally in August 1852 the foundation stone of what would become Margaret's centre of operations and the novitiate of the Order was laid at Stone in north Staffordshire. The story of convent foundations is a relatively familiar and conventional one in Victorian England: of financial struggles, personal

---

4. Drane, pp. 130–1.

hardship and dedication, occasional generous patronage and hostility from society at large. Margaret's organizational skills and capacity to draw support to the work of her new foundations was shared by many women of her time, who were meeting the desperate pastoral and physical needs of the towns and cities in which they lived. The convent and church at Stone were built on a grand scale, with Ullathorne's continued encouragement and support. Yet none of these aspects of Margaret Hallahan's life are what mark her out as truly heroic and unique. Religious life was chosen by most of her contemporaries from a mixture of motives including family and kinship ties which had an early impact on the life choices of young women, education and the formative influence of older religious Sisters as teachers and the personal recommendation or encouragement of clergy. It offered young women a respectable alternative to marriage and family life, combining a spiritual vision with social activism and scope for leadership and influence, and similar patterns are repeated throughout the new foundations of the nineteenth century.

Margaret Hallahan's route and purpose were somewhat different, in that, at the core of her call to religious life was the specific charism of the Dominican Order and in particular of St Catherine of Siena. Her devotion to the Dominican Order was total, and she fought to keep her institute within the Order, preferring to leave England and enter an enclosed convent elsewhere than abandon the Dominican roots which had been planted in her at a young age in Bruges. It was St Catherine who gave Margaret her unique ideal of a form of religious life which was both contemplative and active. Like Catherine, Margaret did not share the great intellectual heritage of the Order of Preachers, but did imbibe from her a spirit of interiority which would bear fruit in her service of the poor. Margaret had little formal education, and, like Catherine, would not produce published works. Mother Francis Raphael Drane compared her written style to that of St Catherine, but also, in its humanity, with St Teresa of Avila. When, after her death, comparisons were also drawn with St Gertrude,

Ullathorne agreed, but insisted that, 'her nature, style of mind and her humour savours more of St Teresa, and her interior heart of St Catherine'.[5] Her spiritual heroism would become known through her dealings with individuals and her immense correspondence of which over six hundred letters survive, which breathes an intensity of passionate devotion to God, the Virgin Mary and the saints of her own Order. She lived a life which was, to an extraordinary degree, constantly centred upon God and detached from the world around, yet which was dedicated to the service of that world. It is true of many of these extraordinary Victorian women that, in the retelling of their achievements in missionary and pastoral work, in building churches and convents and in leading other women and men to a closer relationship with God, their inner lives have received scant attention.

This is particularly true of Margaret Hallahan, who had many of the spiritual qualities which might have led her, in another generation, to being described as a mystic. This surely was the foundation of her deep friendship with Ullathorne, the monk who understood her mind and heart, and sought to correct this lack of attention to her interior life by writing about it after her death. In his Gifford Lectures, *The Varieties of Religious Experience*, published over forty years after Margaret Hallahan's death, William James included her in his list of saints and spiritual heroes alongside Bernard of Clairvaux, Francis of Assisi, Martin Luther, Ignatius of Loyola and John Wesley. These people, James says, show themselves, and everyone perceives their strength and stature. 'Their sense of mystery in things, their passion, their goodness, irradiate about them and enlarge their outlines while they soften them. They are like pictures with an atmosphere and background; and, placed alongside of them, the strong men of this world and no other seem dry as sticks, as hard and crude as blocks of stone or brickbats'.[6]

[5] Champ, Judith, *William Bernard Ullathorne: A Different Kind of Monk*, Leominster, Gracewing, 2006, p. 351.

[6] James, William, *The Varieties of Religious Experience*, New York, The Modern Library, 1902, p. 376.

Margaret Hallahan was certainly a woman of passion with a sense of the mystery of things. Her intense focus on 'God Alone' created her atmosphere which she carried with her, and which is conveyed in the 135 Chapter Instructions which she gave to her community. It is almost certainly the case that, without her influence, Ullathorne would have had the capacity to become 'dry as sticks' and hard as blocks of stone or brickbats. Her humane care as much as her deep spiritual power shaped his humanity and that of the other Victorian clerics with whom she came into contact. She earned the respect of many of the men who led the Victorian Catholic revival, as well as that of other powerful female leaders, and had a spiritual influence which was unusual in its depth and breadth. Her own community, naturally enough, appreciated her spiritual wisdom, preserved in the huge archive of correspondence with a wide range of people and the Chapter Instructions copied down and preserved by those who listened to them. The extent of Margaret's spiritual wisdom and influence is evident from Ullathorne's assurance that, after the death of his 'dear friend and sister', those who lived under her leadership received an immense sense of consolation and of being 'lifted into a higher and more supernatural sphere'.[7] It was not, however, only those closest to her who benefited from contact with Margaret, but also those, like John Henry Newman, who met her only rarely. Her sympathy for, and understanding of him, was extraordinary, and she followed the currents of his life, supporting him with the prayers of her communities through all the many difficulties he encountered in the 1850s and 1860s. When she died, he was surprised and indeed almost embarrassed to discover the depth and consistency of her 'singular tenderness towards myself', realizing late in the day that it was probably due to her influence on Ullathorne that the bishop's attitude to Newman had mellowed and become kinder. Newman described her as 'a wonderful woman, full of faith, devotion and energy, and by

---

7.   Champ, p. 349.

the force of these virtues, possessed of singular powers of influence. Her doings betokened her greatness'.[8]

Those 'singular powers of influence' spread far and wide, as other Dominican Third Order foundations around the world sought to imitate her foundation. In the early 1860s, within a few years of her Constitutions being approved in Rome, Sisters in Switzerland and America were consulting Mother Margaret and asking for copies of the Constitutions for their own foundations, and in 1864 she was asked to make a foundation in California from Stone. This did not happen, but the eventual foundation in California did use the Stone Constitutions, and the biography published immediately after her death found a ready readership across the Atlantic. In 1929, the five foundations of English Third Order Dominican Sisters amalgamated into a single Congregation under the patronage of St Catherine of Siena, adopting Stone as its mother house and noviciate, and a new edition of her biography was published. In 1936, the Congregation proposed Margaret's cause for beatification. Margaret's true heroism lay, like that of her patron St Catherine of Siena, in her intense awareness of the presence of God, which Ullathorne believed had been the core of her life since she was a child of nine. Her life was an expression of that relationship.

8. Newman to Francis Raphael Drane, 28 Mary 1869, *Letter and Diaries*, vol. xxiv.

Chapter 14

Caroline Chisholm

Joanna Bogle

In 1838 the word 'Australia' spelt excitement and opportunity for the young and adventurous. But it also still carried overtones of horror, exile, and tragedy. For many decades it had been a penal colony, where convicts were sent in chains, treated with savage cruelty, and subjected to vicious punishments if they infringed the rules of their servitude. Transportation to the penal settlements of New South Wales for periods of seven or fourteen years had been a standard punishment meted out by British courts for a range of offences including fairly minor forms of theft. Many of those convicted died on the long and dangerous journey from Britain in the ships where food and sanitation were lacking, others during the years of hard labour in the grim conditions that greeted them on arrival.

But in the 1830s a new era was emerging. A young queen had inherited the throne of Britain. New religious and political movements were making an impact. Transportation of criminals to remote regions with systematic brutality was no longer accepted as a necessary part of maintaining order.

And Britain had acquired an empire. Partly by accident, without any initial direct imperial plan, colonies which owed allegiance to the British Crown were attracting young settlers from British towns and cities. Here, in new territory, they could acquire land – or, more modestly, at least find some work and the prospect of a decent home. The colonies were protected by the forces of the British Crown and connected by sea routes protected by her Navy. Men serving in the Army and Navy brought back to Britain descriptions of magnificent far-off places full of exciting opportunities.

On the ship *Emerald Isle,* sailing into Sydney Harbour, were Archibald and Caroline Chisholm.[1] They were an Army couple, and had sailed from India with their two small sons. Archbibald was due for two years' leave and they planned to spend these in the new colony of New South Wales. The ship took them first to Mauritius – where the Indian *ayah* who had been helping them with the children disembarked and would work for another family making the return voyage – then to Adelaide on Australia's southern coast, then Hobart in Van Diemen's Land (now Tasmania) before the final arrival at Sydney.

The Chisholms had met and married in Northamptonshire, where Caroline's family owned a farm, and Archibald, then on leave from the Madras Infantry, had been based at Northampton barracks. The *Northampton Mercury* recorded their wedding in its issue of 1 January 1831:

On Monday last, at St Sepulchre's Church, by the Rev Spencer Gunning (by permission of the Rev B. Winthrop) Captain Archibald Chisholm, of the Honourable East India Company's Service, to Caroline, youngest daughter of the late Mr Wm. Jones, of this place.

Archibald was a Scot, from a Highland family that was traditionally Catholic. Caroline was brought up in the Church of England and converted to Catholicism around the time of her marriage. They would spend the first years of their married life in India, where Archibald was serving. Two children were born to them there.

Arrival in New South Wales must have been a great relief after the long journey. A sea voyage, even travelling as cabin passengers on a good ship, was not something undertaken lightly and safe arrival was cause for gratitude. The

[1.] Bogle, Joanna, *Caroline Chisholm, The Emigrant's Friend*, Leominster, Gracewing, 1993.

Chisholms had contacts among the settlers in Australia, savings from Archibald's Army pay and the modest status associated with belonging to a regiment in the Indian Army. Australia was to be the next chapter in their married life and Caroline was an enterprising young woman who took all sorts of challenges in her stride.

After staying for a while with friends they settled in a small cottage on the rural outskirts of the town. The hot weather would be a trial – though no worse than that of India – and this new land had welcomed them. The children loved it, there would good neighbours and friends around, plenty of fresh food, and everything to make for a happy family life.

But it was not so for everyone, and Caroline quickly discovered this. In Sydney harbour were to be found the flotsam and jetsam of colonial life – the drunkards and the lost people, the girl newly arrived from England seeking a sweetheart last seen being taken off to a convict ship some years earlier, the unsuccessful traveller who had run out of money, the drifter, the dispossessed, all along with the sailors and the merchants and the debt collectors and the brothel-madams and the soldiers and the harbour workers.

For every new settler who arrived with some money to invest and the prospect of a new life with work and prosperity, there were others for whom Australia was offering only misery and hopelessness. Ex-convicts longed to reach their families back in England – perhaps to bring them over so that, now the sentence had been served, they could all settle in this new land – but lacked the means to get a letter there safely. New arrivals were prey to exploitation at the hands of cheats and swindlers. People who wanted jobs lacked contacts and the means to establish them. It was hard to get out of the city and into the farmland where hands were needed.

It was here that Caroline would discover her life's work, and would apply herself to it with such dedication and love that it would earn her a lasting place in Australia's history and even folklore. In years to come, in an Australia unimaginable in those early days, the Chisholm name would be commemorated in schools and even a section of a brand-new capital city, and Caroline's kindly face would peer gently out from the back of a banknote. She would become synonymous with the courage and enterprise of Australian pioneer life, with adventures in leading wagon trains of settlers out into the bush, with establishing farming communities and building up hope in a new land.

How did it start?

With practicalities – Caroline was always an essentially practical person, with a common sense and neighbourliness that was rooted in a deep Christian charity, nourished by prayer and completely free of pomposity or cant.

During the course of visits to Sydney for shopping and other business, Caroline came across girls who were sleeping rough in the harbour district. They had nowhere to go, and no money – they were newly arrived from a ship but there was no one to greet them or direct them to families where they might find work. It was all too easy for them to slip into prostitution when starvation loomed – and a brothel-madam would know this and would hover around, offering what seemed like a welcome and a place to stay.

Often, these girls had very limited education, few ideas about what life in the new colony was like, no funds, and were in poor health after the long sea journey. They had come from poverty in Britain to what they hoped would be a life offering wonderful new possibilities and hope, but needed help to get started.

Caroline began with the simple neighbourly offer of a meal, an overnight stay, some clean clothes, and an opportunity to talk about plans and to find work. She knew that settled families with young children would value an extra pair of hands, and found that it was very easy to get a young woman a good job. Very quickly, she found placements for the two girls she befriended – and had the delight of seeing them well settled, forging strong friendships with the families for whom they worked, with comfortable accommodation and a settled wage.

The first two girls she helped were hugely grateful to her, and talked about her to others. Word spread quickly to each new batch of newly arrived immigrants that here was a Mrs Chisholm to whom a newcomer could go, who would be a true friend and be able to offer practical help and good advice.

It was satisfying work, though it involved a good deal of time and patience. Sometimes, the girls whom Caroline met in the harbour – she very soon took to making regular trips there to look for those in need of help – would be ill or badly under-nourished following the long sea journey. Almost always, they were in need of a good wash and the chance to clean their clothes. And helping them to find work involved talks and interviews, visiting different homes and establishing new contacts. What spurred Caroline on, however, was a recognition that there were so many possibilities in this new colony, and so little need for the misery that seemed to be the lot of too many of the new arrivals. She was by nature a cheerful and optimistic person, and this, combined with a great sweetness of manner and an ability to put people at their ease – regardless of their social background – meant that she was able to establish a really effective network.

As the months went by the work increased and Archibald was a strong supporter. Their own family life was happy, too. Another baby arrived, and a nursemaid was engaged. Everything prospered. Only Archibald's eventual return to India for his next tour of duty loomed to limit their pleasant horizons.

When Archibald's leave was up they decided that Caroline and the children should not return with him to India, but remain in their New South Wales home to await his return. The children were prospering, the climate was good, the life was comfortable and pleasant. And Archibald had warm admiration for his wife's increasing dedication to the cause of the poor and struggling newcomers to the colony, and wanted her to continue. He was proud of her and urged her to continue with her work while he was away.

Army wives in the nineteenth century knew about coping

with farewells, and Caroline had already, back in India, seen Archibald go off on duty to the North West Frontier. Their farewells on this occasion, as on others, were done with courage and faith. Caroline would cope in his absence – and had work to do.

Was she doing enough? The question tormented her. It went into her prayers. At stake were not just lives but souls, and human dignity. Caroline's faith was deep.

She would later describe her activities thus, in a pamphlet explaining how her work had started:

> At about this time, several young women whom I had served, advised others to write to me: I did all I could to aid them in their prospects by advice, or recommending them to situations [ie to families who would offer them work] but the number increased, and I saw that my plan, if carried into effect, would serve *all*. My delay pressed on my mind as a sin; and when I heard of a poor girl suffering distress and losing her reputation in consequence, I felt I was not clear of her sin, for I did not do all I could to prevent it.

What was her plan? To acquire some accommodation – she had her eye on an old building which could be transformed into a clean and comfortable place where girls could stay – and run a small office where prospective employers could come and meet the young people and interview them for jobs.

It was not an easy decision to turn simple neighbourly actions into a full-scale campaign, but it had to be done. The Church spoke to her – not with a nagging voice or a sermon but through its annual liturgical round of the seasons. Lent, and Holy Week of 1841 approached, the Church's time for a searching of hearts and an openness to God's grace. She prayed and, as she later described it 'suffered much'. On Easter Sunday she knew what she must do: she made an offering of all her talents and energies to God, promising to serve anyone in need and 'nor in fact consider my own wishes or feelings but wholly devote myself to the work I had in hand'. She felt a sense of God's blessing on her work though she added that 'It was His will to permit many serious difficulties to be thrown in my way, and to conduct me through a path of deep humiliation.'

With difficulty, she persuaded some other ladies in the colony to support her, and – with difficulty again – obtained, after an interview with the Governor, Sir George Gipps, the use of the old Immigration Barracks as a Home for newly arrived girls. He would later recall that, in agreeing to meet her, he had thought he would be introduced to an 'old lady in cap and spectacles' who would talk to him about the state of his soul. He was surprised to be introduced to 'a handsome, stately young woman, who proceeded to reason the question as though she thought her reason and experience to be worth as much as mine'. Initially opposing her plans, he eventually agreed to her using the old Barracks provided that she signed a statement establishing that there would be absolutely no claim on public funds.

Undeterred, Caroline set about fundraising, and here met further blocks as both Catholic and Protestant clergy, after initially pledging support, backed away. Rumours circulated among some that she was a campaigning Catholic crusader, intent on establishing a 'romanizing' force in the colony. Catholic clergy, on the other hand, seem simply to have seen her as rather tiresome, intent on establishing some wide-ranging scheme for earnest good works which would founder and prove humiliating for all involved.

Finally, however, she obtained the use of the old Barracks. By now, she was more or less alone and she simply had to get on with things by herself, and see who would come to help her in due course. Once in possession of the keys, she would have to move into the barracks and begin work, or her right to be there would be open to challenge.

Fearing infection, she could not bring her own children to live in this large rat-infested building and so she had to leave them with their nurse/governess, a Miss Galvin (who proved more than equal to the task and a true friend). The old barracks were filthy – on Caroline's first night there, she was woken by a rat running across her face and would later describe how she put out some bread and milk for the rodents in the middle of the room, tucked a shawl around her shoulders, and sat with a book till the morning. She bought rat poison and cleaning materials, got to work with energy, and the Home was open for business. Gifts came in as the community began to support her enterprise. Caroline recorded them all gratefully: sugar, tea, rice, bedding.

It wasn't easy. Men arrived to leer. Interviews with prospective employers took time and sometimes tried patience. People were inclined to laugh at the efforts of a do-gooder (and a Catholic, at that – people still wondered about her motives: was she, as rumoured, planning to turn New South Wales into a papist fiefdom?). But the project prospered. Prejudices were worn down. People arrived to sneer but stayed to help. The girls themselves proved the value of the enterprise: the vast majority were not – as some had claim they would be – immoral, drunken, untrustworthy or vicious, but were simply young women who sought new lives in this new colony and were prepared to work hard.

The *Sydney Morning Herald* began to report the success of Mrs Chisholm's venture, listing the number of job placements that had been made, the families helped, the assistance given with food or other necessities. A key part of the venture was efficiency: Caroline made out a contract in triplicate for every job which was agreed, with one copy for the employer, one for the employee, and one for her own records. Wages were written down and agreed, along with details such as food and accommodation. And girls knew that, on their day off, there was a warm welcome for them back at the Home – where many started to come, even walking long distances from outlying farms, with gifts of flowers or cakes.

And more. Out there in the bush there were lonely settlers. The arrival of one of 'Mrs Chisholm's girls' meant the prospect of social life, and a possible bride. News of happy bush weddings began to arrive back in Sydney. Then as now, it was traditional to send out pieces of wedding cake to those unable to attend the celebrations, and Caroline kept a careful account of all that she received, at one point listing a final tally of fifty-one slices of wedding cake along with a number of other wedding tokens.[2]

Earlier humiliations, money worries, derision and even denunciations had given way to popular enthusiasm.

The work grew. The real need now was to help girls to settle on the outlying farms, where pioneers were forging new lives out in the bush. The land was rich and fertile, wheat could be grown and sheep and cattle raised ... but the life was lonely. A married man knew that his wife would lack not merely friends but vitally necessary practical help with the house and the baby. Such married couples were very keen to welcome a girl from Sydney who would be a real help and companion for the wife – and who would very likely marry one of the many bachelor settlers and start a new family, a welcome addition to local life.

But travel out to the bush meant more than merely encouraging a group of girls to go there. It meant organization. The *Sydney Morning Herald* begged farmers, who were bringing carts and drays into the city with wheat and other crops, to offer help in taking girls back to the country districts. The response was generous.

Caroline was a good horsewoman – a country girl who had grown up on a farm and who loved the open air. Among the gifts donated for her work at this time was 'Captain', a splendid white horse. On this, she would ride on the long journeys leading the carts and drays along the bush roads – and a legend was born.

On the way, all the young girls travelled under Mrs Chisholm's special protection. No one molested them. At night, the travellers would gather for a meal cooked over an open fire, and then sleep out under the stars, the girls all gathered together around Mrs Chisholm next to one of the wagons.

It was discovered that Caroline had an unusual and useful

2. Hoban, Mary, *Fifty-One Pieces of Wedding Cake*, Kilmore (Victoria), Lowden Publishing Co., 1973.

gift – she was a water-diviner. In new territory, water was the most crucial item necessary when looking for somewhere to make camp for the night. Caroline's ability to find it fostered the semi-legendary status that was beginning to surround her.

Wherever possible, of course, the travellers would make their overnight stay at a farm, where, on their arrival, there was usually something of a celebration. News would have spread that the wagon train was coming, and preparations would be made for a good meal, a fire lit for outdoor cooking to cater for the large numbers, word sent to neighbours to come along to enjoy the gathering. Over the next days, the arrival of newcomers to the neighbourhood would mean more social gatherings – and, as Mrs Chisholm was famous for bringing young girls into the community, some weddings could be expected. Her name became a byword for matchmaking – although she never actually undertook to provide wives, always cheerfully – and correctly – assuming that settling girls with good families would ensure that in the natural course of things they would establish local friendships and the rest would follow.

When Archibald Chisholm returned to New South Wales from his tour of duty in India he found that the Chisholm name was famous across the colony. His wife was a heroine. Not only had she settled large numbers of people on farms in the colony, but she had built up a great sense of community solidarity – people were proud of what was being achieved. She was also doing something which was to be of great practical benefit as well as establishing fascinating material for historians – she carried out a survey, by asking farmers detailed questions at every place she visited, establishing what could be grown, and what prices they obtained for wheat and other crops. In her questioning, she also asked what help was needed by the settlers – and the overriding message was that they were prospering, the land was good, and the longing was for families to be reunited, for lone settlers to find wives, and for ex-convicts to be given an opportunity to rediscover friends and family members left behind in Britain long before.

It was with this in mind that the Chisholms decided to set out on the long journey back to England. A family visit of their own was long overdue – Caroline had not seen her mother or her other relations for several years. And, in London, she would take to the Colonial Office the pleas of settlers and an accurate picture of life in the colony.

It was a huge task. The journey to England was delayed for some while as they made plans, and when they set out it was not in the best of circumstances as Caroline was now pregnant again. She had to give birth at sea and suffered badly from the poor conditions. But both she and the baby – called Sydney, after the city they had made their own – survived to arrive safely in Britain. Archibald rented a house in London and Mrs Jones, Caroline's mother, came to live with them. After an initial stay in King Street, Covent Gardens, they moved to Islington, renting a terraced house not far from the local Catholic church.

With her accustomed vigour, Caroline started to tackle her immense self-appointed task – beginning by helping to reunite families by tracking down settlers' relatives who wanted to go to Australia. This meant hours of travel to workhouses and orphanages, and a great correspondence with all sorts of people. She had lists of names, and went painstakingly to addresses she had been given, contacting people and sorting out the administrative and other difficulties that got in the way of obtaining them a passage to New South Wales. A particular issue was that of 'bounty migrants'; men who had gone out to Australia (a ship's captain was given a 'bounty' for each man that he took) and who had prospered and now wanted to bring their families over. There was great joy among such families when news arrived that they might be able travel to Australia – but a great deal of work for Mrs Chisholm in making the arrangements, especially where the family was very poor.

How to get these people to Australia? The law allowed for a free passage for the wives and families of convicts, but no such arrangements had been made – or could be expected – for the wives of free settlers. Caroline found that there was a general recognition of the need to send more women out to Australia, but little practical concern for how this could be done. She must mobilize public opinion. It was not just a case of reuniting families, or even of simply sending out single women in order to provide lonely farmers with wives. It was a matter of helping poor people in Britain to find new hope and prosperity overseas.

She published a book, with the unpromising title of *Emigration and Transportation Relatively Considered*, which told the stories of the farmers and settlers from whom she had gathered information in New South Wales. It was written in the form of an open letter to the Colonial Secretary, Lord Grey, and was a plea for generosity in helping people to emigrate to Australia, but because of its vivid descriptions of life in Australia, and message of hope for prospective emigrants, it became a best-seller.

> Is it not a lamentable thought, then, my Lord, that deaths should daily result from starvation among British subjects, while in this valuable colony good wheat is rotting in the ground for the want of hands to gather it in – that tens of thousands of fine sheep, droves after droves, thousands upon thousands of fat cattle are annually slaughtered there and 'boiled down' into tallow for the European market[?] . . .

The booklet – and a companion one with the more catchy title of *Comfort for the Poor! Meat three times a day!* attracted considerable attention. The *Comfort* book had vivid descriptions – taken down verbatim and simply reproduced – of life on Australian farms and was immensely popular. Both booklets were discussed in the press, and sold widely. Caroline was invited to give evidence to a parliamentary committee – the first woman ever to do so – about conditions in Australia, and the economic prospects there. Totally committed to the ban on transportation – the savagery and cruelties of that policy were now beginning to be widely recognized – she saw an urgency in putting forward the true face of Australia, a land of hope and opportunity, a place where the poor and hungry of Britain's overcrowded towns and cities could start new lives. She produced from her reticule some wheat that was grown in New South Wales, and this was solemnly passed around the committee members. She spoke of the good farming land and the great possibilities for growing all sorts of food.

While lobbying for the use of public funds to help the poor to travel to Australia, Caroline also recognized that the best way forward was to show how it could all be done at the practical level. Together with Archibald she initiated the Family Colonization Loan Society – a simple system through which people could contribute a modest (sometimes it was very modest indeed, perhaps just a farthing a week) amount towards their own fare, with the rest being made up by charitable donations. The emigrants would undertake to pay back the money once they had settled and made good in Australia.

This was a massive undertaking – and it would all be run from an ordinary house in Islington, by a busy mother and an Army officer on half-pay. The Chisholms were not rich, and Archibald's years of Army service were now over, so that he was living on the half-pay of a retired major. Their family continued to increase – daughters Caroline (always known as Carrie) and Monica were born during these Islington years, as was baby Sara, who sadly survived only a short while and was buried from St John's church, just round the corner from the Chisholm's home in Charlton terrace.

Carrie, Monica, and the four brothers, Archie, William, Henry, and Sydney, made the house a real family home. Mrs Jones continued to live with the family as a very active grandmother, caring for the children and helping Caroline with the increasing number of visitors, who came to enquire about travelling to Australia.

Caroline was now a public figure – effectively Australia's ambassador in London. She spoke at meetings and rallies promoting emigration, publicized the stories of successful emigrants, and gave huge amounts of time to answering enquiries of all sorts, mostly from very poor people, about the possibility of travelling to New South Wales. With the launch of the Family Colonization Society came much more work – not only the banking and financial arrangements, which Archibald undertook to supervise – but the practical need to help families to get ready for the long journey, to find somewhere to stay in London while waiting to embark, and to learn about how to live in Australia once they arrived at their final destination.

Renting the house next door to their own in Charlton terrace, the Chisholms fitted out one room to resemble a ship's cabin. It proved a huge hit with visitors, and in it Caroline gave weekly talks to prospective emigrants. These always began with Caroline reading aloud from letters sent by settlers describing their lives and conditions, and continued with advice on everything from shipboard health (including the need for huge quantities of babies' nappies, because of the impossibility of washing them) to practical packing. (Use a barrel, not a trunk, she urged – it can be rolled down a plank at Sydney rather than having to be carried by porters, and can later be split into two halves one of which can be used as a cradle!)

Caroline's methods of work induced a sense of hope and optimism. She became known as 'The Emigrant's Friend'. She was tactful when dealing with the needs of individual families – poorer people, just as much as rich ones, deserved privacy when discussing financial matters and the need for a loan to cover the costs of the journey to Australia. She remained a dedicated Catholic, finding in the Catholic faith a daily inspiration for all her work, and she spoke naturally and without affectation about God's providence and generosity: he had provided enough for all, but charity and mutual help were necessary to make sure it was available to everyone.

The press were interested in Caroline Chisholm. She was still comparatively young, she had a young family, she could have enjoyed a comfortable life without unduly troubling herself over the plight of the poor – but she gave hours and hours of her time every day, without any pay or acclamation, to assist needy people. Descriptions of her in the press provide an interesting picture of what she was like – busy, pleasant, cheerful, wearing simple clothes of hard-wearing fabrics and carrying herself with dignity and charm. When impoverished people called at the house she would give them a meal while talking to them and answering their enquiries about Australia – her daughter Carrie would later recall that the family sometimes had their own meals interrupted for this purpose, and the children were expected to help their mother cheerfully and without complaint in serving the visitors.

Author Charles Dickens was among the many people who were influenced by Caroline – he warmly admired her work and his novels reflected a recognition that starting a new life in Australia offered real hope to the poor. (Think of Little Em'ly or the Micawber family flourishing in New South Wales after their travails in Britain.)

Lord Shaftesbury – who was becoming famous for his passionate campaigns on behalf of the children who worked long hours in mills and factories – became a firm ally of Caroline and spoke alongside her at emigration rallies. Florence Nightingale, national heroine and founder of a famous School of Nursing, looked to Caroline Chisholm as an example of a woman working in public life and inspired by Christian principles.

Caroline and Archibald would eventually return to Australia – Archibald and young Archie travelling first and establishing the Australian branch of the Family Colonisation Society and seeing to its arrangements in Sydney, while Caroline continued her work in London. Before that, Caroline's campaigns had extended to shipboard conditions: she lobbied successfully for laws insisting on the provision of essential privacy and hygiene on board, and had a ship designed to her own specifications in which everyone had access to the supper decks and to fresh air and exercise. She travelled to Ireland to help the huge numbers of people there seeking to escape famine by emigration to Australia, and she visited France and Germany by invitation to address meetings there. (She spoke good French, having been well taught by a governess when young.)

The 1850s were really the central years of Caroline's work. By the 1870s, the image of Australia in the public mind in Britain had utterly changed – and this was in no small part due to Caroline. From being a remote land, with a hideous convict past and an uncertain future, Australia had become 'the lucky country', a land of hope and opportunity, where a family could really prosper.

After many more years in Australia, Caroline and Archibald finally returned to Britain where they lived in old age. One son, William, went to Rome to study for the priesthood but had to leave due to ill health. Caroline travelled to Rome to bring him home, and was granted an audience with the Pope, who praised her work and presented her with a commemorative gift in recognition of what she had done for the poor. William returned to Australia and married, but died only a year later and his young wife entered a convent. The other Chisholm offspring also married and their descendants live in Australia and Canada to this day.

Caroline and Archibald both died in 1877 in London. They had been living in Fulham, cared for by their daughter Monica. They are buried at Northampton, where Caroline had been born and brought up and where they were married. Their grave is well tended, and every year in March, on the anniversary of Caroline's death, it blooms with golden daffodils, planted by Australian visitors to honour a woman who gave so much service to their country. In Australia, there are schools, a welfare society, and a suburb named in her honour and she has appeared on a banknote. Hers was a life dedicated to the service of others – out in the sunshine of the Australian bush, on ships at sea, in London lobbying Parliament or meeting prospective emigrants. A life inspired by sincere Christian faith shown in practical service and love, honouring marriage and family and seeing these blessings extended to people to whom they might otherwise have been denied.

Punch magazine paid tribute to her at the height of her fame, urging people to support her work and help people travelling to Australia.

> The ragged pauper crawling home towards a parish grave
> She roused – directed to a home beyond the western wave
> She smoothed his weary passage across the troubled deep
> With food, and air, and decencies of ship-room and of sleep.

The poem hailed her as something of a prophetess, and urged people to support her generously. It recognized Caroline's extraordinary achievement in marrying principles of self-reliance with justice and charity to secure real hope for Britain's poor:

> Who led their expedition? And under whose command
> Through dangers and through hardships sought they
>   the promised land?
> A second Moses surely, it was who did it all
> It was a second Moses in a bonnet and a shawl.

Chapter 15

M. Mary Clare Moore, RSM

Penny Roker, RSM

The painting of Florence Nightingale in the National Portrait Gallery is not called 'Portrait of Florence Nightingale' but 'The Mission of Mercy'. Though it depicts her in heroic pose, bathed in sunlight as she greets the straggling line of wounded soldiers returning from the Crimean battlefields, she does not stand alone. With her we see army doctors and orderlies, civilian volunteers, Turkish dignitaries and the casualties of war. The artist has also painted himself observing the scene from an upper window, bidding us take a yet closer look, for one of the wounded officers inclines his head in reverence, not towards Miss Nightingale, as it would seem at first sight, but to a nun standing behind her. Another wounded officer raises himself from his stretcher, pointing to the wall where sunlight streaming through the hospital entrance has framed the Sister's shadow in a circle of light. Miss Nightingale turns: it has caught her attention too. In real life, as in this painting, she was never so dazzled by her own glory that she could not recognize a halo when she saw one.

This Sister of Mercy was born in Dublin on 20 March 1814 into a Protestant family and baptized Georgiana. Her father died when she was only three, which left the family in financial straits, though her mother did all she could to educate her intelligent daughter. In 1823, the whole family was received into the Catholic Church. Georgiana's first contact with the Sisters of Mercy came when she was fourteen, although they were not actually religious Sisters then. The 'House of Mercy', which opened in Baggot Street, Dublin the year before, was run by a team of Catholic lady volunteers as a centre for homeless poor women and children. The initiative had been driven and funded by the heiress, Catherine McAuley, who employed the shy, young Georgiana as governess to her young wards.

It must have been exciting to be part of a venture which was the talk of fashionable Dublin, and even more so when the idea of the House of Mercy began to evolve. The ladies, playfully at first, started to call one another 'Sister'. Miss McAuley initially opposed the idea of her House of Mercy becoming a Convent but local clergy had concerns about its unregulated status and threatened to hand the whole project over to the Sisters of Charity. Succumbing to pressure from within her own group as well as from outside, Miss McAuley decided to found her own order of active, rather than enclosed, religious women.

After training with the Presentation Sisters, Catherine McAuley returned to her house in Baggot Street in 1831 to found her own congregation. Georgiana was unsure about religious life. Some Dublin Catholics struggled with the idea of 'Walking Nuns' and it was hard for a sixteen-year-old to forego the prospect of marriage. Yet once Sr M. Catherine, as Miss McAuley became, was installed as Mother Superior, Georgiana also received the habit. Known in religion as Sr Mary Clare, she made Profession of Vows on 24 January 1833, one of the first to do so as a Sister of Mercy. To the vows of poverty, chastity and obedience, the Sisters of Mercy added a fourth vow of service to those in need.

Catherine McAuley was by this time fifty-five years old, Clare Moore only eighteen, yet the two became close companions, rising at 4 a.m. to pray, two hours before the others. Both worked as nurses at the Depot Hospital, Dublin, when cholera broke out in 1832. Much of what we know of the Venerable Catherine has been handed down by Clare Moore. Catherine relied heavily on her in preparing the original Rule and Constitutions of the Sisters of Mercy, and it was Clare's own handwritten copy that Archbishop Murray received in 1835. Only just turned twenty-three years of age, Sr Clare was appointed first Superior of the new foundation in Cork. Two years later, she was chosen to be temporary Superior of the first Mercy Convent to be founded in England. She was still only twenty-five.

Dockhead in Bermondsey was a dismal slum area of wharves and tanneries, the poorest parish in the London District. Dickens' *Oliver Twist*, published the year before Clare Moore arrived, described it as, 'a maze of close, narrow and muddy streets, thronged by the roughest and poorest of waterside people'. The energetic parish priest, Fr Butler, had a Catholic church built there, on land given by Baroness Montesquieu, to serve the numerous, though often non-practising, Catholic families. He was supported in his work with the poor by a group of ladies. Nurturing their vocation, he arranged for two to train as Sisters of Mercy in Ireland. With the generosity of one of his pious ladies, Lady Barbara Eyre, he commissioned the architect A. W. Pugin to design a convent for them next to his church – some three hundred years after the destruction of the great Benedictine Abbey of Bermondsey under Henry VIII.

Mother McAuley sent the two English ladies to Clare Moore in Cork for their noviciate. It was just a decade after Catholic Emancipation and news of a new Catholic Religious Order in England could be expected to create a stir, but public attention was distracted by the approaching wedding of Queen Victoria. By November 1839 the newly professed Sisters returned to London, accompanied by Catherine McAuley herself and with Mother Clare 'on loan'. The little party reached their new convent late at night to find Fr Butler seriously ill and the building just a damp shell. Only one room was furnished and the cells were not yet built. The Sisters nevertheless moved in. Catherine McAuley felt entombed by Pugin's idealized Gothic design and complained that no one could stretch up even to touch the windows, much less see out of them. 'The cold pierces my heart', she wrote, though it did not deter her from receiving some distinguished visitors, including the Earl of Arundel and Surrey, later to become Duke of Norfolk.

Less than a month after their arrival a public Solemn Ceremony of Clothing took place in the new parish church for some of Fr Butler's other ladies. Among them was Lady Barbara herself, daughter of the Earl of Newburgh, splendidly attired, her hair arranged by the court hairdresser, and her bridal gown adorned with jewels still proudly displayed in Bermondsey. Many of the Catholic nobility were present. Other young ladies asked to enter and six were accepted during the short few weeks of Catherine McAuley's visit to London.

The Sisters' presence was greatly needed in Bermondsey with poor, sick families to visit, converts to instruct, and children to teach and prepare for the Sacraments. Clare Moore left Bermondsey for Ireland in 1841, but tensions between the Sisters and the eccentricities of their new Superior obliged her to return within the year. She remained in office there as Reverend Mother to the end of her life. During that time, her Sisters won the hearts of local people and Clare was soon able to respond to requests to open other Convents of Mercy in England.

The Convent Annals speak of her 'great liberality' to the poor and 'spirit of prayer'.[1] Thomas Griffiths, Bishop of London, said he 'never saw such maturity in so young a person'.[2] A picture emerges of Clare Moore as a compassionate and practical woman with gravity beyond her years. Rather strict as a young Superior, she nevertheless mellowed over the years: her portrait, now hanging outside the Chapel in Bermondsey, presents a youthful, smiling, bespectacled face. Her many letters to Sisters were full of rather modern-sounding advice, telling them to 'look on the bright side of everything' and to have patience with themselves as well as with other people. 'We are

---

[1.] Annals of the Convent of Our Lady of Mercy, Bermondsey, vol. I, Bermondsey Archives, Institute of Our Lady of Mercy.

[2.] Letter from Catherine McAuley to M. Francis Warde, 30 January 1840, Silver Spring Archives, Institute of the Sisters of Mercy of the Americas.

not angels', she wrote. The letters are affectionate, often teasing.[3]

Underneath the playfulness was a highly capable woman. One of the bishops, probably Thomas Grant, said that 'she was fit to rule a kingdom'.[4] She had already played a pivotal role as trusted companion of the Foundress, and had personally founded several Convents of Mercy, two – Bermondsey and Chelsea – in the capital of Protestant England. In doing so, she managed to attract a number of vocations, ensuring Bermondsey's future as a centre for evangelization during these important years following Catholic Emancipation. Her most important work, however, was still to come.

The Crimean War, which began in 1854, was the first time a Special Correspondent accompanied an army into battle. Britain had not fought a major war since Napoleon's defeat at Waterloo and medical arrangements proved woefully inadequate. Russell, a journalist for *The Times*, awakened public awareness to the dreadful conditions at the Front and compared British nursing unfavourably with the Sisters of Charity caring for French troops. An anonymous letter to *The Times* published on 14 October 1854, asked, 'Why have we no Sisters of Charity?' Government officials resented the interference of the media, especially when *The Times* opened its own fund to procure supplies for the Scutari hospitals, but the tide of public opinion was unstoppable.

This was a public relations opportunity and Thomas Grant, Bishop of Southwark, lost no time in sending Catholic Sisters to the British military hospitals. He knew that he could rely on Clare Moore. As he was later to remark to one of his fellow bishops, 'She has never yet failed me ...'[5] So it was that, late in the evening of the very day *The Times* letter was published, Bishop Grant called to the Convent in Bermondsey. Mother Clare was amongst those who

[3.] Original letters, Bermondsey Archives, Institute of Our Lady of Mercy.

[4.] Carroll, M. Austin, *Leaves from the Annals of the Sisters of Mercy*, vol. II, New York, The Catholic Publication Co., 1883.

[5.] Ibid.

immediately offered to go. Touched by her spontaneous generosity, Bishop Grant did not want to deprive Bermondsey of its Superior and he was still uncertain whether religious would be accepted as volunteers. By Monday morning, however, Mother Clare received a note from him asking her to be ready to leave the next morning with four Sisters. The Government was already organizing an official expedition of nurses and Florence Nightingale would be appointed to lead it. Bishop Grant wanted Catholics to be seen as first to respond in the nation's hour of need.

Bishop Grant came himself that evening to bid a personal farewell to the Sisters. He cautioned them to take ordinary clothes in case they were not allowed to wear the habit, and they obediently packed some black net caps, hoping not to have to wear them. Mother Clare asked if he had any words of advice, but, weeping, he replied, 'nothing, do the best you can'. After his departure they spent until midnight preparing. The parish priest purchased outdoor wear and a small travelling bag for each Sister. They took underclothing and books of devotion but there was no room for a second veil or habit, and new ones were not sent out to them until the following spring. They took a pewter jug (still displayed in Bermondsey) to improvise as an iron for their guimpes, the white collar of their religious habit. Lord Arundel paid for their expenses.

Next morning after Mass and breakfast, Mother Clare blessed and embraced those left behind and the five set out for London Bridge station to catch the 8.10 a.m. train to Dover. Clare was by then forty years old with a very weak chest. Rather shockingly, they travelled unescorted, still unsure whether they were going via Calais or Boulogne. The Sisters each took one of the Five Wounds as a travelling name. They arrived in Paris at a late hour, securing hotel accommodation with difficulty. There they received an instruction from Sidney Herbert, Secretary at War, to await the arrival of the official nursing expedition under its Superintendent. After all the urgency of their departure, they now had to wait a week.

There had been no rush of applicants and it had been decided to increase the number of Catholic Sisters in the expedition to ten. Bishop Grant approached the Norwood Sisters, an enclosed Order which ran an orphanage in Southwark. These and the rest of the party, including fourteen Anglican nuns and Miss Nightingale, eventually arrived, making an expedition which totalled forty nurses from England. Sarah Terrot, who was among them, recalled the five Bermondsey Sisters: '... no gloom, no formality, no self-consciousness apparent: animated, simple, affectionate and humble ... their conduct did much to disarm dislike'.[6]

It was not until Florence Nightingale called to their Paris hotel that they had any notion about conditions of employment. Miss Nightingale presented them with an agreement already signed by Bishop Grant on their behalf which placed them unreservedly under her direction. The Sisters were to take orders from the Lady Superintendent rather than from their own Superior. It also stipulated that Sisters should not introduce religious topics except with Catholic troops – about a third of the British Army was Irish and Catholic at that time. This was a controversial undertaking, for English people still viewed Catholics as potential traitors and expected them to use nursing as cover for proselytising. Catholics were equally sensitive about the rights of a religious Superior being signed away and felt that Bishop Grant had been too anxious to appease anti-Catholic feeling. As it turned out, Clare Moore's relations with the Lady Superintendent were always cordial and Florence Nightingale observed the courtesy of directing the Sisters through their Reverend Mother.

The British Government paid for their onward journey. The party set sail from Marseilles on 27 October 1854 aboard the *Vectis*. A mailbag hold improvised as the Sisters' cabin, with no window or ventilation other than a gap under the door – those in the lower 'berths' were drenched by

---

6. Terrot, Sarah, *Reminiscences of Scutari hospitals*, Edinburgh, Andrew Stephenson & Co., 1898.

seawater. Storms battered the vessel, and Clare Moore became very ill. They arrived in Constantinople on the eve of the Battle of Inkerman, 4 November. They then went by boat across the Bosphorus to Scutari on the Asiatic shore where artillery barracks and a General Hospital had been put at the disposal of the British Army by the Turkish government for use as military hospitals. The Norwood Sisters decided to rest at Galata but the Bermondsey Sisters wanted to push on with Florence Nightingale and the other nurses. After putting ashore at the rickety landing stage they climbed the steep slope. A stench greeted them before they even reached the entrance.

The Barrack Hospital was a colossal square, stone building with turrets at each corner built around a courtyard. It looked imposing from a distance but was very run down. Blocked sewers under the building contaminated the rooms above and moisture oozed from the walls. The floor was so rotten that it proved impossible to scrub clean. Put together, the wards extended a total distance of three or four miles. There were no beds for the patients, just straw sacks on the floor, so close that it was difficult to pass between them. Boots served as pillows and greatcoats as blankets. With only twenty chamber pots available, large wooden tubs, which orderlies were in no hurry to empty, were used as lavatories on each ward. Most patients suffered from fever and diarrhoea so that the distinction between 'sick' and 'wounded' became theoretical. Amputations without anaesthetic were performed in the wards on makeshift trestle tables in open sight of other patients.

Arrivals from the Crimean battlefields screamed in pain as they jolted up the rough slope. They were initially tended in field hospitals at the Front or at the Balaclava hospitals. Survivors sent down to the base hospitals at Scutari endured a 400-mile journey across the Black Sea in crammed vessels awash with blood and dysentery. Some died on the last leg of their journey, others as they lay untended in corridors awaiting admission. Doctors and 'dressers' were too busy to offer post-operative care. Often the sick tended the sick.

It is difficult to comprehend the reluctance of medical authorities in Scutari to accept the help of forty English nurses, but army doctors regarded them as an unwelcome intrusion. When they first arrived, they were refused admittance to the wards. The party was allotted a few rooms in the north-west tower where they remained cooped up for the best part of a week. The Bermondsey Sisters had to share their room with the Norwood nuns, who arrived a fortnight later, five mattresses on each side of the room with a sheet between. The only other furniture was a single backless chair which they used as a table. There was no bed linen. Every window pane was broken. They washed from the same basin and saved the water for their laundry. If soldiers had not shared their rations, they would have gone hungry in that first week. Tea consisted of a few leaves in warm water without milk.

As it happened, the first casualties began arriving from the Battle of Inkerman on 9 November and army doctors had no option but to enlist their help on the wards. Suddenly plunged into activity, 'The Sisters were now almost overworked preparing the wards and beds, and ... as the wounded arrived, helping them, dressing their wounds and comforting them.'[7] The Sisters endured terrible conditions:

> In the severest cold, when the snow lay deep on the ground they never had a fire; their food was so bad and so sparing that they were often faint from hunger ... the want of water was a suffering greater than can be expressed. During the first weeks ... they were parched with thirst ... and they were unwilling to seek remedy or redress as the others did, feeling how important it was for them to give an example of patient endurance and conformity with prescribed regulations.[8]

Two Bermondsey Sisters were sent out each day with other nurses to work in the General Hospital, Scutari. This involved

---

[7.] Annals of the Convent of Our Lady of Mercy, vol. I.
[8.] Ibid.

a walk across a bleak hillside infested with wild dogs. If they were caught in the rain – and sometimes they might be ankle-deep in snow – the Sisters had no option but to go to bed until their wet habits dried. They did not complain about conditions nor, unlike the Lady Superintendent, get into disputes with army officials. Sarah Terrot, who walked with them daily to the General Hospital, later commented on the 'gentle, cheerful manner of the nuns [which] overcame all ... antipathy'. One of them was Sr Gonzaga, who related her experiences in letters home to Bermondsey:

> The other day I was dressing a gangrened wound in a man's leg, and he tried to draw a plan of Sebastopol on it to explain the fighting to me ... Some die as they are carried from the landing place, some as we change their clothes when brought into Hospital.[9]

The other Bermondsey Sisters worked in the Barrack Hospital where numbers of patients varied between 1,900 and 2,500 during the winter of 1854–5. They were given charge of two of the wards and a corridor, a total of 150 beds.

> The Sisters in the wards were ... engaged among the sick until a late hour and after all their fatigue were forced to stay up until near midnight to free themselves from the filth and insects which came on them among the poor sufferers – yet even when they lay down other pests which infected the place allowed them little rest.[10]

The place was infested with lice, fleas and rats. 'Our home rats would run if you hushed them; but ... Scutari rats would not take the least notice.'[11]

---

[9]. Letter from Sr M. Gonzaga Barrie, dated 3 December 1854, copied into the Annals of the Convent of Our Lady of Mercy, Bermondsey, vol. I, Bermondsey Archives, Institute of Our Lady of Mercy.

[10]. Annals of the Convent of Our Lady of Mercy, vol. I.

[11]. Doyle, M. Aloysius, 'Memories of the Crimea' in Maria Luddy (ed.), *The Crimean Journals of the Sisters of Mercy 1854–6*, Dublin, Four Courts Press, 2004.

As winter set in, frostbite took its toll. Cloth froze to the soldiers' flesh and casualties' boots sometimes had to be cut away piece by piece. Christmas 1854 was spent miserably. It was only after their work late at night that Sisters could celebrate by kneeling before a little picture of the Christ-child to sing a carol in hushed voices. From early 1855 cholera added to the miseries of the troops. Clare Moore had seen plenty of cholera before, but a letter home from one of the Sisters described it as 'the very worst type- the attacked man lasted only four or five hours. Oh! Those dreadful cramps; you might as well try to bend a piece of iron as to move the joints'. Survivors were rare: the Sisters tried to persuade orderlies to be certain patients were dead before taking them to the mortuary. Graves were shallow graves and there were no coffins. The air was putrid.

Winter gave way to the overpowering heat of summer. Flies plagued the hospital by day and mosquitoes by night. Mother Clare presented a comical appearance after being bitten on both lips which swelled up like balls. Confined for long hours in the hospital, army doctors became concerned about the Sisters' health and ordered them out into the fresh air: two of them had almost died of fever earlier in the year. Lack of personal space was an additional torment. Sisters ate and worked closely with lay nurses who could be abusive and drunken. Sr M. Gonzaga wrote cheerfully to Bermondsey that 'Revd. Mother is a general favourite with all parties and is invaluable for keeping peace ... the nurses are always wrangling with each other.' But not everyone favoured them: one Matron was openly hostile to Catholics and Sisters felt exposed to the critical gaze of all. They were acutely aware of ' ... the strangeness of their position as Nuns dwelling among more than three thousand soldiers'.[12] Many of these were foreigners. Turks called the Sisters 'Johnny', the name reserved for anyone English.

Clare Moore was made personally responsible for the linen stores and 'Extra Diets' kitchen. This was a mark of

[12.] Annals of the Convent of Our Lady of Mercy, vol. I.

Miss Nightingale's trust, for her main preoccupation was procuring supplies. Hospital stores were shipped with artillery and difficult to extricate. The purveyor created further obstacles since officers viewed troops as animals and mostly disregarded requests for bedding or soup. Miss Nightingale's Free Gift stores and *The Times* Fund were therefore crucial. She had good reason to place the kitchen and stores under the sole charge of Mother Clare as the average daily distribution of hot arrowroot included the contents of 100 bottles of port.

The 'Extra Diets' kitchen was the only means of feeding very sick patients. On the wards orderlies issued lumps of salted meat cooked in gigantic coppers which scarcely reached boiling point. This meant that patients ate almost raw meat, and without cutlery. Orderlies consumed the rations of very ill or sleeping patients themselves. Using portable stoves purchased by Miss Nightingale in Marseilles, Clare Moore was soon dispensing pails of hot beverages and broth to those who could not manage rations. She might have been better deployed nursing cholera patients, but spent her days stuffing pillows, supervising laundry, doling out rations and cutting up the monogrammed underclothing donated by royal and noble households for bandages. Mother Clare wrote, 'I should have more comfort were I allowed to attend to the poor men who are sick or wounded – but I feel very happy in my present employment which scarcely leaves me one moment all day long.'[13]

Florence Nightingale herself was an administrator rather than a nurse. Her reputation as 'The Lady with the Lamp' stemmed from her routine of late night ward-rounds. Clare, too, seems to have used this night-time respite from her normal duties to tour the wards. She spoke of the orderlies asking them to sprinkle men with holy water at night and felt that, 'Our going about in our religious Habit has done much good ... We are constantly told of the many lives we have

13. Letter from Mother Clare Moore to Bishop Thomas Grant, dated 6 December 1854, Bermondsey Archives, Institute of Our Lady of Mercy.

saved – or that the wounds have gone on improving ever since we put a hand to them.'[14] Sr Gonzaga wrote at that time, 'You would be surprised ... [the men] never utter a bad word, nor an oath before us. If any chance to say what the others think too free in our presence the whole Ward cry out "hush".'[15]

Bishop Grant sent £50 to cover Sisters' expenses and told Mother Clare to be cautious about taking more money from Miss Nightingale than they needed for their keep. He need not have worried. Miss Nightingale did not offer payment to volunteers. The distinction between their role as nurses and religious Sisters was harder to maintain for soldiers of all denominations begged them to send money to their families, write letters for them and give them prayer books or beads. The dual role of nurse and nun, strictly defined by the agreement Bishop Grant made with the British Government, was further complicated by the arrival of a second party of Sisters of Mercy in December 1854 from Liverpool, Chelsea, Kinsale, Carlow, Cork, Dublin and Charleville under the leadership of Mother Francis Bridgeman. This group of Mercy Sisters was usually referred to as 'the Irish Sisters' to distinguish them from the 'Bermondsey Sisters'.

Cardinal Manning had been more firm about terms of employment for this second party. Unlike the Bermondsey Sisters, the 'Irish Sisters' were independent of Miss Nightingale's absolute control and were even allowed their own chaplain. Bishop Grant must have felt embarrassed. Having cautioned the Bermondsey Sisters about religious sensibilities at the time of their departure, he was soon suggesting that they raise their profile. He wrote to Mother Clare in February 1855 saying that 'We are anxious that you should always be Nuns as well as Nurses.'

Clare Moore was walking a diplomatic tightrope, especially as Miss Nightingale was infuriated by the arrival of nursing reinforcements and determined that her authority in the military hospitals should not be further undermined. Clare found

14. Ibid.
15. Letter from Sr M. Gonzaga Barrie, dated 3 December 1854.

herself caught in the middle of a dispute between her Superintendent, to whom she was bound by agreement, though not one of her own making, and fellow Sisters of Mercy who deserved a better welcome to Constantinople. Instructed by Miss Nightingale to negotiate with Mother Bridgeman, Clare Moore set off across the Bosphorus in an open boat in a violent snowstorm, shocking the Irish Sisters by her 'soiled and neglected looking' appearance, as Mother Bridgeman later described it.[16] The issue of Miss Nightingale's authority over the second party of nurses remained contentious and the English Sisters suffered by association.

The situation was exacerbated by Miss Nightingale's decision to relinquish the services of the Norwood Sisters, who, as an enclosed Order, found life in the military hospitals more challenging. Catholic chaplains openly criticized the Bermondsey Sisters for continuing to work for Miss Nightingale, and one even refused them Communion. Clare Moore found it very painful to continue her work amidst such loud disapproval, though she never fuelled argument by expressing her views. Mother Bridgeman, free from the contractual bounds under which Clare Moore worked, called her 'a perfect drudge'.

> Amidst the contending feelings of all around them our Sisters tried to pass on humbly and simply. They had undertaken the work expecting to find great difficulty and hardship and they knew it would be wrong to complain, especially as their chief grievances arose from the angry way in which both Priests and Religious looked on Miss Nightingale's Superintendence and their submission to her in the Hospital work.[17]

The loyalty and dignity of the Bermondsey Sisters deeply impressed Miss Nightingale, who urged Clare to send for

---

[16.] Bolster, Evelyn, *The Sisters of Mercy in the Crimean War*, Cork, The Mercier Press, 1964.

[17.] Annals of the Convent of Our Lady of Mercy, vol. I.

more of them. A further three arrived early in 1856. It was Clare herself who impressed her most of all. By the time illness forced Clare Moore to leave for home in April 1856, Florence Nightingale was working at the Balaclava General Hospital. From there she wrote,

> Your going home is the greatest blow I have had yet ... I do not presume to express praise or gratitude to you, Revd. Mother, because it would look as if I thought you had done the work not unto God but unto me. You were far above me in fitness for the general superintendency, both in worldly talent of administration, and far more in the spiritual qualifications which God values in a superior. My being placed over you in our unenviable reign of the East was my misfortune and not my fault ... My love and gratitude will be yours, dearest Revd. Mother, wherever you go. I do not presume to give you any other tribute but my tears ... But I should be glad that the Bishop of Southwark should know and Dr. Manning ... that you were valued here as you deserved and that the gratitude of the Army is yours ... Florence Nightingale.[18]

The friendship of Miss Nightingale and Reverend Mother, as they continued to call each other according to the etiquette of their day, has puzzled some. The two were very different in personality. 'I am not like my dear Revd Mother', Florence later wrote to her 'who is never ruffled'.[19] Alike in administrative ability, however, and dogged devotion to the task in hand, they worked well together. They also shared a love of mystical writers. Florence Nightingale's religious motivation as a reformer is not always recognized, perhaps because she felt and showed little affinity to any church. She was never able to take the step of becoming a Catholic, though Mother Clare must have hoped she might. Florence Nightingale referred to her as, '... the only R. Catholic I have ever known who never tried to convert me'.[20]

[18] Original letters, Bermondsey Archives, Institute of Our Lady of Mercy.
[19] Ibid.
[20] Letter from Florence Nightingale to Benjamin Jowett, 1862, quoted in Sullivan, Mary C. (ed.), *The Friendship of Florence Nightingale and Mary Clare Moore*, University of Pennsylvania Press, 1995.

When, in late July 1856, Florence Nightingale came home at the end of the war, she drove directly to the Bermondsey Convent, though it was still only eight o'clock in the morning, before taking the train back to Lea Hurst where she lived. She remained a regular visitor and correspondent for the next eighteen years. Roles were now reversed: Reverend Mother, her assistant in the Crimea, became the wisdom figure Florence Nightingale turned to again and again. Clare Moore saw and brought out a side of her she rarely showed: a vulnerable, generous and reflective side. She supported her throughout long campaigns to reform medical training and workhouse management, and helped her explore her personal interest in spirituality.

In contrast to the adulation surrounding Miss Nightingale, the Sisters received no honours until Queen Victoria bestowed a belated Royal Red Cross on the surviving Crimean Sisters at the Diamond Jubilee celebrations thirteen years after Mother Clare's death. Yet the reputation of their work brought a number of requests for Mercy foundations and nine convents were founded from Bermondsey during Clare Moore's time in office. For Mother Clare herself, life quickly returned to normal. 'After we came home' wrote Florence Nightingale, 'I found her one day cleaning out a gutter with her own hands.'[21]

Bishop Grant did not let her lie low for very long. As early as 15 July 1856, while she was still convalescing, he confided to Mother Clare Dr Manning's plan to use Crimean Sisters for the first Catholic Hospital in London since the Reformation. Four months later St Elizabeth's Hospital for Incurables opened with Sister Gonzaga from Bermondsey as its Superior. Later transferred to St John's Wood, it became the famous Hospital of St John and St Elizabeth. Bishop Grant used Clare and her Sisters as a personal secretariat, delegating to them his copying and translation work. It was Clare who personally nursed him night and day while he was dying. However busy her itinerary, poor people remained

---

21. Ibid.

the priority. She wrote to Florence Nightingale in 1862:

> I went to St George's Church this morning, to bring my writing to the Bishop ... on my way back I felt I must go out of my way to see a poor family; the children have been obliged to stay from school on account of smallpox – five had it – one died – a dear child of six – her younger sister greeted me by pulling out from a dreadful piece of rag a half penny for the poor – 'for Katie's soul!' I could not well describe their own wretchedness, for the father has been in a dying state for months. We had five shillings to give them – a small fortune – but I could not help feeling it was the dear child's self-denial & faith which drew me there, for I hesitated to add to my walk – already very long for me.[22]

Clare Moore died of pleurisy on 14 December 1874, aged sixty-one. She had been anxious about the opening of a school for poor girls in Eltham and had been travelling back and forth in bitter cold weather to buy clothing and furniture and to arrange credit from local shopkeepers for the new Community. 'What an anxious charge for us! ... I have been there six or seven times – no little cross to me, who do not care for travelling. We must accept our cross whatever it is made of, even a railway carriage.'[23] This was a different kind of courage to the frontline soldier facing Russian cannons, a different kind of heroism to Florence Nightingale's lifelong offensive against vested interests and institutional red tape. There were no trumpets or headlines for Clare Moore. Hers was 'a humble, unobtrusive life' as the parish priest said in his eulogy, 'doing far more for [God] and suffering humanity than the accumulated acts of many others, who with much noise and stir win the applause and glory of the world'.[24]

[22.] Letter from Mother Clare Moore to Florence Nightingale, dated 13 October 1862, quoted in Sullivan, Mary C. (ed.), *The Friendship of Florence Nightingale and Mary Clare Moore*, University of Pennsylvania Press, 1995.

[23.] Annals of the Convent of Our Lady of Mercy, vol. I.

[24.] Ibid.

Chapter 16

Frances Wootten

Dora Nash

If you are lucky enough to visit the lovely Oratorian house at Rednal, once a village near Birmingham but now engulfed by its suburbs, you will certainly wish to see the little graveyard to the north of the building. Rows of plain mounds with small crosses mark the burial places of the Birmingham Oratorians from the 1850s until the present day: including Cardinal Newman himself. Look behind you before you go and you will see two other graves: one a layman, and the other a woman 'in that last resting place of celibacy'.[1] It is the grave of Frances Wootten, whom Newman had known since his Oxford days, and to whom he turned in 1859 when he needed a helpmate *'Fortis et Sapiens'*, as the epitaph he gave her reads on the tombstone.

What is known of her early life is soon told. She lived in Oxford and was the wife of a well-known and respected local physician, Dr John Wootten of Lincoln and Balliol Colleges, who in 1830 moved to number 40, Broad Street and was elected physician of the Radcliffe Infirmary. He was described as being 'in the forefront of Oxford medical practice'.[2] Amongst his patients in the early 1840s were Newman and the group of like-minded friends who accompanied him to Littlemore, withdrawing from university life to consider their future in the Church of England. It is apparent that his

[1.] www.newmanreader.org/biography/meynell/chapter6
[2.] www.headington.org.uk/oxon/doctors

wife knew this circle too, since one of them – later Fr Nicholas Darnell – described her in after years as having been 'his second mother'. The Woottens were friends of the Puseys and had become Tractarians: those Anglicans who believed they would like to be 'Catholic without the Pope'.[3]

John Wootten died in 1847, just short of his forty-eighth birthday, leaving his wife childless though not without money. Newman and his great friend Ambrose St John – whom Frances was destined to know very well indeed – were in Rome, newly ordained and learning to become Oratorians. By 1850, Frances Wootten had left the Pusey circle and Oxford and followed Newman and the Littlemore group into the Catholic Church, and we next find her relocated to Birmingham as a devout member of the new Oratory parish. She put herself at the service of the Birmingham Oratory fathers, helping out when they were short of money and being a hostess to female visitors.

It was in 1859 that she was called to take part in one of the few still-surviving enterprises that John Henry Newman undertook, taking on a new and important role in her late middle age. Newman had had an unusual request. Educated converts to Catholicism, who had themselves attended the best public schools in England, were now looking for somewhere to send their sons. They – and their gently-born convert wives – did not consider the seminary-type training and the spartan atmosphere of the existing Catholic schools to be a good education for the laymen of the future which would fit them for engagement with the world; a good liberal education, but in a truly Catholic ethos, was what they required, and they only really trusted Newman to provide it. He knew that the right kind of feminine presence would be a vital ingredient, and who better than his loyal benefactress and friend who had a talent for caring for young men and, presumably, some familiarity with medical practice from her married life, to become the Matron, or Dame.

Rooms for the school, and for Mrs Wootten, were built on

[3.] Newman, J. H., *Loss and Gain*.

to the Oratory fathers' house on the Hagley Road; a head-master – that same Fr Darnell – was appointed, and on 2 May 1859 the new Oratory School opened to nine pupils.

Mrs Wootten's role was to be *in loco parentis* to the boys in the school, dealing with illness, homesickness, cleanliness and any problems which arose, often writing to anxious mothers about her charges. She was obviously very effective as Dame: too effective for the taste of the headmaster. Fr Darnell clearly did not share Newman's vision of the school and Mrs Wootten did. Amongst other things, he favoured flogging the boys, whereas Newman said that 'their persons should be sacred'. Darnell was hoping to move the school away from the Oratory site with himself independent of Newman and with no Mrs Wootten, to create something more like an ordinary public school. Mrs Wootten knew of his plans and tried to dissuade him, urging him to obedience and opposing the scheme 'with all her might'.[4] What became known as 'the Darnell affair' must have been deeply upsetting to her. Harsh criticisms and accusations poured from Darnell about her: she was a 'princess regnant with a back way to the emperor' (Newman), she 'sneaked off and retailed everything' to other Oratory fathers, and was 'an insolent perverse and blindly frantic woman'.[5] All falsehood, and this about one who, he admitted, had been his 'unselfish benefactress'.[6] His supporters, mainly lay staff, also claimed that 'the boys hate Mrs W, love Darnell and care nothing for Newman whom they never see'.[7] This was clearly untrue: the boys knew perfectly well what was going on in the school and showed their support for their Dame by deliberately going to visit her during the feud.

The climax was reached on 28 December 1861. Newman read a paper to the General Congregation of the Birmingham Oratory defending Mrs Wootten's contribution

4. Trevor, Meriol, *Newman: Light in Winter*, London, Macmillan & Co. Ltd, 1962.
5. Ibid., p. 250.
6. Ibid., pp. 248–50.
7. Ibid., p. 256.

to the school: 'The mode of conducting the great schools of Eton, Winchester etc. necessarily end in subordinating religion to secular principles and interests ... and ... this consequence would ensue in ours but for the presence of Matrons of a high class, and spiritual directors.' He said, moreover, that whilst 'the parents have intrusted their children to me', Mrs Wootten had been a real cause of the school's growth.[8] Not long afterwards Fr Darnell left, along with all four lay masters, and Newman had to re-staff the school before the next term began. The faithful Ambrose St John became the new headmaster. The verdict was that Mrs Wootten had behaved 'with restraint' unlike Darnell, and that it was really her championship of Newman which had made her such enemies. He himself concluded that he could never have banished from the school such a loyal friend and benefactress 'at the dictation of a lot of men'.[9]

All this time, Mrs Wootten feared she was dying: she was coughing up blood and was sure she had not long to live, though she did not make it public. In the event she lived to be Newman's Dame for another decade and more, always concerned for her boys and always in support of him. She was assiduous in keeping contact with the boys' mothers, who much appreciated her maternal care and her consultation of them. She seems to have had a certain wisdom in the care of the young, balancing firmness with tender solicitude at the right times. Everyone preferred her ministrations to those of other stricter matrons who succeeded her; they did not have 'Mrs Wootten's motherliness'.[10]

Her ordinary round of duties in the school have left few traces in the literature. Newman did not need to write to her, as she was very close by, so she does not figure large in the vast collection of his letters. He did praise her to others, though, and perhaps felt about her what he said about other friends, that he had not sufficiently expressed what he felt

[8.] Ibid., p. 253.
[9.] Ibid., p. 261.
[10.] Trevor, p. 537.

he owed. Not a demonstrative person, he tended rather to rejoice quietly 'in the confidence of an everyday relationship'.[11] One small and telling glimpse of her is seen when she gave him £20 to go on a much-needed holiday in Kent when he was beset by financial worries and the loss of friends. She also sent to him there a huge hamper of food – more than he could possibly use – when she believed him to be hungry.

Mrs Wootten did not live to see the cloud of suspicion and rejection which had always hung over Newman lift for ever when he was made a cardinal in 1879. She died three years before, in January 1876, interested in the boys until the end, so much so indeed that no one knew she was in her last illness. She talked to boys from her sickbed and was 'so bright and alert in manner that the boys did not guess how ill she was'.[12] She was attended by a local Protestant doctor who was 'impressed with her fortitude and cheerfulness',[13] and Newman wrote of her: 'Mrs Wootten died on Sunday night … All along she had no fear of death but was cheerful and joyful, and we could not tell the moment when she went.'[14] She was buried at Rednal under snow.

Wherein lies her heroism? Certainly she did not in any sense die for her faith, or convert the heathen as a missionary, or sacrifice herself to a life of enclosure as a holy nun. She will never be canonized. But I think she deserves inclusion amongst a roll-call of English Catholic heroines because she exemplifies a number of qualities which ordinary women can recognize and appreciate and which are taken for granted, or even scoffed at, by the world.

Firstly, she is the archetypal 'helpmeet', an idea which comes from that seminal text in Genesis 2, but is not only to be found in the married relationship. The complementarity of the sexes can work in other situations too, and here she

[11.] Ibid., p. 528.
[12.] Sugg, Joyce, *Ever Yours Affly: John Henry Newman and his female circle*, Leominster, Gracewing, 1996, p. 271.
[13.] Trevor, p. 536.
[14.] Sugg, p. 271.

was in effect a colleague of England's foremost Catholic educator, carrying out his principles and plainly understanding very well why he held them. How many priests have relied on the chaste friendship, loyal support and womanly wisdom of a female ally who is content to be in their shadow? Such women could adopt a worse 'patron saint' than Frances Wootten.

Her loyalty to Newman would have been a good model for Darnell, evidently not willing to subordinate himself to the ideas and ministry of his spiritual father. Her offer to quit her role in the school if it would solve Newman's quarrel with his headmaster was typical of her lack of self-interest. Newman recognized this trait in her when he said: '[She] in many ways has sacrificed herself for us.'[15] He knew that she had been an important factor in the success of the school, shortly after the Darnell crisis writing:

> If she had gone, there was a chance of all the school going – for her care of the young boys and popularity with the mothers have been the making of the school – as I know full well if I did not know it before, by what the mothers have said to me since the row.

Newman also valued her opinion of the boys highly and appreciated her dedication. Indeed the latter worried him rather. He wrote to one of the mothers that Mrs Wootten did too much: 'She is more like a saint than most people you come across.'[16]

She could also be seen as a model for Catholic women who have no children of their own. Quite late in life – in her fifties, when most ladies, even if they had any employment, must have been looking forward to an easy old age – she was called to take on a heavy responsibility, which involved mothering young and teenage boys not her own: her original brief had been to be 'Guardian of the children'.[17]

[15.] Trevor, p. 258.
[16.] Sugg, p. 254.
[17.] Ibid., p. 254.

This was a remarkable 'second career' for a Victorian widow.

In her dealings with the boys and their parents she was putting into practice Newman's principle, *Cor ad Cor Loquitur:* Heart speaks to Heart. The implication is that Catholic education and formation, coming to know God, happens through personal influence, rather than through argument, indoctrination, didactic methods. Though not perhaps typical of educational ideas of the mid nineteenth century, it is very much in line with those of the founder of the Oratorians, St Philip Neri, though the Latin quotation is adapted from St Francis de Sales. Newman chose it as his official motto on becoming a cardinal: it is still the motto of his school. Mrs Wootten had understood it well.

Another of her admirable traits, which incidentally she shares with Newman himself, is her forbearance under vitriolic criticism. Accused of being insolent, hated by her charges and panicky, she refused to reply in kind or to gossip but, ill as she was, carried on with what she knew Newman needed from her. His admiring and supportive comments about her role indicate that he knew what he owed her.

She could sometimes be over-fussy in her attentions to others, and was on occasion indecisive when unsure of what other people wanted of her, but these are faults of generosity. A more tangible and positive result of her generosity was her gift to the Oratory of £10,000 which was an enormous sum in those days, something over half a million pounds in today's money. A benefactress indeed.

It is somehow fitting that she now lies in the shadow of the Rednal house: it reflects her relation to Newman's life and work. Every year, in the summer, Oratory boys go to visit and pray at her grave to remember and thank her for her care of their predecessors. How much does the Church in every age need women like her: *Fortis et Sapiens.*

Chapter 17

M. Elizabeth Prout, CP

Dominic Savio Hamer, CP

The remains of Elizabeth Prout are interred in the shrine of that great Apostle of England, Blessed Dominic Barberi, CP, in the Church of St Anne and Blessed Dominic in Sutton, St Helens, Lancashire. They lie to the right of his tomb and opposite the remains of another illustrious Passionist, Father Ignatius of St Paul of the noble house of Spencer. Elizabeth would never have aspired to such a unique distinction. She simply tried to respond to the Will of God in her everyday life. Following the Royal Road of the Holy Cross, however, not in any spectacular martyrdom but in faithfully corresponding with God's Will, she attained both heroism and sanctity, whilst socially as well as spiritually raising countless men, women and children above the thraldom of the Industrial Revolution.

Elizabeth was born on 2 September 1820 in Coleham, the industrial suburb of Shrewsbury. Her father, a non-practising Catholic, worked as a cooper in the Coleham Brewery, making the barrels that would carry porter along the River Severn and the network of England's rivers and canals. Her mother Ann (Yates) was a devout Anglican. On 17 September 1820 Elizabeth was baptized into the Anglican Communion in St Julian's, Shrewsbury. Whilst it is impossible to establish where she was educated, it is probable that she attended the National School at Coleham Head, which at that time was favoured by upper working-class parents because it offered a wide curriculum and admitted girls as well as boys. The pupils were also instructed in the Anglican catechism and attended Sunday morning services in Shrewsbury's Benedictine abbey church.

By 1836, however, the brewery had closed and by 1841, when a census was taken, Elizabeth and her parents were living in a house belonging to Joule's brewery in Stone, Staffordshire, where Edward Prout continued his work as a journeyman cooper. At twenty-one years of age, beautiful, 'refined, intelligent and gently nurtured', as a later annalist described her, Elizabeth was a respectable young lady of the artisan class, knowing 'nothing but the love of devoted parents, a comfortable and happy home and bright prospects for the future'. Her parents might well have expected that an eligible suitor would soon seek her hand in marriage and they would live happily ever after.

Such was not, in fact, the case. Instead, on 18 February 1842, Blessed Dominic Barberi opened the first Passionist monastery in England at Aston Hall, about two miles from Elizabeth's home. On 22 July that year he was joined by a young Italian priest, Father Gaudentius Rossi. On 21 December 1846 Father George Spencer entered their noviciate to emerge in January 1848 as Father Ignatius of St Paul (Spencer). By then, in a momentous meeting, Elizabeth Prout, the future Foundress of the Congregation of the Sisters of the Cross and Passion of Our Lord Jesus Christ, had encountered Blessed Dominic Barberi. She had heard him preach. She had imbibed Catholicism in the context of Passionist spirituality. During a Benediction service she had experienced an extraordinary insight into the Real Presence in the Blessed Sacrament. Finally, she had become a Catholic, although she knew that she might well be ostracized by former friends.

About July 1848, on the recommendation of Father Gaudentius, she entered the noviciate of the Sisters of the Infant Jesus in Northampton. It was a precious experience, for there she received her own noviciate training, as well as learning how to conduct a workroom for seamstresses and how to teach in both day and evening schools. She also discovered that the Passionist spirituality she had imbibed in

Stone was further enriched by living a Rule which, although directed towards Our Lord's Infancy, also included devotion to His Sacred Passion. A fervent novice, esteemed by her superiors, Elizabeth was very happy in Northampton. By late January 1849, however, she had tuberculosis in her knee. The doctor said she would never walk again. It was clear that life with the Sisters of the Infant Jesus was not for her. She returned home to Stone. Her Catholicism had cost her her health.

In fact, her mother nursed her so well that she did walk again but if her mother thought she would abandon her Catholic faith she was quickly proved wrong. Only a few minutes' walk from their home Blessed Dominic had built a church school. As soon as she could, fasting from midnight according to the custom at the time, Elizabeth limped to morning Mass. Her mother left her without breakfast. Elizabeth continued to go to Holy Communion. As her mother's anger increased, she raised her voice and finally her arm. Elizabeth realized that, if she wished to keep her Catholic faith, she could not stay at home.

She applied to a convent in Belgium in the hope of retrying her vocation and she sought advice from Father Gaudentius. Earlier that year he had given a mission in St Chad's, Cheetham Hill, Manchester and knew that the priest, Father Robert Croskell, was looking for a schoolmistress. As a result, in September 1849 Elizabeth arrived in Manchester, to discover that people were dying on the streets from cholera; that her school was no more than a battered old warehouse with a hole in the roof; and that in her class she had more than a hundred pupils from eight to thirteen, a mixture of full-timers and part-timers, factory children with cotton fluff in their hair and tiredness in their eyes. She saw that Manchester was the frontier town of an industrial revolution that was reducing handloom weavers to destitution and mill workers to physical slavery. As the health-conscious wealthier people moved out of their smoke-ridden, three-storey houses near the town centre, the most criminal members of society, the poorest, the least educated and

Irish refugees from the Great Potato Famine moved in, with even several families sharing each fever-prone cellar. Elizabeth not only stayed; she also accepted the priest's suggestion that she should undergo a Government Inspection of her teaching, so that he could apply for a Government Grant for a new school building beside the new St Chad's church. She also looked after the sacristy and she started a quasi-youth club for the girls who worked in the mills.

In the meantime, Fathers Gaudentius and Croskell had made another suggestion: that she should be the foundress of a new type of religious Order. Their idea was to provide consecrated religious life, with choir observance for all, for those young girls and women who felt that they had a religious vocation but could not afford the dowry required by the existing Orders and did not wish to be lay Sisters. At the same time, Elizabeth received a reply from Belgium inviting her to enter a noviciate there; and she also received a marriage proposal. She would not hear of the latter. In a radical option for the poor, she surrendered her chance of religious life in an established convent, in order to co-operate with the two priests in providing religious life for the poor. Her first two companions were Irish, one a power-loom weaver and the other a domestic servant. As other postulants arrived, most of them had neither money nor qualifications and so had to become seamstresses. Only two of her first group of six were able to join her in teaching.

With hundreds of Irish children to be educated in Manchester, in addition to their English counterparts, the clergy were looking for established teaching Orders, who would provide a steady stream of competent teachers for the indefinite future. The Notre Dame Sisters were invited to take charge of the new St Chad's, for which Elizabeth Prout had earned a building grant of £620, as well other grants for books and equipment. The Faithful Companions of Jesus were invited to teach in St John's school, Salford, which Father Gaudentius had expected to be given to Elizabeth. Instead, she was asked to take charge of St Chad's woefully substandard infant school at the heart of Angel Meadow, Manchester's worst slum, and to teach in St Chad's night school when the Notre Dame Sisters were absent.

In this context, however, she found herself playing an important role in the battle for Catholic education then raging in Manchester. Anxious to provide free education on the rates not just for the poor but for the children of tradesmen, shopkeepers and small businessmen and knowing that they could not possibly afford to give free education to all the Catholic children in Manchester, a group of prominent men, secularists, political economists, Anglican Evangelicals and Wesleyans, tried to debar Catholics from their scheme by stipulating that the Authorised Version of the Bible must be used in all schools maintained on the rates. They also proposed to build new schools in any areas where they did not already exist. The Catholic clergy, anxious to safeguard the Catholic faith of their parishioners, were desperate to have a Catholic school in every parish. As a result, when a postulant arrived who could take her place in the infant school, Elizabeth was asked to take charge of St Mary's school off Deansgate. Thus that area, described by one of the priests as 'a locality noted for wickedness and crime', had a Catholic school. She taught there in the day and Sunday schools through the winter of 1852–3, limping backwards and forwards from her convent at Cheetham Hill six days a week, until she became very seriously ill.

When she was recovering, she was asked in 1853 by Father Stephan, the French priest in charge of the new St Joseph's parish, to open a school for him in the temperance guild hall that served as his church. As described by Father Gaudentius, it was 'at the centre of a densely populated part of Manchester where the majority were poor Irish Catholics'. Again she obliged, although the school had no desks, no books, no slates, no equipment and no stoves for heating. She even agreed to a Government Inspection to try to win a building grant. It was too poor to receive a grant but its very existence prevented the anti-Catholic Manchester and Salford Education Committee from claiming that there was no school in that area. At the same time, she and her Sisters were visiting the homes of the parishioners to encourage them to attend Mass and to offer them whatever assistance and consolation they could. In late 1853, however, all her Sisters succumbed to the fever that raged through Manchester's slums and a few almost died.

Bishop William Turner, therefore, provided her with a convent, a converted old farm building, at Levenshulme on the outskirts of Manchester, where he was establishing the new St Mary's parish. There she opened the parochial elementary school and also provided a girls' boarding school in the convent, to provide for those Catholic children of tradesmen and shopkeepers who were so much in need of suitable education. It was in St Mary's, Levenshulme on 21 November 1854 that Bishop Turner received the vows of Elizabeth Prout and her first five companions. From then she was 'Mother Mary Joseph of Jesus'. With these professed Sisters and a number of novices, on 1 January 1855 she was able to make a second foundation, at Bishop Turner's request, in turbulent and fanatically Orange Ashton-under-Lyne. There she opened an elementary school in St Ann's church and she and her three companions continued the parish visitation they had done in Manchester.

In the spring, she was invited by the Passionist Rector of St Anne's monastery in Sutton, St Helens to make a further foundation there and to take charge of the girls' school. This invitation signified far more than stepping into a second diocese and extending both her Congregation and her educational apostolate. It indicated that the Passionist Congregation in England recognized that her Order had a special relationship with the sons of St Paul of the Cross. Later in 1855 she was invited by the Misses Orrell of Blackbrook House, St Helens to take charge of Parr Hall Young Ladies' Seminary and to open a new elementary school on their land behind St Mary's church. She and her companion, a pupil-teacher, went to live in Sutton in July 1855, lodging with the Catholic landowner, John Smith, who had built the church, the monastery and the schools. They moved to Parr Hall in August. After that they walked to Sutton each day, although staying overnight with the Smiths in very bad weather. By 5 September 1855, however, Elizabeth had acquired a cottage in Peckers Hill Road in Sutton. She called it 'Holy Cross Convent'. It was officially opened by Fathers Gaudentius and Ignatius Spencer on the feast of St Paul of the Cross, 16 November 1855. In Parr Hall, calling the Ladies' Seminary simply 'Holy Family School', she reduced the fees, so that parents of the lower middle classes could afford to send their daughters to it and she began to admit day girls as well as boarders, which meant that upper working-class girls living at home could also attend. Thus she opened Catholic secondary education in that area to numerous girls who would otherwise have been deprived of it. In late September, when it was clear that the Blackbrook building would not be ready for some time, she opened the elementary school in Parr Hall.

By 1857 there were so many children attending St Anne's school in Sutton that it was too small. The Rector, Father Bernardine Carosi, CP, wanted to apply for a Government Grant to build a new school. Elizabeth Prout had to face yet another Government Inspection of her school. She did very well, for Father Bernardine was awarded a building grant of £754 towards the cost of a new school. He built it at neighbouring Peasley Cross in 1857 and her Sisters took charge of it, to the great satisfaction of the parents.

In the meantime, however, in November 1855 Father Gaudentius had been sent to North America, leaving Father Ignatius Spencer to take his place as co-founder. Although a charming person, Father Gaudentius had been difficult to work with but he was the prime founder and Elizabeth had always given him his place. Unfortunately, the superior in Levenshulme had regarded him rather than Elizabeth as her superior. When he left for North America, she became restless and finally in 1857 she left, taking a number of others with her and leaving a large debt behind her. Deprived of these Sisters' work and wages, Elizabeth could not afford to support four houses and seven schools, nor could she pay the Levenshulme debts. Sadly she withdrew her Sisters from Ashton-under-Lyne, where they were very much loved, and also from Parr Hall and Blackbrook, retaining only two convents, Levenshulme and Sutton and four schools, Sutton, Peasley Cross and the two in Levenshulme.

That did not pay the debts and so with Bishop Turner's permission and a first donation from him, she set out to quest through the towns of Lancashire. There was a cotton slump at the time, however, and so the people had nothing to give. Then, with the help of Father Ignatius Spencer, in late November 1857 she crossed to Ireland to quest in Dublin, Co. Tipperary and further south, especially in Co. Cork. Returning to England in late January 1858, she discovered that the Sister whom she had left in charge had neglected the Sisters while preparing to transfer to a Cistercian convent. A few months later a young novice died. This was the first death in the Congregation and Elizabeth felt it keenly. The ex-Sisters in the meantime were spreading rumours that the Congregation was going to be suppressed. On 31 May 1858 Canon Croskell informed her that he wished to withdraw from its affairs: it was an economic disaster. On 2 July he informed their retreat master, Father Bernard O'Loughlin, CP, that the Congregation was going to be suppressed. It was Elizabeth Prout's darkest hour.

There had been complaints about the new Order since the first clothing ceremony in November 1852. Although the Sisters wore a mantle to conceal their habits when they went out, the people knew they were religious. They complained that nuns should not be seen on the streets. Even worse, Elizabeth and her companions were sometimes seen on omnibuses and the new-fangled railways. Moreover, Manchester and Salford seethed with 'popular Protestantism', fomented by the notorious Canon Stowell. In the Stockport riots of 1852, Catholic churches had been destroyed. Throughout the 1850s there were demands in Parliament for a bill to inspect convents and for a Royal Commission to investigate them. Finally, people said, the Sisters, unable to teach, were 'just a lot of factory girls', who could not support themselves. Unaware of the facts and overwhelmed by the large, Catholic, urban population in Manchester, the local clergy considered this new religious institute a liability they could not afford.

Expecting to receive novices' vows at the end of the retreat, Father Bernard ascertained the truth from Elizabeth and then went to see Bishop Turner. The Bishop then appointed a canonical enquiry to be held immediately, on 6 July, in Levenshulme convent. To his credit, Canon Croskell, who was the Vicar General, asked Father Bernard to be present. The next twenty-four hours must have seemed the longest in Elizabeth's life but at the end Father Bernard, on Bishop Turner's orders, led her community in a *Te Deum* of thanksgiving. The canons who had taken part in the enquiry now had the greatest admiration for her. Thus her Congregation survived but it was still desperately poor, struggling on amidst difficulties and opposition. Mainly thanks, again, to Father Ignatius Spencer and other Passionist Fathers, however, in the next few years a number of excellent postulants entered the noviciate.

When Elizabeth had had to withdraw her Sisters from Ashton in 1857, the parishioners had been so very upset that she had promised that, if it ever became possible, she would bring them back. When a slump in the cotton industry, following the American Civil War, caused the Lancashire Cotton Famine, most of the people in Ashton-under-Lyne were out of work and starving. Then the Government decided to open sewing schools and to pay the mill workers for attending them. Father Cromblehome, the parish priest of St Ann's, asked Elizabeth Prout to come back to Ashton to take charge of one of these schools for his Catholic parishioners. In November 1862 she brought four Sisters. They taught about 600 girls and women in St Ann's industrial school, which became known as the best in the town. Father Ignatius Spencer was there at the same time. While in Rome in 1857, he had presented Father Gaudentius Rossi's Rule for the approval of the Holy See. He had been told that, whilst its content was excellent, its style was too diffuse. It needed to be revised according to the Rule of someone whose sanctity was already recognized. For Elizabeth and Father Ignatius that person could be no other than Blessed Paul of the Cross, Founder of the Passionist Congregation and patron of her own. In designing the habit that the Sisters would wear, Elizabeth in 1854 had already taken as much as she dared of the Passionist Sign. Now, with the Passionist Rule in front of her for the first time, she realized that Father Gaudentius had based their Rule, diffuse as it might be, on the only Rule he knew and practised, that of Paul of the Cross. Removing all its 'trimmings' into regulations for novices, she and Father Ignatius made the Rule distinctly Passionist.

When he returned to Rome in 1863 Father Ignatius took the revision with him. He returned with its immediate approbation, written permission to hold the Congregation's first General Chapter and indulgences for both the Sisters and the young women who would live in their Homes. The provision in the Rule for Homes for the girls and young women who worked in the mills was Elizabeth Prout's personal response to the conditions they had to endure in the common mixed lodging houses. She was offering them not simply a refuge, nor even just a home, but a type of religious life, a modified version of her Congregation. They would wear secular dress, continue to work in the mills and retain their wages, whilst living a religiously orientated community life, in the same house as the Sisters, although not within the enclosure, and without binding themselves to a lifelong commitment to monastic observance. She hoped to found the first of these Homes in Ashton-under-Lyne. Father Cromblehome, the parish priest, would build it, if Lord Stamford would donate a piece of land beside the church and school. Father Ignatius Spencer went to Dunham Massey to ask him and was refused. Stamford supported the Orangemen.

Elizabeth did not live to see her first Home opened in Bolton in 1865. When she had arrived in Ashton in November 1862, she had discovered that Father

Cromblehome had provided practically nothing but an empty house. He did not realize how very poor the Sisters were, so poor that they had no bedclothes to bring with them. There was a bitterly cold wind. Elizabeth caught a bad cold, which in her tubercular condition was very serious. She never recovered. In 1863 she was very ill with consumption. The doctor, fearing for her life, ordered her to France. With Bishop Turner's permission and possibly with Mrs Smith's companionship and charity, she went to Paris. When they returned, John Smith suddenly became ill. His wife was too shocked to look after him. Elizabeth therefore unstintingly spent her restored energy in nursing her benefactor until he died and then another fortnight in caring for Mrs Smith in Levenshulme. By her annual retreat in July 1863 she was physically prostrate, although overwhelmed with joy at the news of the approbation and both mentally and spiritually alert. On 17 August, with Rome's permission, Bishop Turner canonically established her Congregation. In October she was unanimously elected as the first Superioress General but she had been too ill to travel to Levenshulme for the Chapter. On 21 November she made her final vows. She was sinking, however. In mid December she received the Sacrament of Extreme Unction. On Christmas Day she called all the Sisters to her room. She encouraged them to perse-vere and to be faithful to their vocation. Then she blessed them. 'God bless you, Sisters' were her last words to her Congregation.

Like Father Gaudentius, she had consistently emphasized the contemplative dimension of Passionist spirituality as she had first received it from Blessed Dominic. It was that emphasis on the contemplative nature of the Congregation that permitted the variety of its active apostlolates. Their success, however, depended on the quality of the Sisters' contemplative life. Their union with God was the dynamic force behind their activities. Their prayer was the source in which they daily renewed their apostolic strength. Fittingly she died, almost imperceptibly, as the Angelus bell called them to prayer on 11 January 1864 and as Father Ignatius

Spencer gave her a final Absolution, She was forty-three. Father Ignatius informed Bishop Turner immediately. The Bishop replied, 'Well, she did a good thing in her life by establishing the Institute and I trust she is now enjoying the rewards of her labours.'

During Elizabeth Prout's lifetime the Congregation was called, 'The Institute of the Sisters of the Holy Family', the title given to it in December 1851 by Father Gaudentius, who, of course, had no right to confer on it the Passionist title. Shortly after Elizabeth's death, however, the Passionist Father General visited England for the first time. Father Ignatius Spencer brought him to see the Sisters in Sutton and to be present at a clothing ceremony. He watched intently, listened and finally invited them to take the title 'Sisters of the Cross and Passion of Our Lord Jesus Christ', for, he said, everything about them was Passionist. Next he suggested they should be formally aggregated to the Passionist Congregation. Finally, in 1874, when the process had passed through Rome, the Passionist General Chapter awarded them the privilege of wearing the full Passionist Sign. Thus Elizabeth Prout's dearest wishes came to fruition. Her mother, too, had visited her over the years. She had become a Catholic before her death in 1862 and Elizabeth's father had returned to the Church before he died in January 1863. Elizabeth Prout had made heroic sacrifices but God had not been outdone in generosity.

Chapter 18

M. Elizabeth Hayes, MFIC

Pauline J. Shaw, MFIC

On a beautiful sunny morning in Guernsey a bright young girl, accompanied by an older woman, walked through the colourful Candie Gardens. The girl's name was Elizabeth. She was undecided whether to find a shady tree so that she could sit and read her book or to go down to see again the tall ships moored at St Peter Port harbour. Choices, decisions, what's new? Life in the nineteenth century, while different in many ways from today, produced teenagers who were full of curious anticipation and who dreamt of challenging years that lay ahead. Elizabeth had visited London with her family, yet for the time being she delighted in living in Sausmarez Street and attending her Aunt Sophie's ladies school in Allez Street which was only a few minutes' walk from her pleasant hilltop home.

Elizabeth Hayes was born in 1823 of English parents on historic Guernsey in the Channel Isles, an island closer to France than England. Guernsey's port and town, St Peter Port, were named after St Peter the Apostle and 900 years of living history are to be found in the 'Cathedral Church' of the islands. It was here that Elizabeth was baptized into the Anglican faith. Part of the church, once cared for by French Catholics, dates back to eighteen years before the Battle of Hastings (1066), and the exterior is practically still the same.

In her outings around Guernsey, Elizabeth was often accompanied by her former nurse, a French woman, as was the custom in her time when parents were financially comfortable. Elizabeth's mother was frail in health and so when in the company of her French companion, they spoke in French. Elizabeth developed a great command of French as well as the English language and throughout her life this would have significant consequences. Through her companion Elizabeth experienced her first awareness of Catholicism for she heard the story of the French Franciscan friars who once lived on the island until they were deported by Henry VIII when monasteries were dissolved. In jest, Elizabeth's father loved to call her 'his little French girl'. Mr Hayes, or rather, Reverend Philip Hayes (1781–1841) was headmaster of a college where boys were prepared for matriculation. He had been a chorister at Magdalen College, Oxford, gained his BA, and became an Anglican clergyman yet preferred the teaching profession, educating London boys before migrating with his wife and first child. The family grew and Elizabeth's parents lovingly cared for six surviving children of whom Elizabeth was the youngest, her father's blue-eyed 'precious one'.

From the back windows in the three-storied house, Elizabeth could look out to the islands of Sark and Herm, and she heard the cry of sea birds as they circled overhead. Closer to the port, she observed the thirteenth-century Castle Cornet, the sea and the golden beaches. Elizabeth knew that the quickest way to the town's covered markets below was by the stone-walled Clifton Steps. When her parents arrived in 1811, the town was described as 'insanitary but picturesque' yet soon it grew into a delightful and intriguing place. In the nineteenth century, St Peter Port changed from a small quayside settlement into a large town of wealthy merchants since privateering, smuggling and legitimate trade had brought prosperity to Guernsey. New buildings became the symbol of wealth and houses in Elizabeth's street were part of these developments.

Elizabeth's older siblings enjoyed Guernsey's social life while love of reading became her passion. One wonders what she read in the 1830s. What was available to a clergyman's daughter and a young lady of her class? Elizabeth may have accessed works of William Blake, Robert Burns, William

Wordsworth, Sir Walter Scott, Jane Austen, Thomas Carlyle, Edward B. Pusey or John H. Newman. Family reading, besides family musicals, was part of orderly life in the Hayes home, so this encouraged her early love of literature. Besides books, there were also plenty of journals to which a new generation of writers was contributing. By 1829, the young William M. Thackeray was already a contributor to the famous *Edinburgh Review*; the nineteenth century would become known as the 'The Age of Journalism' and in time Elizabeth would be caught up in a rapidly expanding media movement.

When Elizabeth was fifteen, she experienced intense grief through the death of her mother whom she loved dearly. Then only three years later in 1841, her father on whom she centred so much affection also died. To this day one can visit her parents' grave in Candie Cemetery. From the grave it is possible to look seaward; in the following years, Elizabeth decided to cross those blue waters and begin a new life in England. Her parents had inspired her to have faith and trust in God, so between 1843 and 1845, she said farewell to Aunt Sophie and immediate family members. As St Peter Port and its beautiful harbour faded into the distance Elizabeth wondered what God had in store for her yet she bravely faced the unknown.

Biographers differ as to where Elizabeth first lived in England but had I been in Elizabeth's shoes, my special attraction would have been to visit first the place of forebears and for Elizabeth this was Oxford. It is interesting to try to identify with Elizabeth in the 1840s. Where were our forebears living at this same time and what were they doing? Were they country folk or town people? Elizabeth's parents had told her stories of Oxford and she could see for herself the records and paintings of her famous Hayes musical forebears who lived in the previous century. St Mary's University Church had witnessed her great-grandfather, Dr William Hayes, and then his son, Philip, excel at its organ for fifty-six years; they were appointed organists with exceptional talent. Her relatives had attended a number of the colleges yet her family favoured Magdalen College. The Anglican Bishop of Oxford was Samuel Wilberforce, son of the slave-freeing advocate, a clergyman with conviction about the importance of providing trained teachers for parish schools in his diocese.

The Oxford Movement, through which the Anglican Church of England hoped to renew and revitalize itself, was initiated in 1833 and growing. In 1841, Marian R. Hughes under the guidance of Dr Edward B. Pusey had taken religious vows; she later became a firm friend of Elizabeth. Tractarians, as Oxford Movement members were often known, were bravely encouraging a new venture that saw some women deciding not to marry but live together in small communities so as to better provide service to others. One service included assisting at St Katharine's Hospital where Elizabeth's cousin, Reverend William Hayes, was chaplain. He not only introduced her to the Anglican Sisters but also to Dr Pusey and Revd John Keble who were the remaining leaders of the Oxford Movement for by this time Dr Newman had become a Catholic. In the late 1840s Elizabeth's interest in the Puseyite sisterhoods grew, she interacted with them and resolved to join one of these pioneer groups.

Tractarians, a name derived from reading the tracts written or edited by Dr Newman and the initial men of the Movement, saw the importance of distributing reading material at a time when 'literary London' was captured by new developments in the press world, in advancements in publishing newspapers and journals as well as books. Yet for every book there were far more journals so it is not surprising that the nineteenth century was called the 'Age of Journalism'. Elizabeth's love of reading had continued to grow and now she shared in the excitement of the time as more and more people and children were able to learn to read and write. Education through schools became more urgent and Elizabeth found work to support herself through teaching.

In 1848 in Wantage, a town outside Oxford, a young

married Anglican clergyman, Revd William Butler, decided to establish a parish project to assist poor children who needed education and to help women who were in distress. He approached a lady, Elizabeth Crawford Lockhart, and she with a friend agreed to implement Revd Butler's ideas. The pupils arrived, yet within two years, Miss Lockhart, whose brother William and also her stepmother, Martha, had previously converted to Catholicism, decided that she too would convert. Many Tractarians/Puseyites, be they in London or in Oxford, knew one another. Dr Pusey recommended to Revd Butler that a lady who could ably fill the vacant position in Wantage would be Elizabeth Hayes. Hence in 1850 Elizabeth not only joined the Wantage project but over a period of five and a half years she lifted the standard of education, established a number of departments, gained further education to be a fully trained school principal, and engaged pupil teachers which in turn increased income. In July 1855 Elizabeth became a religious Sister and was publicly installed as the Mother Superior of the School Community by Bishop Samuel Wilberforce. In the eyes of many people this was a heroic undertaking for it was still at a time when many Anglicans regarded the taking of religious vows by women as being wrong; it was too close to what had been seen in England before the Reformation when thousands of Catholic women chose to serve God and the poor by living together in convents throughout the country.

Elizabeth Hayes had been given authority by the bishop to rule over the educational complex but apparently Revd Butler still believed that he was in charge of everything. Up until the instalment ceremony Revd Butler wrote nothing but complimentary words about Elizabeth in his diary but by early 1856 the situation had completely changed, and by April Elizabeth decided to resign and follow another path. In the Jesuit Mayfair Church, better known as Farm Street, where many, many new converts were received into their new faith, Elizabeth took the mighty leap of leaving behind the strong traditional faith of her parents and forebears to enter into a new phase of her personal faith journey.

Religious reading played a major role in her decision to do this; for years she had studied the great mystics and the lives of English martyrs. Elizabeth prayed for guidance and looked for a community where she could live and work for God. Having considered joining the Franciscan Poor Clares or Catherine McAuley's Sisters of Mercy, she was led to a Rosminian Community of former Anglican Sisters and other convert women in Greenwich. They were under the capable and gentle leadership of the same Elizabeth Lockhart whom she knew from earlier days. After a while, Elizabeth asked to become a postulant with the intention of re-affirming her religious vows in a Catholic sisterhood.

At this time in England there was a new growth of Catholic religious communities, for since the Catholic Emancipation Act of 1829, many Orders returned to England from Europe. In this period of great religious ferment and renewal, some new groups were desirous of following the Rules and Constitutions of ancient Orders. Dr Henry Manning, another famous convert from Anglicanism, had known Elizabeth Lockhart in Chichester when she and her stepmother assisted him in his Anglican parish. He had decided that the Franciscan way of following Christ was best for him, not as a friar but by belonging to what is traditionally known as the secular Third Order of St Francis of Assisi. In his work in Glasgow and Inverness, he was impressed by the life and work of Franciscan Sisters of the Immaculate Conception. He counselled the former Greenwich Community, now living in Bayswater, to look toward the Franciscan way of life and mission. So some of the Bayswater Sisters and the postulants who desired it, planned to go to Glasgow and learn from Sisters whose Franciscan roots dated back to fourteenth-century Angela of Foligno. Before a group set out in November 1858, Elizabeth Hayes received the habit of St Francis in a London ceremony in which Dr Manning was the celebrant, and during which she promised God to follow her new path as a Franciscan novice. Elizabeth was always interested in the foreign missions and knew that the Glasgow Franciscan Sisters had a mission in Jamaica; this made her all the more certain that God was calling her for further spiritual training before being missioned to the West Indies.

Life for Catholics in Glasgow was challenging. Catholicism was only gradually being re-established, but it was gaining strength because of the large number of Irish who fled their homeland in the 'hungry forties'. It must have been a tough existence for Elizabeth yet she was able once again to serve others by contributing her educational skills. Franciscans taught children in parish schools by day and returned again in the evening to help the needy youth. Elizabeth's health was weakened when she returned with her Sisters on cold foggy nights to their Charlotte Street Convent. The time came for her to make her profession of religious vows in Glasgow's Cathedral where the public found it inspiring to see women, English, Irish and Scottish, promising their lives to God despite the hardships that surrounded them.

During her time in Jamaica, Elizabeth recorded some of her personal thoughts and struggles. It has been called a diary but strictly speaking it is not a day-to-day account. It reveals to us something of life in a religious house which was governed by outdated regulations that did not often suit a missionary situation. The Sisters were expected to spend much time alone in their 'cells' – small, very hot and poorly-ventilated bedrooms – when not teaching in the classroom, praying in the chapel, eating in the refectory, or participating in a community activity. During Elizabeth's years in Jamaica the leader, Sr M. Veronica Cordier became ill and was forced to return to Tourcoing in France. Regarding the voting for her replacement, there was Jesuit interference in the person of Crimean War veteran Fr Sydney Woollett. An account of this provides insight into Elizabeth's character for she spoke out and would not tolerate injustice. During 1863 Elizabeth gained permission from the Vicar Apostolic in Jamaica, Monsignor Dupeyron, to depart from the island and to join another Franciscan Community, possibly in France, or to begin anew in the diocese of a bishop who would accept her as a religious with vows of poverty, chastity and obedience.

On her sea journey to France Elizabeth passed through London, later had an interview with Archbishop Darboy of Paris and she was invited to serve in two other dioceses. On selecting Orléans, her bishop – the famous Felix A. P. Doupanloup – discovered the need for revision in the Glasgow Franciscan Rule and Constitutions that she intended to use. Immediately Elizabeth set out for Rome to have the matter clarified. For two years, in Rome's uncomfortable extremes of cold and heat, living as a parlour border in a convent of another community, Elizabeth showed her outstanding skills for reading, researching and writing under difficult conditions, yet courageously persevered in her task. The Franciscan Sisters over in Bayswater, London, and in Glasgow where she had once lived, wrote to her and asked that her work, the identifying of a more authentic Third Order Regular Franciscan Rule and the accompanying Constitutions, be used for their religious communities as well. Elizabeth facilitated their requests and during August of 1866 she was able to return to France. Events however had happened during her absence and now she accepted from the Bishop of Versailles, a modest house, chapel and chaplain, with his blessing to establish a boarding school and a noviciate in Sèvres, outside Paris.

Elizabeth opened a school for young French and English girls while also providing assistance to English converts. Around this time Elizabeth found friendship with the Honourable Mrs Fanny Montgomery who had an apartment in Rue St Honoré in the heart of Paris, besides keeping in contact with numerous English friends whom she knew in Rome, including Monsignor George Talbot (Rector of the English College in Rome and well known to Pius IX). However with the outbreak of the Franco-Prussian War in 1870 and since Sèvres was in the path of the advancing Prussian army, she had to abandon the work and ask French girls and women to return to their homes. A few had English passports, the novice Sr Clare Peet, a ward named Annie Rosalie S. Thomas and of course Elizabeth herself. She could have headed for 'England's green and pleasant land', instead she realized that there would be suffering and opportunity to render assistance in war zones, so accompanied also by her friend, Fanny Montgomery, they headed by train in the direction of Nancy, a city between Paris and Strasbourg. Along the way, the child Annie was given into care while the remaining three, taking advantage of the good railway system, moved on to the city of Saarbrücken in southwest Germany and finally to Berlin. After becoming accredited members of the Red Cross and receiving their arm-bands, they moved northwest to Spandau where many French wounded soldiers needed assistance. They worked alongside the famous German-Jewish convert, Fr Herman Cohen, a Carmelite priest known in London for his holiness and musical accomplishments – he had been a favourite pupil of Liszt. The three women, interested in music, literature and poetry, never forgot their Spandau experience, especially the final hours of Fr Cohen's life in January 1871, for in ministering to others he contracted smallpox himself and died.

After gaining passports signed by Lord Augustus Loftus, as British subjects travelling on the Continent, the companions left Berlin travelling through Germany and France for months. It appears from a broad examination of events that during 1871 Franciscanism and literary interests guided some of the activities of Elizabeth and her companions. Franciscan hospitality was freely given when travellers knocked on convent doors, including ones in Düsseldorf and Fulda where English visitors were always made welcome. Research suggests that probably Mary Ward's 'English Ladies' gave them shelter, as well as numerous Poor Clares and other Franciscan and religious convents that were scattered throughout Germany and France.

Finally having resettled young Annie and saying farewell to Fanny, Elizabeth (known as Sr M. Ignatius) and Alice Peet (Sr M. Clare) were in Marseilles ready to venture out on another foreign mission, this time to the Island of St Thomas in the West Indies. Elizabeth and her companion had accepted the invitation of Fr Louis de Buggenoms but it proved to be a short-lived experience for though the mission looked worthwhile, on arrival at the port where passengers were quarantined, Elizabeth was allocated a room in which the former occupant had died from yellow fever. Weakened in health and finding insurmountable difficulties at the Redemptorist mission, it was necessary to move on. Elizabeth knew that many German Catholic families had migrated to the State of Minnesota which was in dire need of the service of religious women. Thousands of brave religious women were working for Christ and God's people all over America in poor and demanding circumstances; their commitment enticed others to do the same so Elizabeth and Clare caught a ship bound for New York. Before long Elizabeth signed a deed for a portion of land in the Wild West in a small town called Belle Prairie in Minnesota. The biggest adventure of their lives was about to begin; it was September 1872.

Travelling by rail and stagecoach, the two Franciscans reached the tiny outpost of Belle Prairie; children stared in wonder at the unfamiliar apparition of women in long brown habits with faces appearing out of white headgear and heads draped with black veils. One biographer many years later would describe Elizabeth as 'commanding but not demanding' and it seems to capture the woman Elizabeth who was confident and capable yet warm and personable. It was the practice of the early settlers to gather in a log cabin erected on church property for the celebration of Mass when a priest rode into town. Belle Prairie – serviced by German-born Fr Joseph Buh – had been no different, but by 1872 parishioners had built a church using mainly stones from the nearby Mississippi River. The log cabin stood empty so this was the first shelter of the Franciscan Sisters. Elizabeth set to work immediately and although their first winter was one of the coldest that Minnesotans experienced, she ensured that there would be a building ready to welcome children for the start of the 1873 school year. The buildings around an inner court continued to take shape as the year progressed and the number of pupils continued to grow. Aware that another town further north was likely to become a large railroad centre in the near future, Elizabeth opened another school in Brainerd. However on failing to gain a donation of land, she and Sr Clare, who had many gifts including music and foreign languages (French and German), gave their full attention to the Belle Prairie school known as St Anthony's Academy.

During the summer holidays of that first year, Elizabeth set out for the old Franciscan mission of Santa Barbara on the west coast. She travelled the long route to California partly by the Northern Pacific Rail Road and by coach, and having reached San Francisco she visited the gold fields in order to gain finances for her Belle Prairie projects. Elizabeth had entertained a dream for some time about joining the emerging group of Catholic writers and publishers who understood the call to the Apostolate of the Press in a time when the printed word was greatly influencing what people thought, said and did. She had come to Santa Barbara to discuss her plans with Father José M. Romo because she knew that while there were Franciscan journals being published in French, Italian and Spanish, and she was abreast of them, no Franciscan journal was available in English in America or even in England. Confirmed in her intentions, she returned to Belle Prairie and made communication with Morris Russell, a respected printer in Brainerd. Through her incredible industry and her sheer determination, January of 1874 saw her first publication, the *Annals of Our Lady of the Angels*, roll off the press. At the beginning of the venture distribution of the monthly journal was carried out by a secular woman but gradually this changed. It was to become the work of the Sisters who were given the appropriate yet unusual name of 'Zelatrices'.

As a woman of faith, courage and conviction, Elizabeth's career developed. Through her successful publication of the *Annals of Our Lady of the Angels* there exists the proof of her mission in Catholic journalism for twenty-one years, and after that others would follow for another seventy-nine years. In different parts of the world, religious Sisters of hundreds of other congregations were focused on providing service through education and nursing, yet Elizabeth dared to follow a different path. She understood the need for Catholic journals and so she strongly and absolutely committed herself to the Apostolate of the Press. Why did Elizabeth embark on an editing-publishing career when this was so difficult for women writers? Because she read 'the signs of times'; she wanted to respond to certain external social factors that were active in nineteenth-century society.

More and more people were able to read but not everyone could afford books. Newpapers and journals, called periodical literature, were in great demand for they were not only affordable to poorer people but through the introduction of the serial, a reader could enjoy parts of a book as it was printed daily, weekly, monthly or whenever. Elizabeth perceived the power for good and evil in periodical literature. She recognized this power of the press and watched how the thinking of those around her was being strongly influenced by what they read in journals, newspapers and books. So in her mind, as in the thinking of a group of her international literary friends, she believed the best way to counteract pernicious literature was to provide a wholesome alternative. Elizabeth saw a mission that meant working for the restoration of the kingdom of Christ by means of the Press, a ministry that basically hoped to help others find Truth, find God, in a society in which science was fast replacing God and where religious faith was challenged on every side.

Today people witness the impact of contemporary journalism and its relation to the wider processes of change. We can look back with hindsight on the history of English literature and be enlightened by what happened in the nineteenth century and the changes that evolved. It can be surprising to learn that the development of the periodical actually outpaced the growth and popularization of the novel, which for so long was considered, along with poetry, the distinctive characteristic of nineteenth-century English literature. Elizabeth was able to see in the changing milieu that surrounded her, a need for a sub-genre of periodical literature, a need for a particular kind of Catholic journal.

She was well grounded for the literary challenge she set herself. Love of reading had accompanied her throughout her life and, with the assistance of different circles of literary friends, she was always surrounded by good literature. Having internalized what she read, Elizabeth wanted to spread the essence of her reading through her *Annals,* motivated by what became known as the 'propagation of good books'. She knew that she had the literary talents and aptitude for bringing to birth the world's first Franciscan journal in English, so she set out bravely to achieve her goals.

In mid 1874, with the approval of Bishop Grace, Elizabeth travelled to the East Coast and across the Atlantic to Europe for the purpose of gaining Franciscan helpers who would join the Belle Prairie community. She had shouldered the responsibility of the school, ensured that new building projects were underway, maintained her periodical and prepared well for forthcoming issues. However the need for more personnel was critical. Elizabeth failed to find Italian religious women free to join her; she was directed to Fulda in her effort to gain a friar as a chaplain and finally two Poor Clare nuns, Annetta and Costanza Bentivoglio, volunteered to accompany her. After many obstacles and struggles with key ecclesiastics – concerned for the nuns' safety – the pope gave his blessing to the enterprise. Elizabeth was forced to be in Europe for around eighteen months and during the first six months she continued to edit and write for her journal and send material to her printer in Brainerd.

Arriving back in New York, a new set of circumstances confronted Elizabeth, for the Franciscan priest decided to stay and help other friars. The pope had specifically named the friar as spiritual director so the two nuns felt that they were unable to accompany Elizabeth to the west, and so she returned to Belle Prairie without more helpers. Elizabeth was unaware that one day she would be acknowledged as the one who brought the first permanent Poor Clares to America. At the time, though terribly disappointed, Elizabeth determined not to be foiled and after 'recharging her batteries', she prepared to travel again. She moved north to

Canada desperate to find new recruits for her mission; even staying with the Benedictine Sisters in Chicago. During the stop-over she talked to a young working woman called Angela Swiss Chaffee who asked to join her. Elizabeth promised to call back for her on the return journey when she hoped to bring with her other women who presently belonged to a group of secular Third Order women in Montreal. God was certainly on Elizabeth's side for Angela would become an important factor in the history of the first Franciscan journal in English to be printed in the world; this woman had the experience of working in a Chicago printery and her contribution to the fulfilment of Elizabeth's dream to build up the Apostolate of the Press was enormous.

When Elizabeth courageously commenced her Franciscan publication in Minnesota, not only was she embarking on an undertaking that was considered mainly a male profession, although she knew of the achievements of a group of English Catholic women writers, but there were only six Franciscan journals in existence. The French friars produced two (the first beginning in 1861 in Paris), the Italians claimed three, while in Barcelona the Spanish friars had commenced one in 1873. At the same time, Minnesota was not a backwater as far as newspapers and printing houses were considered. St Paul, the leading city in the territory, boasted in 1849 about Goodhue's Press and its successful newspaper, the *Minnesota Pioneer,* while the printing houses of St Cloud's, not far from Belle Prairie, were well known. Elizabeth advertised her academy in the St Cloud newspapers but for the first eighteen months of her illustrated publication, it was Mr Russell of Brainerd who printed it. Mention was made to the fact that Elizabeth had to travel to Europe and for the first six months of that time she was the mobile editor. Then she was forced to make a pause in the *Annals,* the only one ever, for once she had more helpers in Belle Prairie, the third volume appeared in January 1878.

Another very popular leading American Catholic periodical at the time was the *Ave Maria.* Today, the former religious house of the Holy Cross Fathers, and nearby Sisters, is better known as the University of Notre Dame, Indiana. Elizabeth and another Sister visited the campus in the early half of 1878 and Hudson described her *Annals* in the *Ave Maria* publication on 8 June 1878 as follows:

> *The Annals of Our Lady of the Angels* is the title of a neat little monthly magazine of thirty-two pages published at Belle Prairie, Morrison Co., Mn., by the Sisters Regular of the Third Order of St. Francis. It is well edited and neatly printed – being, by the way, exclusively the work of the Sisters themselves. It is, we see, in its third year, although new to us, for until now we had not been sent a copy of it and saw no notice of it in the Catholic Press. The subscription price is $1.25 a year. Contrary to what its title would seem to indicate, *The Annals* is not an exclusively devotional or ascetic work; a great portion of its contents is made up of interesting stories and sketches which cannot fail to make the magazine attractive to the general reader, and thus in a measure to counteract the growing appetite for nonsensical trash. The Contents of the present number are: I, The Gifts and Graces of Mary; II, Clare, or the Child of Our Lady of the Angels; III, Hail Mary; IV, Thoughts of a Tertiary Priest; V. California a Century Ago; VI, A Convert's Gratitude (Poetry); VII, Life of Mary Cherubina Clare of St. Francis; VIII, Alone in the Far West; IX, Franciscan Record.[1]

While it is fascinating to look at Elizabeth's *Annals* in contemporary religious journalism in the countries where she lived and toiled, namely England, France, the United States of America and Italy, this article has to be very selective. Analysis of non-Catholic as well as Catholic journals has coalesced to highlight the significance of Elizabeth's contribution which was situated in a period of time when religious leaders of different creeds encouraged the faithful to take up the pen and fight for Christian principles and values. For Elizabeth to have lived at a time when the pope was himself

[1]   Hudson, Daniel E., 'The Annals of Our Lady of the Angels', *Ave Maria* XIV, no. 23 (1878), 370.

committed to and outspoken about Franciscanism, proved a bonus for one wanting to share her own Franciscan experiential insights. The situating of Elizabeth's *Annals* in the arena of nineteenth-century Franciscan journals opens up new possibilities.

Elizabeth Hayes joined in the risky business of women who put their lives on a journal's page to claim the importance of a lived experience. For Elizabeth, it was the experience of being 'a Catholic, a religious, a Franciscan' so Franciscan ideals, spirituality, history and mission news were high on her *Annals*' agenda as she presented the big picture to her readers. In examining Elizabeth's contribution to Catholic journals, it has been possible to lift a veil of obscurity and allow her to take her place as successful editor and publisher. Through a study of Catholic journals, new light has been thrown on the network of Elizabeth's international interests, concerns and communications. Her selection of Catholic articles reveals her dedication to finding and publishing the truth, some reflecting an element of sacrifice, for cost what it might, she and her readers were to be 'on God's side always'. Through research and the building of a new nineteenth-century Franciscan journal directory, Elizabeth has emerged not only as the first person to publish a Franciscan journal in English but also as the first Franciscan woman editor and publisher of a religious journal.

Through her commitment to the Apostolate of the Press, Elizabeth added her zeal to that of others who earnestly waged a war against what they believed were the evils of the Press in their time. She chose her *Annals* content for both the general reader and for Franciscans; for the former she provided original tales, historical and biographical sketches and the lives of saints and contemporary holy people. Elizabeth's readers appreciated accounts of pilgrimages, stories of missionary enterprise and articles on devotions and general Catholic life. New research has resurrected the *Annals*' thematic content that engaged the Franciscan readers. This revolved around the major Franciscan saints, especially Francis, Clare and Anthony, and around traditional Franciscan literature, stories and devotions.

Through research on Elizabeth's *Annals*, it has been made possible that from obscurity, sometimes through just a person's initials, flesh and characteristics have been given to a list of contributors who initially appeared lost in time. Now they can again speak to readers with words of wisdom and stir their hearts. The forgotten poetry of a Dublin Poor Clare nun or the freshness of the Honourable Fanny Montgomery's prose are examples of contributors' work that Elizabeth commissioned and whose authors are now identified. Be the contributors women religious, clergymen, members of the secular Third Order Franciscans or other committed laity, the investigation has found that Elizabeth could collect their contributions, edit them well and disseminate the resulting literature to her many readers on both sides of the Atlantic.

Elizabeth understood that her first responsibility as a baptized Christian was to spread the name and reign of Christ more widely every day and this she hoped to achieve through her publication. Elizabeth used the power of the periodical press for evangelization, for the building up of the reign of God on earth. A new investigation has counterbalanced earlier biographers' references to the *Annals* as being merely an instrument for raising funds without sufficient attention to the primary reason for production, namely adult faith education and the enjoyment of reading good literature. When so many other journals failed or became ephemeral, evidence shows that Elizabeth's strategies for success consisted of the high quality of the *Annals*, the regularity of the publication and the distribution method involving the Sister Zelatrices. Circulation of Elizabeth's publication through her Sisters was crucial to ensuring that countless homes welcomed the *Annals*.

Elizabeth's project was enormous for it embraced not just reading widely, extensive correspondence and editing but also the responsibility for overseeing production and distribution. She achieved her twin aims of providing literature of interest to the general reader and of presenting the Franciscan Order's progress and development. Elizabeth was an insightful and intelligent woman who clung to her belief in the *Annals'* power for good, despite the painstaking heroic work it demanded. This is affirmed also through the unpublished writing of Mother M. Chaffee who deeply admired Elizabeth and who recorded some of the story of Elizabeth's *Annals* and its influence.

By comparative research into contemporary journals, not only has Elizabeth's success been enhanced but also new scholarship on nineteenth-century periodicals has been opened up and presented. Investigation of Elizabeth's *Annals* contributes to the growing scholarship on outstanding Victorian women, especially those now forgotten for their contribution to the periodical literature component of journalism so popular at the time. Elizabeth's application to research, her literary talents and her capacity for works are obvious, yet her pen recorded that journalism alone would not overcome evil. Rather she believed that journalism could facilitate God's reign only when accompanied by the spirit of love, prayer and service. In Elizabeth Hayes one discovers not only a competent religious woman but also a true Apostle of the Press who achieved a mission of heroic proportion through journalism.

Finally, the woman editor herself: Elizabeth alone was the initiator of her project. It has been a concern of feminist historians, who are writing women back into history, to discover women like her who held their own in a man's world. Elizabeth had enough confidence in herself to assume confidence as an equal when dealing with leading male figures of her time including Oxford Movement leaders, Catholic bishops, popes, clergymen and academics. She won the respect and admiration of her colleagues. Many great women lived in the aura of a particular eminent man; Elizabeth's life gives no evidence of this.

The personality of Elizabeth is that of an intelligent, informed and confident woman, her own woman, whose path followed neither over-conservatism nor liberalism, yet like a bee collecting the best nectar for the hive, she knew the purpose of her mission in journalism and remained steadfast. The extent of the challenge she offered could at times prove too much for some who were unable to share her broad vision. Passionate, talented, self-contained and focused on her objectives – enough to frighten some who lacked her integrity when hard work and courage were necessary – she balanced her approach to others with consideration, cooperation and spiritual support. Elizabeth was a woman who had the capacity to elicit great loyalty in the public sphere as well as among her early Sisters. Elizabeth is a Franciscan woman infinitely more interesting than the nineteenth-century dominant stereotype of woman as subservient, male-dependent and debarred from the public sphere. Hopefully this account has revealed her personality, her outstanding courage and her great service in Catholic journalism, one truly worthy of being called an English Catholic heroine.

Bibliography

Ahles, Veronica (Sr M. Assumpta), *In the Shadow of His Wings: A History of the Franciscan Sisters*, St Paul, MN, The North Central Publishing Company, 1977.

Chaffee, Angelica (Mother M. of the Angels), 'Memories of the Life and Works of Mother Mary Ignatius of Jesus, Foundress of the Institute of the Missionary Franciscan Sisters of the Immaculate Conception', c.1912, unpublished typescript.

Hayes, Elizabeth (Mother M. Ignatius), ed., *Annals of our Lady of the Angels* I–XIX, 1874, 1875; 1878–94. Held in the Roman archives of the Missionary Franciscan Sisters of the Immaculate Conception and on CDs in Australia by P. J. Shaw.

Shaw, Pauline (Sr M. Francine), ed., *Diary. Sister Mary Ignatius of Jesus (Elizabeth Hayes)*, Brisbane (Queensland), Missionary Franciscan Sisters of the

Immaculate Conception & Rapid Offset, 1994.

Shaw, Pauline J., Ph.D. thesis, 'Mission Through Journalism: Elizabeth Hayes and the *Annals of Our Lady of the Angels*', Brisbane (Queensland), Australian Catholic University, 2006. Available online through ACU.

Shaw, Pauline J., *Elizabeth Hayes: Pioneer Franciscan Journalist*, Leominster (Herefordshire), Gracewing, 2009.

Chapter 19

M. Riccarda Hambrough

Simon Caldwell

Nearly a million European Jews survived the Holocaust because of the efforts of the Roman Catholic Church under the guidance of much-maligned wartime Pope Pius XII, who embarked on a huge, and generally clandestine, humanitarian enterprise in hiding Jews from the Nazis, helping them to escape to safe countries and, in some instances, persuading the leaders of occupied nations to resist Adolf Hitler's orders to round up Jews for deportation.

Among those who took part in this gigantic work of charity was an English nun who was living and working in Rome during the Second World War. Mother Mary Richard Beauchamp Hambrough is credited with playing a vital role in saving the lives of more than sixty Jews by smuggling them into her convent, the Casa di Santa Brigida, where they hid from the Gestapo. Although she was obeying the orders of the Pope and her abbess, the Bridgettines, the order to which she belonged, believe she lived a life of such heroic virtue that in 2008 they applied to the Vatican for permission to open her cause for sainthood. Her case is clearly compelling because a favourable announcement from the Vatican is expected to be made in 2009.

Mother Mary Richard – known to her fellow nuns as Mother Riccarda – was born Madaleina Catherine in London on September 10 1887 and was baptized in the Church of St Mary Magdalen in Brighton, Sussex, when she was four years old after her Anglican parents, Windsor and Louise, converted to the faith. At present, little is known about her childhood but it is certain that as a young woman she fell under the influence of Father Benedict Williamson, a London-based Benedictine monk, and in 1912, at the age of twenty-four, she travelled to Rome to become a nun. She was following a group of three other English girls who had set out a year earlier to join the Bridgettines, a fourteenth-century Order which had all but died out until it was re-established in 1911 by Blessed Mary Elizabeth Hasselblad, a Swedish convert from Lutheranism. Taking the religious name Mary Richard, she was soon chosen to be the assistant to Blessed Mary Elizabeth, the abbess. In the following decades Mother Riccarda was at her superior's side as the order won canonical approval from the Pope and, attracting an increasing number of vocations, began to open religious houses in Sweden, India, England and Italy.

In the 1920s the Order also acquired a mother house in Piazza Farnese in historic Rome, a grand building standing on the site of the house of the order's original founder, St Bridget, an aristocratic mother of eight children who, after the death of her husband, became a nun, a mystic and eventually a patron saint of Europe. Within years of moving into the new home war broke out and the activities of Mother Riccarda, as she was known to her fellow nuns, were soon concentrated on helping the victims of the conflict.

When Italy changed sides in 1943 it became an occupied country and the Germans began to round up Italian Jews. On 16 October of that year the Gestapo arrested 1,007 Jews in a sweep of the city for deportation to Poland. Pope Pius XII, through his Secretary of State, Cardinal Luigi Maglione, protested vigorously to the German Ambassador, Ernst von Weizsacker, and asked for their release but not a single person was freed. Seeing the futility in trying to reason with the Nazis, Pius then secretly ordered the religious houses of Rome to lift their enclosures and to shelter Jews and others fleeing persecution. His policy enabled nearly 5,000 Rome Jews – about eighty-five per cent of the city's population – to escape certain death. Hundreds of these were given refuge in the Vatican itself, while in monasteries and churches Jews were disguised as priests and equipped with faked baptismal certificates. In one convent the nuns slept in the crypt so that Jews could have their beds.

Mother Riccarda and Mother Mary Elizabeth were among those who willingly gave refuge to scores of Italian Jews, Communists and Poles fleeing for their lives. The Bridgettines are unwilling to publicize the activities of Mother Riccarda until the decree from the Vatican on her cause for status has been formally issued. But the Sisters of Casa di Santa Brigida have confirmed to reporters that Mother Riccarda was very much involved in hiding refugees, a strategy that carried the risk of death if discovered. One of them said: 'We were helping many Jewish people during the war and Mother Riccarda was helping Mother Elizabeth to hide them.' Another, Sister Elisa Famiglietti, the vicar general of the Bridgettines' Order in Rome, in a brief interview with *The Catholic Herald* in February 2009 described Mother Riccarda as a 'wonderful woman' and 'an angel who did so much to help our Jewish brothers during the war'.

I know they want to honour her as well. There are about a dozen or so sisters here in the convent in Rome who remember her and we are all very excited at the fact she is being considered for sainthood. Mother Riccarda was full of the spirit of God and was a very humble woman, she sang beautifully from the heart and she was devoted to God and she left a mark on all of us. Mother Riccarda was humble and discreet and she provided safety and charity for our Jewish brothers during the war but she very rarely spoke about it. 'What I always remember about her is that despite living for so long in Italy she never forgot she was English and always spoke English to us.

She said she believed the formal opening of the cause would be 'such a great honour for England'.

Mother Riccarda's role in saving Jewish lives may feature strongly in persuading the Vatican that she is a saint – as it was a factor in her abbess's swift beatification. This was apparent when Pope John Paul II declared Mary Elizabeth

'Blessed' in 1999, noting in his homily the 'care and concern' Mother Riccarda's abbess had shown to 'the persecuted Jewish people' and 'those who suffered because of racial laws'.

A year after the war the Chief Rabbi of Rome, Israel Zolli, who was known to both Mother Riccarda and Blessed Mary Elizabeth, converted to the Catholic faith – partly because he was so impressed by the efforts of Catholics to save Jewish lives. He took as his Christian name Eugenio – after Pope Pius, the previous Cardinal Eugenio Pacelli.

In 2004 Blessed Mary Elizabeth was recognized by Yad Vashem as one of the Righteous Among the Nations for her work in saving Jews from the Holocaust. She died in 1957 and Mother Riccarda succeeded her as abbess until her own death on 26 June 1966 at the age of seventy-nine. The pair are buried in the same grave in the convent church where they hid people from persecution.

A prayer for the beatification of Mother Riccarda has already been drafted ahead of the Vatican announcing her status as a Servant of God. But even as Mother Riccarda progresses to sainthood it is unlikely, however, that she will be honoured as a Righteous Gentile. This is because it is the policy of the Commission for the Designation of the Righteous Among the Nations, an independent body comprised of Holocaust survivors and historians and chaired by a retired Israeli Supreme Court Justice, to honour only the mother superior in those cases where Jews have been hidden in convents.

'It is the head of the institution that bears the responsibility and makes the decisions, and the nuns are bound by the vow of obedience,' explained Estee Yaari, a spokeswoman for Yad Vashem. 'In the case of Mother Mary Riccarda Beauchamp Hambrough, Yad Vashem's Department of the Righteous Among the Nations does not have material on file that sheds light on her case. As in all cases, Yad Vashem would be very happy to receive any documentation and material that would illuminate this story.'

Chapter 20

Elinor Brent-Dyer

Joanna Bogle

I am honestly not absolutely confident that we can class Elinor Brent-Dyer as an English Catholic Heroine. But I wanted to include her in this collection because she contributed a whole image of heroines to our culture. Elinor Brent-Dyer, a fairly ordinary Catholic Englishwoman, was crucial in creating a classic type of fiction, that fostered an important self-image for huge numbers of girls: The English Schoolgirl.

It has become so much a part of our culture that it is a cliché: whether it is the hearty wholesome figure in a classic school story ('Gosh', said Amanda, 'we must stand up against bullying and cheating, for the honour of the Lower Fourth ...') or the glorious horror of St Trinian's (remember Joyce Grenfell in those black-and-white films of the 1950s?).

The 'school story', a completely unique British concept, was produced by many authors. It is generally agreed that the real inventor of girls' school stories was Angela Brazil, whose first books set in girls' boarding schools were published in the late Edwardian period and during the First World War. They certainly contributed to, and in turn were influenced by, the changing attitudes towards women from the 1900s onwards. Angela Brazil's heroines were courageous, lively, articulate, and energetic. They enjoyed sport – this was the beginning of the 'jolly hockey sticks' style – and they loved being out of doors. They were fiercely patriotic. They wanted to 'Do the Right Thing', and were regular churchgoers, took part in various charitable activities for the poor and needy, and despised those who cared only for personal luxury or adornment. They were ripe for later membership of the Girl Guides and the Women's Institute. They would never be Victorian stay-at-homes.

The genre, once created, was capable of mass reproduction. In a later era, among the most popular were the 'Malory Towers' and 'St Clare' series produced by Enid Blyton. By now the stories were set in post-Second World War Britain: the girls travel by car, use telephones, work for public exams, look forward to having careers. But the stories are still set in a sort of timeless sub-culture – no pop music or television as yet intrudes, boyfriends are non-existent, structures of parental and school authority are unquestioned save for harmless 'tricks' played on teachers with the aid of joke materials such as a device set beneath a dinner plate to make it wobble. Enid Blyton's books are essentially derivative – she is working to a pattern, and when she wrote the books she knew the form: her readers wanted a set structure, and the story had to develop within the set limits of the school with its term-times and its uniform, its rules, its characters, its own traditions and jargon. The geography of the school, and what its pupils wore and what they ate, was important – essential to the tale was the sense of it all being set within safe and organized limits, a small world to which readers could belong.

But if Angela Brazil produced the first school stories, and Enid Blyton worked to a pattern by then well established, the key person in creating and fostering the real and lasting school-story was Elinor Brent-Dyer. She gave us the *Chalet School*.

In creating the idea of an English boarding school, set in the Tyrolean mountains and with pupils coming from many nations, Elinor Brent-Dyer was giving her readers a sort of ideal vision of what a school could and should be.

The *Chalet School* series – an almost unbelievable sixty-two books in all – takes us from the first establishment of this school and its earliest pupils, through their various adventures and activities down through to the next generation. The extraordinary mixture of a stunning Alpine setting – which also provides all sorts of wonderful opportunities for adventures with snowstorms, avalanches and the like – with a strictly structured school life, gives a mixture which has a compelling appeal. For children, it is almost the ideal mix: out there is the beauty and the terror of the mountains, the forests, the strangers coming and going, the snow or fierce summer heat, the possibility of getting lost or of falling into danger. Immediately adjacent, and comfortingly secure, is the school with its rules and structures, its regular meals and insistence on good behaviour, its uniforms and little customs, its *mittagessen* and freshly-brewed coffee.

And the pupils are all, ridiculously, somehow believable even though they are not particularly well-drawn characters and some are really one-dimensional. But there they all are, centred on Joey Bettany, the first and key pupil, whose career we follow as she grows to womanhood through the books, marries a doctor at an Alpine clinic (of course!) and has offspring, with daughters who will become Chalet School pupils in their turn. Everyone at the school – the wise and kindly matron, the slightly stern teacher whose formal approach masks a deep personal warmth and integrity, the bubbly small pupil eager for new projects, the shy new girl needing support and encouragement – is in danger of being a walking cliché, but somehow it doesn't work that way. Instead, we find that the story is readable, that the characters and their activities maintain our interest – above all, that we wish we were there, eating pastries or walking through the snow or learning French or struggling with a crisis alongside them all.

It's important to understand that Elinor Brent-Dyer's books were mostly read, not by girls who were attending boarding school, or even likely to attend one, and certainly not by girls for whom travelling to the Alps was likely to figure on their annual agenda, but by girls from much more modest backgrounds.

The typical reader would be a girl attending a state school and living in a very ordinary home. It was quite likely to be a home where many of the things that the Chalet School pupils enjoy – tasty meals served by cheerful cooks, good social connections, possibility of becoming fluent in two or three languages, music lessons – simply did not figure at all. Undoubtedly part of the attraction of the books is precisely that the lifestyle in general seems extremely agreeable. But there is much more to the charm than that. The books exude moral certainty. The pupils struggle with genuine human difficulties. They make mistakes due to bad temper or loneliness. They fall out with friends and have to make up. They pray, and cry, and try to do what is right in complicated circumstances – or fail to do so, and suffer the consequences. They make and break promises. But around and beneath all of this is a sense that life is sustained by a loving Creator, that there is a moral law, and that what we do and think and believe matters very much.

Sometimes the books descend to the preachy, and often to the trite. But all the time, in the very air that the characters – and the readers – breathe, is a sense of the great reality of things. God is real and the world that he has made has a fundamental order, structure, and purpose. Learning itself has value. Life matters. In order to achieve great things, we can and must sustain ourselves with knowledge. We might even achieve real wisdom. Because there is a sense of order, things can be achieved: relationships can be sorted out, sick people can be made well (or can learn to cope with a disability, their burden alleviated by the care of others), people can meet and marry and establish families, great events can be celebrated and enjoyed.

So who was Elinor Brent-Dyer and how did she come to write the *Chalet School* books?

Her life was certainly not remotely like that of the girls she created for her books. No childhood spent among alpine scenes, no secure social status, and no good-looking, noble-minded husband.

She was born Gladys Eleanor May Dyer in 1894, and grew up in South Shields. Her family background was complicated. Her father, Charles Morris Brent Dyer, had been married before, and already had a son, Charles. This son however did not come with his father when the new marriage, to Eleanor Watson Rutherford, who was to become Gladys' mother, took place. Instead, Charles senior and his new wife established their own small family – in addition to Gladys there was a boy, Henzell. But when the children were still very small, Charles left again. He went to live with another woman and had another son by her (extraordinarily, also called Charles).

It must have been clear to Gladys – who changed her name to Elinor when she grew up, so I will from now on use that name for her – that she would have to work hard and make her own way in the world, and probably provide for her mother as well. The First World War had robbed many women of her generation of their chances of marriage. She trained as a teacher – one of the few careers open to girls at that time – at a college in Leeds, and then returned to South Shields to work. At the age of twenty-eight, in 1922, she had her first book published. It was called *Gerry Goes to School* and was a modest success. She went on writing. *The School at the Chalet* was published in 1925, and from then one she wrote a *Chalet School* book every year. The early ones were: *Jo of the Chalet School* (1926), *The Princess at the Chalet School* (1927), *The Head Girl of the Chalet School* (1928), *The Rivals of the Chalet School* (1930).

From the start, the *Chalet School* series had a theme of health and healing: Madge Bettany needs to find somewhere suitable for her sickly younger sister, Jo, to stay and regain her strength and decides on the great adventure of founding a school in the Austrian Alps. The idea of fresh air and sick people becoming well is a constant in the books, along with images of the great beauty of the Alps and the charm of the local customs and traditions. There are lots of mentions of the girls' curtseying to the teachers, of delicious Austrian cakes and pastries served with morning coffee, of clear starry icy nights and the joy of arriving safely in a warm snug building.

It is clear that Elinor Brent-Dyer fell in love with the Austrian Alps when visiting there on holiday. But that it was no passing romance is also clear: she became deeply immersed in the culture, came to know the language (although there is no evidence that she spoke it fluently), and went on loving all things Alpine for the rest of her life.

In 1930 she became a Catholic. This was no light decision – then, as now, Catholicism meant commitment to a set of doctrines which Catholics believe have been revealed by God as true. Commitment to this truth means living by its precepts, and central to these is the regular worship of God – daily prayer, Sunday Mass. Although in the England of the 1930s, churchgoing in general was certainly regarded as more normal than it is now, and the Church's teachings on, for example, sexual morality, were also more widely recognized as being a useful standard for life, there were other prejudices which could make life difficult for the convert. The Church was in many places dominated by Irish communities – or seen as being so – and regarded by some people as being somehow alien and 'un-English'. Ecumenical activity was non-existent, and Catholics were urged by their own Church to shun any invitations to participate in non-Catholic church services – indeed it was generally regarded as sinful to take part in these. Thus, a Catholic could face complications when seeking to go to a relative's wedding (sometimes a priest would say this was all right, sometimes not) and there could be hurt feelings and awkward family discussions. Such things as Armistice Day parades, town festivals, and Christmas events saw Catholics on the sidelines, and they were expected to excuse themselves when attending any activity which might involve joint prayer with others.

For a single lady, even a successful author, this situation could add to social isolation at times and the decision to become a Catholic certainly marks out Elinor Brent-Dyer as someone who was prepared to make a decision about religion and then live by it, even if the decision brought some difficulties.

Was her initial interest in the Catholic faith sparked by her visits to Austria? Possibly, indeed probably. But if she first met the Faith in the mountains, she certainly lived it out in the everyday life of a busy schoolteacher in Britain. The Catholicism of the North of England was of a much bleaker variety than the version she encountered in the baroque churches and picturesque villages of the Alps. Whereas in Austria, a whole culture is permeated with the Faith, at least historically, in England the reverse is true – Catholicism has been wrenched from its natural place and put into new structures, with a dramatic sense of that break being evident at every turn. But she seems to have embraced the whole of the faith with enthusiasm, and lived out the rest of her life as a dedicated member of the Church.

It is interesting that in her school stories, she invariably establishes that provision is made for both Catholic and Protestant girls to attend regular worship – separately – and emphasizes regular daily prayer as being something that should be done as a matter of course. At no point does she actually emphasize Catholicism over other faiths, and indeed a genial Anglicanism is what chiefly emerges from her books. There is no specific mention of, for example, girls going to confession or praying the Rosary.

It is clear that the books, although successful, did not initially provide an adequate income. Elinor was supporting her mother as well as herself. In 1933 they moved to Hereford, and not long afterwards she founded a small school there, naming it in honour of St Thomas More's daughter, Margaret Roper. But this little Margaret Roper School was not to last long – it barely saw out the war years and closed in 1948. By that date, however, Elinor Brent-Dyer was at the height of her fame, and the books had a life of their own. Following the closure of the school, she became a full-time writer, and went on producing books until she died in 1969, her mother having died some five years earlier.

The saga of the *Chalet School* matched that of the times in which it was written. Passionately anti-Nazi, the school evac-uates to the Channel Islands and from there to the English-Welsh border (the territory Elinor knew well, living in Hereford). It finally moves to Switzerland, back to moun-tain territory.

As we follow the lives of the various girls, always centred on Joey Bettany, we are also immersed in innumerable adventures: spies, royal princesses, illness, accidents, heroism, dramatic rescues. Former pupils of the school, especially those with whom we have become deeply connected, tend to marry well, and to have large numbers of children (a sad little wish here, perhaps, from an unmarried lady of the 1914–18 generation). Health and sickness continue to be centrally important issues – at one stage there is even a clinic attached to the school. And in due course the school assumes a significance even on the world stage, with pupils and ex-pupils playing a role in wartime escapades and in plans for post-war goodwill between nations.

Elinor Brent-Dyer was no heroine in the sense of being a martyr, or laying the foundations of a great work, or organizing projects of caring for the poor and sick. But in producing a large number of books – I have focused only on the *Chalet School* series, but there were a great many more – that celebrated ideas and ideals of real worth, recognized the greatness of God and his place in our lives, and offered a message of hope and gladness, she did something of lasting value. Today, her books are still read with pleasure. She influenced an uncounted number of lives – her books are no mere escapism, they are uplifting, readable, and have enough reality in them to give a young mind much that is nourishing on which to feed.

It is fun to laugh at the 'jolly hockey sticks' tradition, and we certainly shouldn't take the Brent-Dyer version too seriously, or place it too high on the list of 'must read' literature. But in an age when childhood innocence is being widely violated, when teenage suicide is on the increase, when girls lack wholesome and positive role models, when faith in God is mocked and reading material for adolescents too often focuses on the sordid, crude, sexually explicit or violent, here is an example of someone who used her writing talents to offer something of good cheer. I venture to suggest any young girl could benefit from entering, however briefly, into the world of the Chalet School, where she will not only discover some heroines but come to value the ideal of heroism for herself. To have given girlhood that possibility is a worthy achievement. The world would have been the poorer without the work of Elinor Brent-Dyer.

Bibliography

Brent-Dyer, E., The *Chalet School* series: *Jo of the Chalet School*, London, W. and R. Chambers, 1926 to *Althea Joins the Chalet School*, 1969.

Fisher, Margery, *Who's Who in Children's Books*, Weidenfeld and Nicolson, London, 1975.

Wikipedia, free Internet encyclopedia.

Chapter 21

Caryll Houselander

Leonie Caldecott

Caryll Houselander (1901–1954) was a writer and artist whose creativity overflowed into a life of prayer and spiritual friendship. Hers was a highly individual apostolate which, while rooted firmly in what can only be described as a mystical vision of the faith, was carried out in the midst of the world. In some ways she is comparable to St Catherine of Siena (one of her favourite saints), though she carries the marks of a very different age and culture. Caryll's parents separated when she was nine. Her father was distant and her mother was an eccentric and unreliable source of affection. Constantly moved from one school to another, with health so frail that she was never able to keep up academically with her peers, Caryll became something of a misfit, and by her own admission, a neurotic soul.

At her birth on 29 October 1901, she was not expected to live more than a few hours, and thus was baptized Frances Caryll by the doctor who delivered her, who happened to be her uncle. Francis was her uncle's name, and Caryll the name of a yacht of which her mother was fond. The origins of her Catholic identity are as unconventional and roundabout as her physical birth. Her mother, under the influence of Dr Paley, the son of an Oxford Movement convert they got to know when the family moved to Brighton, and of another friend, decided to have her two daughters baptized as Catholics. Caryll's sister Ruth was ten at the time, she herself was six. Thus she came to call herself not a cradle Catholic, but a 'rocking-horse Catholic', the title of her posthumously published childhood memoir. Caryll's mother Gertrude came into the Church after her daughters. One of the powerful influences in Caryll's early life was Mr Justice Bower, dubbed 'Smoky' by the family, who though an avowed agnostic himself, was so convinced that the Catholic Church was the only legitimate expression of Christianity, that he brought Gertrude to the same conclusion. He argued his case, noted Maisie Ward in her biography *Caryll Houselander – That Divine Eccentric,* as though it were a legal brief. He also supplied Caryll with most of her early intellectual formation, introducing her to everything from Shakespeare to the romantic poets.

This was just as well, as Caryll's formal education was woefully mismanaged. Before and during the First World War, she attended a convent school run by French and Belgian nuns, where she imbibed a mixture of classical French piety, devotion to beauty as a spiritual path, and her first real experience of spiritual motherhood, through the nuns who were her teachers and mentors. Whilst there, she had the first of three mystical visions which were to inform her later development. One of the lay sisters in the convent came from Bavaria. There was terrible anti-German feeling because of the approaching war, and the sister must have suffered because of this. One day Caryll happened upon her as she was cleaning shoes, and approaching to offer to help, suddenly realized she was weeping. More than this. On the head of the afflicted Sister, the child 'saw', quite clearly, the crown of thorns.

In her early teens, Caryll's health (a badly infected appendix, among her other ailments) caused her to be withdrawn from this school and brought home. Later she was sent to St Leonard's Mayfield, under the care of the Holy Child nuns, a much less happy experience. This was because by the time she arrived at this rather grand boarding school, the teenage Caryll had become so conscious of her own eccentricities, not to mention her lack of good looks (she wore thick glasses) or social standing, that she never really felt at home with the other pupils. In *A Rocking-Horse Catholic,* she insisted that this was not the fault of the Sisters who ran the school, who showed remarkable patience with their difficult and rebellious charge. An incident from this period is telling. Caryll had written a furious letter to Smoky, who still occupied the fatherly role that Caryll's real father evidently did not, speaking of her classmates and even one of the nuns, in very uncharitable terms. All letters had to be posted through this same woman, and so she called Caryll into her office.

Caryll wrote later:

> There are moments in life, the most critical moments, when one's whole self is in the state of a statue that has been cast in clay and is about to set in a permanent material. Just before the hardening or setting takes place, a single flick of the finger can alter the whole expression forever, but let that moment pass by so much as a second, and the mould is fixed beyond change. Nothing can be done then, if change is desirable, but break it to pieces and begin again. It was one of those moments that this nun gave me – just that flick of the finger which prevented my life from setting in the ugly shape of my adolescence. Handing the letter back to me, she said, quite gently, 'I won't let this go because I cannot allow you to say such unkind things about the children that I love. I love them and Our Lord loves them ...

About herself, it seems 'Mother so-and-so' was not so concerned.

'You are right,' she told Caryll with a little smile. 'I am the cock of the walk here, so there is nothing to be done about that but make the best of it.' Yet with consummate wisdom, this same nun, after Caryll had re-written her letter more charitably, decided not to read or censor her letters to Smoky, judging that the child needed the outlet of a trusted parental figure, for the sake of her psychological health. This perceptiveness on the part of an authority figure was later described by Caryll as 'a stroke of genius' which 'did more than almost anything else in my school life to save my faith'.

This sense of being a person never entirely at home with herself or the world around her persisted throughout

Caryll's youth, and her emotionally irresponsible and yet demanding mother did little to help with this. For several years during her young adulthood, Caryll left the Church. This was partly due to something that often scandalizes young people: the fact that, as she put it later, the Blessed Sacrament is 'put into the hands of sinners', sinners who do not let it transform their lives as it should. She had lost enough of the prickly arrogance of her teens to know that she too was a sinner. But her observation of what you might call the unleavened parts of the body of Christ, particularly the gossip and lack of charity displayed by her fellow Catholics in the face of human weakness, began to rankle. Finally there was a specific incident at a fashionable London parish, where it was the custom to ask people for a financial contribution for sitting in certain pews. Arriving late for Mass on account of having to do chores for her mother, Caryll was unable to find a 'free' seat at the back of the church. When she knelt, exhausted, in another pew, the verger approached and demanded sixpence, which she did not have (she had walked quite a distance as she didn't even have the money for the bus fare). When he insisted, her frustration with the human face of the Church came to a head. She walked out and was not to approach the sacraments again for some years.

During this period she mixed with a Bohemian crowd she got to know whilst attending art school, soon living for the first time away from home. However, she never quite lost the sense of Christ's presence in her life. The second of her formative mystical experiences occurred during this time of spiritual turmoil and alienation. On her way to buy potatoes in July 1918, she suddenly found herself rooted to the spot in the street, as an extraordinary vision of Christ crucified, dressed in the robes of a king, unfolded before her. The following day, the front pages of all the newspapers were filled with pictures of Tsar Nicholas II of Russia, who with his family had been murdered at Ekaterinburg. The face of the Tsar was the face Caryll had seen in the suffering features of Christ the King gazing down at her the day before.

After this Caryll developed an interest in eastern Christianity and Russian culture. Through her involvement with the expatriate Russian community, she met Sidney Reilly, a spy of Russian-Jewish extraction, who had worked as a double agent for the British government, among others. It is said that this man was the original model for Ian Fleming's James Bond. Reilly took an interest in her art, selling paintings for her through his extensive network of contacts. He also seduced the impressionable and lonely young artist. Whether he broke it off, or Caryll did, as she turned back towards the Catholic Church, is uncertain. Shortly afterwards Reilly married another woman, before going back to Russia to try and work for the overthrow of the Bolsheviks, a mission which finally cost him his life.

There is a fascinating scene in *Reilly Ace of Spies,* a television dramatization of this strange and complex man's life, in which Reilly's widow goes to see Caryll after his disappearance in Russia. The artist shows her a painting she has done of the place and circumstances under which Reilly had been executed by the communists. Whether the specific incident is true or not, Caryll is on record as writing to a friend at the time Reilly was imprisoned in Russia, describing how she had seen his circumstances as she prayed for him. Her first biographer, Maisie Ward, is very down-to-earth about this gift of 'seeing' and intuiting things at a distance, pointing out that Caryll herself never made much of it, using the visions, whether of actual events or of divine realities, simply as grist for the mill of her deepening prayer life.

To a large extent, it was Caryll's sense of humour, not to mention humility, which kept this mystical bent in proportion. She would always relate stories against herself, and her correspondence is full of references to her own faults and peccadilloes. Hence the story of the confession through which she returned to the Church. Perhaps not having fully taken on board her admission of the lapsed years, the priest commented: 'And you've done all this in a week? I congratulate you on your vitality!' (One interesting fact revealed by this story is that an early twentieth-century penitent would be frequenting the sacrament of penance on a weekly basis.) It is impossible to credit the good that Caryll did later in her life without the knowledge that this impetuous and some-times imprudent woman – most especially, she admitted, in the area of guarding her tongue – stayed on the side of the angels by dint of weekly confession and daily communion.

From this moment on, Caryll developed not just her artis-tic gifts but also the vocation of writer, through which she was to touch the lives of an increasing number of people. This happened partly because of her involvement with a lay organization called the Grail, whose founder, Yvonne Bosch van Drakestein, encouraged Caryll to write for their journal. As well as earning her living through woodcarving, she went on to write poetry, fiction and a host of articles which were published on both sides of the Atlantic. She also wrote and illustrated children's stories for the *Sacred Heart Messenger*, edited by Fr Geoffrey Bliss, SJ. Indeed when he became ill in the late forties, she often wrote the whole of the magazine by herself. Caryll also published fifteen books with Sheed & Ward. She was a true original when it came to conveying the faith she had re-embraced, whether through a fresh take on scriptural passages or expressing its relevance to her own generation. 'She seemed to see everything for the first time,' wrote Monsignor Ronald Knox, 'and the driest of doctrinal considerations shone out like a restored picture when she had finished with it ... she seemed to find no difficulty in getting the right word; no, not merely the right word, the telling word, that left you gasping.'

The first book that Sheed & Ward published came out of Caryll's experiences during the early years of the Second World War: *This War is the Passion* (1941). In this book she brings together the fears, anxiety and deprivation she was sharing with her countrymen and women, bombs falling, nights kept awake fire-watching on the roof of Nell Gwynn House, with the core of her faith: the focus on the crucified and suffering Christ. Many of her readers were sustained through those difficult times by Caryll's ability to enter into the darkness with them and remind them of a horizon of hope. This book was published in an amended edition after the war, under the title *The Comforting of Christ* (1947). For Caryll, the war might have been over, but with the dropping of the atom bombs and the continuing contempt for the weak and defenceless whether in abortion or other killings, the spiritual war was still very much on. Only the incarnation and passion of the Redeemer could answer to those never-ending challenges.

One of the interesting tensions in Caryll Houselander's life was between the desire to care for souls and the need to create art. Any artist or writer knows that these two vocations, whilst spiritually complementary, can make uncomfortable bedfellows on a practical level. If I were to sum up the overriding vision which motivated everything Caryll did after her return into full communion with the Church, it would be that she was shot through with a sense of the Mystical Body of Christ, both Eucharistic and human. At the end of *A Rocking-Horse Catholic*, she describes the third and most powerful of the mystical experiences of her youth, the one which without doubt was involved in the renunciation of her love affair, and which was to fire her re-discovered faith with an apostolic zeal which never left her.

> I was in an underground train, a crowded train in which all sorts of people jostled together, sitting and strap-hanging – workers of every description going home at the end of the day. Quite suddenly I saw with my mind, but as vividly as a wonderful picture, Christ in them all. But I saw more than that; not only was Christ in every one of them, living in them, dying in them, rejoicing in them, sorrowing in them – but because He was in them, and because they were here, the whole world was here too, here in the underground train; not only the world as it was at that moment, not only all the people in all the countries of the world, but all those people who have lived in the past, and all those yet to come.

This realization, a 'setting on fire' of her imagination which henceforth powered her faith, actually lasted for several days, and affected her at every level. Not only did she overcome her fury against the pharisaical Catholics whom she had judged so harshly before (every bit as harshly, she admitted, as they judged her!), but she also overcame the rebellion itself, *within herself.* The vision of Christ in man, the vast invisible mystical body of the Church, actual and possible, spread through the core of humanity, brought with it an understanding of sin.

> Although it did not prevent me ever sinning again, it showed me what sin is, especially those sins done in the name of 'love', so often held to be 'harmless' – for to sin with one whom you loved was to blaspheme Christ in that person; it was to spit on Him, perhaps to crucify Him. I saw too the reverence that everyone must have for a sinner; instead of condoning his sin, which is reality his utmost sorrow, one must comfort Christ who is suffering in him. And this reverence must be paid even to those sinners whose souls seem to be dead, because it is Christ, who is the life of the soul, who is dead in them; they are His tombs, and Christ in the tomb is potentially the risen Christ. For the same reason, no one of us who has fallen into mortal sin himself must ever lose hope.

Caryll was never to marry, nor have children of her own, but she was sustained through close friendships and had a number of godchildren with whom she was closely involved. Iris Wyndham, whom she got to know during this period and with whom she was to share a home for many years, had a daughter who gave birth to a child. The baby, named Clare, was sometimes cared for by her grandmother and Caryll, who took it in turns to watch her. Caryll derived many of her intuitions about the meaning of infancy and childhood from these experiences of looking after Clare as a baby, then a toddler, then a little girl. Along with the sense of the Mystical Body, Caryll had a spirituality which focused, like that of St Thérèse of Lisieux, on the infant Christ. This in turn informed her devotion to the Blessed Virgin. *The Reed of God* (1946), her powerful meditation on the gestation of the Saviour and the meaning of advent, is one of the modern classics of English Marian devotion.

Another paradox of Caryll's is that whilst she was able to write sublime prose on Our Lord, his mother and the saints, she herself was far from being in some plaster-cast mode of holiness. For most of her life Caryll smoked like a chimney; she was apt to swear and she liked a drink. As Margot King has written of her:

> There are, alas, too few saints with whom lay people can identify. They are virtually all members of religious orders; their lives might inspire admiration but never a shock of recognition, awe but never giggles. God, after all, can only work with the materials at hand. The wonder of Caryll Houselander is found in her humble willingness to suffer with Christ, to let him transform her flawed and sinful nature into a divine work of art.

There was certainly nothing sugar-coated about Caryll. She once prayed to St Peter: 'Dear Saint of Impulses, pray for me that I may stop cutting off people's ears.' As she grew older, she had to exercise patience and forbearance all the more, since her writing brought her an ever-increasing amount of correspondence to deal with. Some of her correspondents became friends. But many people who wrote to her or even knocked at her door were somewhat more burdensome. In a letter to one friend, after relating the difficulties of getting on with her work whilst assailed by needy souls, 'doubting Anglican clergymen, repressed Catholic nuns, neurasthenic nurses, and the uncountable multitude of weeping free-lance virgins', Caryll breaks into a hilarious disquisition.

> I truly believe that the best way to benefit humanity is to make faces in the bus – slightly mad faces, or puttings out of the tongue suddenly at the person opposite. Think of the thrill *that* gives to countless uneventful lives to whom nothing ever happens. They can tell everyone for weeks that they saw a mad woman on the bus, and they can exaggerate this to almost any extent. This form of charity can be practiced on the way to work.

At the same time, Caryll was capable of consoling souls in distress with a sensible, measured spiritual counsel reminiscent of St Francis de Sales or the Abbé de Tourville. 'The only thing that I can see that will help you is to learn to love yourself,' she wrote to one young friend towards the end of the war, 'to forgive yourself, to be kind to yourself, by looking outwards to God, by accepting the fact that you are infinitely loved by Infinite Love, and that if you will only cease to build up notions of the perfection you demand of yourself, and lay your soul open to that love, you will cease to fear, and you will cease to be exhausted as soon as you stop fighting one part of yourself with another.'

This side of Caryll can only be called spiritual motherhood. In an article called *Mothers of the Unseen Christ*, she wrote about this in a way that corresponds exactly to what Pope John Paul II later wrote about the dignity and vocation of women in *Mulieris Dignitatem.*

> For some marriage is a vocation; it is a superb vocation, on it depends not merely our race going on, but the Christ-life going on in the world. But there are others who have the vocation to be spiritual mothers. Sometimes they are married women too and learn this spiritual motherhood from their own children, but sometimes they are unmarried, either from choice or circumstance. I say 'circumstance' because it is a cruel mistake to suppose that if a woman would honestly like to marry but circumstances make it impossible, that she is merely frustrated and should devote her life to toy dogs, bazaars and acidity. Circumstance is the *one* reliable test of God's will for us, and a clearer indication of vocation than any 'attraction' we may feel.
>
> For the woman, then, who does not marry, is motherhood a vocation? It most certainly is, and God forbid that anyone shall read into those words the condoning of that fussy, grasping interfering attitude that passes so often for 'spiritual motherhood'. The first essential thing is this, that the mother instinct, the capacity for love, be awake, alive. This means suffering. It is easier in the long run to dry up the life in us than to develop and direct it. The woman who will be truly a spiritual mother will feel in herself, in her body and in her

soul all the desire and the necessity for a child of her own. In this very passionate longing, in this aliveness of love her purity will consist. Indeed it is the essence of virginity, for we do not lay dead ash on the altar of sacrifice but burning fire.

For all her struggles with herself, indeed precisely because of those struggles, Caryll possessed a psychological acuity which complemented her spiritual vision. Her longest, and in some ways most fascinating book, *Guilt* (1952), is a study of neurosis in the light of original sin and the modern alienation from our religious roots. 'The great repression of our age is the repression of Christ in man,' she wrote in *Guilt*. 'If Christ in man were simply an idea, or something contrary to human nature which man could acquire and somehow add to himself by his own efforts, this could not be true; we can only repress that which is so much a part of us that we cannot cast it out or get rid of it ...'

Caryll's capacity for insight into the damaged human soul was recognized not just by her co-religionists, but also by people such as Dr Eric Strauss, the President of the British Psychological Society. He sent a number of his patients to Caryll for what we now might call counselling, though it more closely resembled spiritual direction. 'She loved them back to life,' he later told Maisie Ward. Given that in our day, a nurse can be suspended for even offering to pray for a patient, this arrangement seems extraordinary. Yet the woman whom Dr Strauss referred to as 'that divine eccentric' knew how to lay a healing hand on a wounded soul. More than anything else, Caryll knew that the true healer of such radical wounds in the personality is Christ himself.

She also knew that one of the abiding handicaps of the neurotic is fear, and the paralysis which it engenders. She had an interesting way of challenging herself on this front, immersing herself in war work, visiting psychiatric hospitals, seeing both her difficult parents (who now lived at opposite ends of London) as often as she could, frequenting insalubrious areas in the east end of London. Some prostitutes, thinking she was trying to ply her trade alongside them (whether out of insecurity or for some other reason, Caryll often wore heavy make-up) started trying to advise her how to dress more smartly to attract customers. While she had got over her more 'socialist' resentment of the rich, Caryll instinctively found herself drawn to the poor and marginalized rather than the 'respectable' elements of society.

Nowhere is this made clearer than in *The Dry Wood*, the one full-length novel she wrote (published in 1947). At the heart of the novel are the figures of a holy priest who has just died, and a disabled and dying child who becomes the focus of all the lives that surround him. Wanting and needing a saint to call their own in the midst of their difficult lives, the people of Riverside spontaneously start a novena to the priest for a miraculous cure. All Caryll's favourite themes are interwoven in the novel: the mystical presence of the Church at the core of lives which otherwise would be without beauty or hope, the contrast between grinding poverty and sated affluence, her dislike of 'elite' Catholic groups, and of course the redeeming touch of the infant Christ, suffering in the person of the weakest, most seemingly pointless of human lives.

It was in the retrieval of spiritual childhood that Caryll herself found the strength to undertake the often burdensome tasks she set herself. Her writings are shot through with the sacramental vision, the wonder and delight that a child takes in the world around it. Her poems, which she insisted were no more than simple 'rhythms', use both her artist's eye and her writer's gift of association.

> Some lift the blossom up,
> like the torch in the runner's hand,
> and shower its petals down
> like stars in the darkness.
> Some are folded upon it:
> devout, like the child on the bus
> home from the one day in the country,
> her white face closed in sleep
> and a smile of ecstasy
> burning quietly through the closed
> sad eyes.

Her soul
and her thin body
fending the faint blue light of harebells,
brought from the green woods
to fade in the city.

'The Flowering Tree', 1945

In her early fifties Caryll was diagnosed with breast cancer, only a few years after her own mother had died from cancer herself. She worked on through her treatment, which came too late, still comforting and cheering those who came to her, still pouring herself out until she was too weak to do anything except suffer. She died on 12 October 1954. Hers is a voice which will always be relevant for those tempted to despair, or for whom the teachings of the Church need to be made more incarnate, more actual and graspable. In short, for all of us who, like the flock of which Christ said are like a sheep without a shepherd, the flock He so longs to gather to His Heart.

Odd though this image may seem when applied to someone who was a cat lover, Caryll Houselander comes across as one of those sheepdog souls who are so essential in the modern Church. These souls reach out in prayer and love, finding and herding stray members of the flock towards the Shepherd, occasionally nipping at their heels, but always guiding the stragglers back to the safety of the fold. She confronted some wolves in her time, took her share of battle scars, but never gave up that slow, exacting instinct to guard and cherish fragile souls: an instinct which is inseparable from the dog's ability to hear and respond to the Shepherd's commands, called out to her attentive ears across the mission field.

Chapter 22

Helen Asquith

Emily Keyte

In an age where much is made of the breaking down of distinctions in race and religion, we forget the fertile exchange of friendship that occurs as hands join across the generations. The old have a vital role in inspiring the young and in standing as witnesses to a life of faith. If Helen Asquith is little known today, it is because the limelight was of no interest to her, but she was a significant figure in Catholic education and well known in her work caring for the sick in Lourdes, as Chief Handmaid of the Society of Our Lady of Lourdes for fourteen years. She was awarded the papal medal *Pro Ecclesia et Pontifice* in 1989.

She was born in 1908, the elder daughter of Raymond Asquith, the Prime Minister's eldest son, who was killed in France in 1916. Her mother was born Katharine Horner, and her home, Mells Manor House, had been acquired at the Dissolution of the Monasteries. Ironically, Katharine, and later her two daughters, returned to the Catholic faith four centuries later, in the 1920s, largely inspired by the Dominican Father Vincent MacNabb, and by family friendships with Hilaire Belloc and Maurice Baring. Even more ironically, the last male Horner became a Benedictine monk at Ampleforth.

Helen went to school at St Paul's in London, and went on to Somerville College, Oxford. She then taught Classics at a secondary school in Clapham until 1938 when she joined the Inspectorate of Schools. On retirement, aged sixty, she went back to teaching, this time at St Mary's, Shaftesbury, while caring for her mother, who was by now in a wheelchair at Mells. She kept up with a host of former pupils, and after finally retiring at the age of eighty she continued to coach a lucky few until her death in 1999.

When I met Helen I was twenty-three and she was eighty-six. My grandparents were long dead and I knew no one of her generation. I was barely ready for life and she was longing for hers to come to an end. I was at a critical point of my life where decisions about how to live, what work to do, were weighing heavy with me and I was sensing the inadequate nature of my studies and how utterly ill-equipped they left me for the challenges of adult life. I suppose I was looking for some model of life to follow and the chance to glimpse the fruits of a long life, which I quickly realized was one of pious devotion, seemed a wonderful opportunity. Might she be a witness to me of what a life of faith meant?

There are many details surrounding Helen's life that are full of beauty, natural and artistic and this was a large attraction for me. Helen's life was centred around the enchanting village of Mells in Somerset and it was my discovery of this gem of a village that became the first step on my path to meeting her. After university my parents had suggested I do a month's cookery course at Whatley Vineyard, as the final cap to the long years of my education. After a morning of ice cream-making, I took a walk past the great scars of the stone quarries with lorries coming and going down narrow lanes, into another world.

Mells is an otherworldly place. Snug in a valley below the Mendip hills, it is a village all of a piece and looking much as it would have done 400 years earlier. The beautiful perpendicular church was a natural stop. Inside there was a tapestry based on a design of Burne-Jones, a carving by Eric Gill and a bronze horse filling the whole of a side chapel by Munnings. This was a surprising artistic collection to find in a Somerset church. Yet each piece recorded a tragic loss: Edward Horner, the last direct heir to the Horner estate, killed in 1917, age twenty-nine and Raymond Asquith, the Prime Minister's son, killed on the Somme in 1916, aged thirty-eight. The wooden crosses that once marked their graves in France are preserved in the chapel. The place seemed filled with sadness. The facts I'd studied in my school history lessons suddenly took on a human reality, the consequences of which reached into the present.

When my husband and I lived in Winchester recently, Raymond Asquith's name headed the long list of pupils from the College in the memorial cloister who also lost their lives. What might have seemed a mere record of the remote past, took on instead a fresh relevance. Later, when I accompanied a school trip from South Hampstead High School to the First World War battlefields, the coach made a special stop at his grave to illustrate the levelling effects of war, where the Prime Minister's son was laid to rest in a grave no different from those of the soldiers he fought with. Outside the church in Mells, the yew tree cast its shadow wide over the graveyard. Here were more names to recognize: Seigfried Sassoon and Ronald Knox.

I must return to telling you about that summer afternoon and confess to trespassing up the drive of the beautiful Elizabethan manor house that stands behind the wall of the church. I later learnt that this was 'the plum' given to Little Jack Horner when Henry VIII dissolved the monasteries. With the presumption of youth, I walked into the garden and looked at the house. To my embarrassment there was the owner, an elderly man who I later realized was Lord Oxford, Helen's brother. He generously invited me to linger on my own in the more cultivated garden behind the house. For a little while I stood in the loggia, looking ignorantly at the plants and flowers and entranced by seeing and hearing further away, a child on a swing – singing. After a while the elderly gentleman came to walk with me and pointed out the plants, naming each one and then reminding me of their place in Milton's *Lycidas*, 'Yet once more, O ye laurels, and once more/ Ye myrtles brown, with ivy never sere,/ I come to pluck your berries harsh and crude,/ And with forced fingers rude,/ Shatter your leaves before the mellowing year', in a gentle, urbane voice, before graciously saying farewell. I returned to Whatley with a song in my heart and a spring in my step, feeling I had set foot into another world. Here was art, beauty, history and village charm hard to rival.

A few months later I had picked up a job in a publishing company, Kingfisher Books, in London. I was planning to do a research degree (clinging on to what I knew), so was filling in time. I mentioned to a colleague that I wanted to learn Latin again, feeling with the absurd idealism of youth, that I would be better equipped to study the English Renaissance if I brushed up on the Classics and got Latin under my belt. My colleague, Camilla Hallinan, an old girl of St Mary's Shaftesbury, recommended a woman she described as 'her remarkable Classics teacher', Lady Helen Asquith, who would be very old by now but might be interested to take me on. She lived in Mells; of course, I hadn't forgotten the place and couldn't resist an excuse to re-visit.

I wrote to her on 10 October 1993 and this was the letter I received six days later:

Dear Miss Robinson [my maiden name],

How nice to hear from you – any friend of Camilla's is most welcome. Please forgive the delay in answering. I'd be delighted to help you with Latin if I possibly can and I'm always glad of any opportunity to teach Latin or Greek which I love doing.

How can it be managed? I fear I'm v. crippled at the moment – walking on 2 sticks – & slightly deaf, but otherwise quite compos. Also I have no transport except what taxis & kind friends provide! Can you get to Mells? From London? From Minterne? Once a week? Twice a week? If so all is easy. I have a good deal of free time and something, but preferably not everything, could be done by correspondence.

Perhaps you could ring me up, but if you ring be very patient because, tho' this isn't a very large house, it does take me a v. long time to get to the telephone, even if it's only across the room!

I shall look forward to hearing from you & shall be delighted to help if I possibly can. Yours sincerely, Helen Asquith.

During the next six months I used to visit Helen on occasional Saturdays and then continue to my parents' house, about twenty miles away in Dorset. These few hours were a haven of peace after the harsh pace of London life. In this deeply civilized and beautiful room my fragile spirits were strengthened and ideals kept alight. Present concerns seemed less important; the remnants of the past more revealing. In his biography of Ronald Knox, Evelyn Waugh relates Knox's dilemma when settling down to finish the translation of the Old Testament from his study in the manor house at Mells: 'I don't know how I shall manage to work in a place where life goes on so dreamily ... I never want to do anything here but sit still and wait for the next time the church chimes will go off.' She wouldn't accept payment for lessons, urging me to spend the money on books instead. There was nothing self-interested in the time she gave to me, apart from her obvious delight in exercising her classical skills. I never felt she was dependent, rather there was a detachment in her self-giving which enabled me to breathe intellectually and spiritually.

The door was usually open and I would call, 'Hello', as I made my way into the sitting room to find Helen seated by the fire. There were books on small tables and stools; jars of flowers propped on shelves. Above the fireplace was a mysterious painting, which Helen liked to quiz me about possible interpretations. She hoped the figures in it were carrying the ciborium and patten. Above the green-painted bookshelf was an inscription in Latin about bees *'libavent'* – lightly touching, or kissing – flowers. Beyond the low windowsills was a well-kept garden with borders of flowers.

Here we sat and began to read *The Aeneid* together, *'arma virumque cano'* and the early stage of that hard and huge task of founding Rome. I remember the thrill of reading about jealous Juno, determined to thwart the Trojans' founding of Rome, by raising a storm, before Aeneas and the seven surviving ships find rest in a cave. Aeneas, tired of war and duty bound, is sick at heart, but feigns hope for his friends; they must have courage and be done with fear and sorrow. Aeneas' cloud lifts when he looks at the court of Dido; Venus breathes beauty on him, and puts a gallant light in his eyes. The royal Dido's long-slumbering heart is awakened by Cupid to love ...

How I wish we could read this all again together, but it became impossible for me to keep up with Latin.

In warmer weather we would sit outside and I would be given a lesson in the garden. She was very stooped when she stood up, having to tilt her head sideways to look at me. Her face was strong, but pallid with age; her voice was clear and firm, sometimes gruff, but she enjoyed a chuckle. There was always an opportunity to teach me something: if a bird was singing, I had to give its name; on a tour of the flower beds, I tried to memorize the names of the plants before my next visit. I have found my notebook where I listed their names in earnest: catmint, salvia, mulberry, medlar, agapanthus, peony, macleaya, myrtle, plumbago, dwarf cyclamen, lark-spur, tobacco plant, phlox. I asked her to suggest possible plants for my window boxes in London and she carefully considered the options, suggesting snapdragons and pansies, then saying she would meditate on it. I was sent on my journey with a sprig of verbena or a cutting of honey-smelling lemon roses.

At four o'clock we would go to the kitchen to make tea. Helen had strict rules about how this was to be done. The kettle could be filled from the hot tap, but the teapot must be warmed well before the kettle boiled. The amount of tea was always considered carefully and the right cup had to be on the tray. Whilst there was an austerity about her habits, I began to see that they reverenced the smallest details of life as gift, that even menial chores were worthy of respectful attention. Shortbread and Viscount biscuits would come from the larder. I would then carry the tray into the sitting room and put it on a stool by the fire, the sweet smell of bluebells on a table by my chair. Helen would declare when the tea was brewed. After a concentrated session of Virgil, we relaxed over tea and talked about her family, literature, teaching, sometimes religion. I loved her strong judgements about people and as we had no friends in common these were always about writers: Vera Britten was petulant, with a chip on her shoulder, I'd do better with Winifred Holtby's *South Riding*. Bloomsbury were waspish; Iris Murdoch nasty; Evelyn Waugh, a close family friend, was overly satirical, not rounded as a novelist; Graeme Greene was the greater writer. She wanted me to give my opinion – I hardly dared! Once I was reading a biography of Shelley and after she exclaimed, 'Poor Shelley!' she told me I shouldn't be too interested in the Romantics; but wouldn't it be lovely to travel and write as he did, I said, but she replied, 'It's not quite enough, though, is it?' What more was there, I wondered to myself; what underpinned her convictions?

If I came in the mornings, coffee, already brewed, would come from the Aga and she would defend it for its nourishing qualities. When we heated milk, I was given firm instructions to watch over it, learning in the process a new term for the top of the heated milk, 'the plop'. She took a childlike delight in these pleasures – there was nothing Puritan about her – and food tasted better when shared with her. Once I stayed for supper and we drank Vermouth with scrambled eggs, which I had to stir with vigilance to prevent them sticking to the pan. Afterwards, we had strawberries and cream and I had to frame an opinion on whether they were nicer with sugar or not. Cutlery had to be dried as soon as it was washed, but cups needed only a wipe and could dry off in the cupboard.

Once I arrived and was told that her Italian help, Maria, who was herself in her late eighties, had been making gnocchi in the morning and after lunch she made us zabaglione, which I had never had before and seemed a wonderful luxury. All this was shared in the simplest kitchen. In fact when I first visited Helen in 1993 she was facing the intrusion of plumbers who were fitting central heating *for the first* time in her house.

Although she was so eager for my visits and lamented how everybody seemed behind time and hungry to catch up, there was a point after tea when she expressed concern for my onward journey. I wonder now whether the splayed pages of her prayer book on top of the basket of logs were calling her attention. After she died her 'help', Linda, told me that Helen was always praying and this frightened her. I never saw Helen pray, but I'm sure her disciplined time-keeping was to do with this.

It became harder to visit during my year at Oxford and then working in London. Helen was assiduous about keeping in touch and her regular letters over the next six years became a constant presence in my life. In many ways, writing letters was Helen's chief occupation in later retirement (she retired from teaching aged eighty) and I was just one of many people she wrote to. Her close interest in all my endeavours gave me encouragement when I was most doubtful and helped me to persevere when jobs were tough.

There was a steady stream of nearly sixty letters or cards sent during these years. Their length at times and their frequency were generous with time and ideas. They were signs of companionship on my search for a vocation, both professionally and spiritually. They are full of practical, everyday situations, often witty and self-deprecating, but hidden beneath the lines was mediated to me the love of Christ. I want to quote from some of them to give you a sense of her guiding presence, particularly in my role as a teacher.

My first month in Oxford was miserable, and she offers sympathy,

> In my own life I have always found major changes of work and/or environment profoundly depressing to begin with – & then imperceptibly found myself adapting to and finally wholly enjoying the new ambience. So take heart – this may well happen to you.

It didn't and I turned my back on research and all academic business for honest work in London. I thought I would try teaching. She writes,

I'm delighted that you're wanting to teach. My very un-modern HM at St Paul's always called it 'the' profession & to me it has always been that.

The early days of teaching were quite hazardous, but she reminds me of its value,

> You never know when you've sown a seed in someone, even when you think you've failed, sometimes you find out much later but not always.

She loved to hear about the nuts and bolts of the classroom and her advice is brimful of her thirty years' experience as an HMI (His/Her Majesty's Inspector), the superior (in her mind) precursor to OFSTED (Office for Standards in Education),

> Spelling etc … My mother used to insist that spelling is a convention & varies down the ages (she used deliberately to spell Balliol differently every time she wrote to my brother in college) that it's not important. But I fear it is, in a worldly, professional sense!
>
> General knowledge [I was teaching *Little Women* and could not explain to the girls its context in history] – one can't set up to be omniscient these days so I'm sure it's always better to admit ignorance – *and* seek to remedy it. I had the same gap about the American Civil War for years. With Little Women (which I almost knew by heart in youth) it never bothered me – it should – I think I was stirred by a rather 2nd rate thriller called Gone with the Wind. But it is a fascinating subject & almost the only interesting bit of American history, so worth researching. Abraham Lincoln is to me a glamorous character.
>
> Metre. How I sympathise! Some people find it quite easy. I never have in spite of a classical education! I hope you are more successful than I've ever been. I shd have thought that for your age groups a sense of rhythm was enough – & learn-ing by heart (which no one does now!)
>
> Good that CS Lewis goes well – & I'm so glad you agree with me about Greek myths. I think they're v. important – apart from the pragmatic value of saving a lot of boring drudgery when one comes to read Milton, or indeed

Shakespeare. My v. eccentric gardener has just stumbled on a copy of the Kingsley's 'Heroes' & has been reading it to his 8 yr old daughter, pupil in an ordinary Frome primary school, & found her enthralled – so the language need not be a problem to able children – especially if read aloud with judicious skipping explanation.

In my teaching practice I was given, as often happens, the class that nobody else wants to teach. There were only nine girls in the class: three were Koreans who had just arrived in the country, eager to learn, but speaking no English; the rest were the streetwise, 'mouthy' ones whose interest was in designer jeans, not school. I wasn't sure I was cut out for the job after all. Helen gives excellent advice:

> I do sympathise about the discipline problems … of course to devise activities which are profitable as well as 'tranquilising' is the crux – but it can be done – so don't despair! And don't worry too much about your motives for teaching. Did I ever tell you that when I was interviewed for my first teaching job (which I got!) I was asked why I wanted to teach. I said in my blunt, tactless way, 'Because I couldn't think of anything else to do' which happened to be the truth at the time, but was an incredibly inept & tactless thing to say! I've always blessed my HM for having the courage to take me on. I think you will get hooked, as I was – but even if you aren't, teaching is a worthwhile activity in itself, & you can't ever gauge the value of your work at the time tho' with luck you may find out long after.

She concludes this letter,

> But it's time I stopped. I'm interested you enjoyed V.Woolf. She was a v. remarkable woman – but rather cruel I think. Did you ever come across a collection of her essays called the Common Reader? They are v. good I think. There is a lovely one called 'On not knowing Greek' which you would find relevant. Come at $1/2$ term if you can. Much love, Helen.

Helen had modern, liberal ideas about teaching methods, which are often surprising.

> I've always held that it was useless to expect that with younger children the study of 'formal grammar' wd make any differences to 'correct' writing which I'm sure at that stage has to be 'caught' from adult conversation plus reading, both to oneself & aloud.

At my first parents' evening a mother had been furious that I was asking her eleven-year-old to learn a speech of Viola's from *Twelfth Night* by heart. She was trained as a psychologist and did I have any idea how damaging it could be for her daughter to be told what eunuch meant! Helen trumpets my cause:

> Don't worry about your tiresome psychologist mother and her complaints about Shakespeare. If you find your Shakespeare lessons go well stick to them! 'Understanding' is a v. odd thing. Of course 11 yr olds don't understand every word of Shakespeare (nor do many adults) – but they can catch enough general sense to satisfy them – and I think that one can assimilate meanings in an odd way just through constant repetition without any explanation or definition! I can remember enjoying Twelfth Night at a school I attended at the age of 9.
>
> ... And I have since seen the same interest and enthusiasm generated in young children of perhaps less 'educated' backgrounds than ours. 1st yr pupils of an evacuated E. End grammar school in 1940 revelling in Julius Caesar's murder and Antony's inflammatory speeches 'and Brutus is an honourable man?'; a class in an 'elementary' school in the Forest of Dean (a peculiarly inbred and backward area) enjoying clown scenes in M/Dream; 4th yr Sec: Modern C Stream boys doing Falstaff bits of Henry 1V with their v. humane HM.
>
> ... It can be done if one has the knack and self-confidence and treats it as fun, not as a vocabulary lesson in a foreign language! I think most children have a great capacity for enjoying words, even when they can't give a dictionary

meaning to them – twas brillig and the slithy toves … ! And that's why learning by heart's so valuable – I still find fresh meanings in passages of verse I've known all my life – (and new subtleties in Jane Austen) The one thing one must avoid is Shakespeare being thought boring – the worst term of abuse by modern young!

And I suspect that as some members of a class enjoy it fashion dictates that everyone will!

I suspect that you were more upset by this stupid parent than you need have been, or would have been if you hadn't been tired! Dismiss her from your mind! …

I was v. interested in your reading lists which seem excellent and v. all embracing to me – tho' I have a few personal reservations – I've never liked the Greengage Summer (Rumer Godden) and I don't think Brighton Rock very edifying reading! I think there is a stronger case for Animal Farm than 1984 – which I found so frightening, as an adult!, that I wouldn't let my mother read it. I always find it odd that RL Stevenson's St Ives is so little read tho' it's a v. exciting and un-sexy story. I also have a great admiration for the Master of Ballantrae. I suppose Treasure Island (which is far better than Kidnapped) is assumed to have been read earlier? I wonder if any modern child could stomach the Swiss Family Robinson – tho' I loved it in very early youth (7/8). Incidentally Decline and Fall is by Evelyn, not Auberon Waugh. I remember long ago one of my cousins being forbidden to read it at Winchester and his parents thinking the veto applied to Gibbon and being deeply shocked!

I really mustn't use another page! Would love to see you round Christmas. I'm sure there are plenty of 'slots'. Much love, Helen.

One of the most enjoyable aspects of her letters and conversations was hearing which authors she loved and why. Kipling, Captain Marryat, R. L. Stevenson, Rumer Godden, Belloc – all too old fashioned for my education, but I loved discovering them. She admits to knowing little about current interests for pupils in secondary schools:

I wd find it hard to recommend reading for adolescent girls – but have plenty of views on books for the younger children –

no doubt many of them too Victorian for today ... I think a good test of the quality of a book for children is whether it can be enjoyed by a grown-up – but then I have rather childish tastes!

This is excellent advice.

It was fun to discover the authors she didn't know and to be reminded of the fleeting fashions of literature: 'I'm afraid I haven't read Frost or John Fowles & am not sure if I've even heard of the latter! But I've always been a slow reader & now can only manage a few paras at a time. This brings you much love, Helen.'

But she was never closed-minded and suggests for a future visit that we barter our knowledge: 'Next time you come you shall teach me some 20th Century literature & I will teach you some botany! Much love, Helen.'

All this time I had been reading more about the Church and talking to people. I knew I wanted to make faith the centre of my life and I was ready to make a commitment. A decisive moment came the one night I stayed in Helen's house, which meant I was able to go to Mass with her in the morning. The room upstairs where I slept had been her mother's, and I was conscious of the cross she bore in the long years of her widowhood. There was a beautiful Italian Renaissance painting of the Madonna suckling Jesus; I began to imagine what comfort this image must have given in the lonely hours. I barely slept a wink, so cold was the room. The next day I drove Helen down the road to the Manor House and sat beside her in the tiny chapel, a converted bothy.

At the Eucharist I checked with her that I wasn't meant to receive communion and she asked why not, 'I'm not Catholic', I said. 'Oh, my dear, you mustn't', she said in alarm. She was sad afterwards to discover that I wasn't Catholic, then mortified about all the things she might have said about the Anglican Church. Knowing that it really mattered whether I was or I wasn't Catholic was vital in persuading me to be sure of my position.

I had once glimpsed the crucial nature of this choice when

I had written to share the news that a friend of mine was being ordained as an Anglican priest. Far from seeing this as a cause for celebration she is sorry: 'I'm afraid I'm very un-ecumenical so it saddens me to hear of ordinations to the C of E. But, no doubt, that is my un-regenerate self!' Being Christian was not enough. At the time this seemed a little harsh, but Helen's attitudes were formed in a climate of often sharp hostility to Catholicism in the social circles in which she grew up. Her Asquith uncles were unfriendly to the Church; and Helen was once verbally abused by Lady Astor for joining it. Catholics of the 1920s could be forgiven for feeling besieged.

I had been asked to take on some religious education teaching at the girls' grammar school I taught in and she expresses surprise: 'I couldn't begin to teach RE and am surprised that neither you nor the school think it odd! But I suppose "mere Christianity" now seems even more important than "denominational" differences.' Indeed Helen's early diaries record the deep wrangling that went on during her sister, Perdita's, engagement to Billy Hylton. Enormous pressure was put on Perdita to renounce her intentions to bring up her children as Catholics. I had no experience of these prejudices; faith itself was the issue at stake, but faith alone, I knew now, was not the only consideration.

I had begun to think that I would seek instruction to become a Catholic and then at least I could make an objective decision. I followed the excellent advice of Fr Bernard Green, an Ampleforth monk whom I had met on a Greek course, who told me to ask for instruction at the cathedral rather than in my parish. I was extremely fortunate to be seen by Father Christopher Colven, who generously gave me unlimited time over a period of two months. I had a joyous sense of pieces of a jigsaw falling into place and a picture emerging.

Still I had doubts – might it not all be a grand hoax? I was reading John Bailey's memoir *Iris* and they thought ironically that there would be laughter in Heaven over man's gullibility. Fr Colven simply asked me to consider whether it rang true and my heart at last knew how to respond. Hadn't the shining guide and friend in my life for the last five years been Helen; wasn't it her, as well as my parents, who had steered me from various pitfalls during my vulnerable twenties? The doubts returned: was I too impressionable, copying the footsteps of someone simply because I couldn't find my own way? Later on verses from the Bible reassured me: Tobit tells his son, 'Ask advice of every wise person; never scorn any profitable advice'; St Paul tells the Philippians: 'Whatever is true, whatever is honorable, whatever is just, whatever is pure, whatever is lovely, whatever is gracious, if there is any excellence, if there is anything worthy of praise, think about these things.' I knew where to recognize these things; the love-liness of old age was praised by John Donne: 'No spring, nor summer beauty hath such grace, /As I have seen in one autumnal face.' The fruits of that long life I knew I had drawn strength from and I knew I had no excuse to be asking for more witnesses.

Once she knew that I was enquiring into the Catholic faith she was delighted and she suggests various books by Ronald Knox to clarify things. His *The Belief of Catholics* was a great help. She later sent me his last, unfinished writing:[1]

> I'm glad you liked RAK [Ronald Knox]'s pamphlet and I'm delighted that you're being received so soon – that's excellent news and a great joy to me. It will be lovely to talk about it. I think you'll find everything different when you are inside and there will be so much grace awaiting you ... This brings you very much love – I am so rejoiced, Helen.

Learning the ropes was exciting, but daunting. I relished the chance to ask her questions and seek her opinions.

I sympathise about Confession. I still find it difficult and

[1.] This was an outline of an apolgetic which he never lived to complete: 'Proving God, A New Apologetic', with preface by Evelyn Waugh, in *The Month*.

disagreeable after 70 yrs – but I suppose it's meant to be penitential.

I think it's important to remember always that religion isn't ever a matter of feeling – which indeed may be deceptive – but of something much deeper and more fundamental which is strengthened by prayer & the sacraments – that's why Mass is so important – but in your demanding life you obviously can't get to Mass a often as I was able to do in far more leisured times!

Since her death I have had privileged access to the diaries she kept for sixty years and it is remarkable to see the regularity with which she attends Mass, fitting it into busy days of travelling to inspect schools or after an early morning milking cows, when during the war she took on the running of a farm that had belonged to Conrad Russell. I love to think of her ploughing the land and churning the butter! Barely a day goes by without Mass being mentioned. The diaries, however, are not in any way confessional and her spiritual thoughts remain private. What the reader sees is a succession of busy, purposeful, social days from a time far different to our own, when waiting for an hour for a train was quite normal and when novels were read aloud in the evening to each other.

Conversations on my infrequent visits became more personal during this time. While the kettle boiled she told me: she read Classics because she wanted to be like her father; her devotion to her mother, who was widowed at thirty-one, with three small children; how the war created a break when she might have married, that marriage was the highest aim, but teaching second best; how religion had kept her on the rails; how the supernatural goes against the grain and so the need to practise it frequently – ten minutes a day; Protestantism being a cut-off branch from the tree of faith – 'long in dying'; had I read the Acts through, to see how the fisherman disciples became so eloquent and determined?; her quiet-spoken longing for death, and her fear of the last moments.

In the year before her death, aged ninety-one, she is vigilant about reminding me to organize my Easter. She writes on 5 February,

> My dear Emily
>   ... I am chiefly writing – in some haste – to urge you to make sure of attending the Holy Week liturgy, in particular on Holy Thursday, Good Friday & the Easter Vigil on Saturday night – also of course the Easter main Mass. It's the culmination of the Church's year and as performed in Cathedrals & monastic houses is incredibly beautiful & moving. ... You should also acquire a prayer book, which will set out the liturgy in the church & give it some study & seek explanations. Really the whole of Lent, which will soon be upon us, is meant to be a preparation for this whole celebration ... do plan your Easter. Much love, Helen.

One element that persuaded me in my faith was Helen's certainty about Truth. When I first met her and heard her modestly referring to the Truth I was repelled, so strong was my aversion to anything more than the relativistic notions of Truth dominant at university and in the secular world. Yet I came to recognize that her certainty was not the arrogant, triumphalist kind, but the quiet, patient confidence, which is the fruit of years of faithful obedience.

The other aspect of her life, which lay behind much of my thoughts when I was with her, was how the tragic early death of her brilliant father, beloved by her mother, could be redeemed or transformed. Her family's suffering seemed to represent the losses of our nation, and this was something we all have a share in and a duty not to forget. Her mother's desperate years of mourning were what brought her across the threshold of the Church. Helen followed of her own accord some years later, when she was nineteen. Her father wasn't religious, but she thought the patriotic ideal that led him to the Front when he had an office job lined up instead, was to him a sort of religion. I never sensed her father was a heroic figure in her life, after all she was only eight when he died, but her devotion to her mother and service to the sick during forty years of pilgrimages to

Lourdes revealed a dedication to charity that had much in common with her father's ideals of duty to his country.

Her last letter to me was on the 11 February 2000, an important day in Helen's life:

> Today is the anniversary of Our Lady's First apparition at Lourdes – I wonder if you got to the service & procession in W Cathedral this evening. It is a very moving occasion.
>
> Forgive this dictated letter – I am really quite well – only deaf, semi-blind & forgetful!
>
> Very much love, Helen.

Later that year I went to Lourdes with my Putney parish and experienced the beauty of one of the many places holy in the faith.

Helen gave me two things as gifts after I was received into the Church: a rosary, which she brought out of the pocket of her apron, and which she had had blessed in Lourdes, and a book of sermons by Ronald Knox, called *From Heaven to Charing Cross*, given at Corpus Christi, Maiden Lane. The sermon she remembered most fondly was called, 'Behind the Wall', a meditation on the Song of Songs. The voice of the Beloved, in the person of the country lover, is heard all of a sudden amid the distractions of Solomon's Court. The analogy Knox makes is to the Host in the Tabernacle calling us back to freedom, to the glory of our inheritance. The light we see shining from the monstrance is not just a reflection of the candles, but is the light from the window of another world. After all the seriousness and intensity of my search for Truth, Knox's sermon was reminding me, indeed all Christians, that the gift we receive is a loving one, that awakens and fulfils our most profound desires.

The glory, Knox tells his congregation, is something human eyes cannot bear to see; Moses has to put a veil over his face to prevent the people's eyes being dazzled by him after he has talked to God on Mount Sinai. We are not able to see the Truth in all its clarity, but must approach it in its hidden aspect;

We hear above the noise of the world the call, 'Come away ... into the wilderness of prayer ... learn to live with the innermost part of your soul.' We are shrinking from the act of confidence which would throw the whole burden of our lives on our Lord.

If we would reach those friends whom Death has taken from us, we must pierce beyond the veil; must live in Christ if we are to be one, consciously, with those who sleep in him.

It was a great regret to me that I couldn't attend Helen's funeral. I had booked a visit to friends in New York and in the airport I thought about cancelling my flight. Amid the noise and misdirected energy of the travelling masses my heart swelled in gratitude to her. I knew that friendship cut short by death was not ended. When I returned I visited her grave.

Helen is buried in Mells' graveyard. The Latin inscription on her gravestone reads: *'Ecce ancilla Domini'* – here lies the handmaid of the Lord. This inscription speaks eloquently of the life that lies beneath. The words make explicit in their beautiful concision the hidden goal of her life, the object of her heart's devotion.

Notes Contributors

Joanna Bogle
Joanna Bogle is an author, broadcaster and journalist living in London. She writes a weekly column for the *Catholic Times,* and contributes to various publications in Britain and the USA. Her books include various historical biographies, and *A Yearbook of Seasons and Celebrations,* with ideas on celebrating the various feasts of the Christian year, which has become a television series broadcast by EWTN.

Leonie Caldecott
Leonie Caldecott has contributed to the *Catholic Herald, Touchstone, Communio* and the *Chesterton Review* among other publications. With her husband Stratford Caldecott she edits *Second Spring,* an international review of faith and culture. She is the author of *Women of Our Century* (BBC, 1984), *What do Catholics Believe?* (Granta, 2008). She lives in Oxford with her husband and three daughters.

Simon Caldwell
Simon Caldwell is a freelance journalist, part-time news editor of the *Catholic Herald* and contributor to the Catholic News Service, press agency of the US Conference of Catholic Bishops. He has written for the *Daily Mail, The Times, Sunday Times, Daily Telegraph, Sunday Telegraph, Daily Mirror, Observer, The Independent, The Spectator,* and London's *Evening Standard.* He is married and lives in London.

Dr Judith Champ

Dr Judith Champ is Director of Studies at St Mary's College, Oscott, where she teaches Church History. She has written numerous articles on aspects of English Catholic history, and published *The English Pilgrimage to Rome: a dwelling for the soul* (2000) and *William Bernard Ullathorne: A Different Kind of Monk* (2006), both by Gracewing.

Mgr Antony Conlon

Mgr Antony Conlon studied at the English College in Valladolid, Spain, and at the Pontifical Gregorian University, Rome, and was ordained in 1979. He is currently chaplain at The Oratory School, Reading and a contributor to various Catholic journals and magazines.

Dame Etheldreda Hession, OSB

Dame Etheldreda Hession, **OSB** was born in Ilford and educated by the Ursulines of Brentwood, Essex. She spent four years in the WRNS and worked as a secretary before entering Stanbrook Abbey in 1964. There she has been prioress and worked as kitchener, habitmaker and portress.

Sr Dominic Savio Hamer, CP

Sr Dominic Savio Hamer, CP is a member of the Historical Commission appointed in 1994 to investigate the life and virtues of Elizabeth Prout, the Foundress of the Sisters of the Cross and Passion, and she prepared the documentation required by the Holy See. Her book, *Elizabeth Prout, 1820–1864: A Religious Life for Industrial England*, (Downside Abbey, 1994) is soon to be republished by Gracewing.

Patti Fordyce

Patti Fordyce was born and educated in California. Before marrying and settling in London, she represented the USA as a professional tennis player, reaching the Wimbledon Ladies' Doubles Final in 1969. She lives in London with her son Patrick and is currently reading for a Theology degree at Heythrop College.

Sr Andrea Fraile

Sr Andrea Fraile was formerly an editor before becoming a Sister of the Gospel of Life in 2000. She has degrees in philosophy, theology, Hispanics and publishing and now works in crisis pregnancy care with the Cardinal Winning Pro-Life Initiative in Glasgow.

Emily Keyte

Emily Keyte attended St Antony's Leweston School and graduated from Edinburgh University with an English degree. She also studied at Leuven and Oxford universities. She has taught English in secondary schools for ten years and lives in London with her husband and son.

Mac McLernon

Mac McLernon is a teacher of science at a London school. She is a single woman and took private vows of dedication in 2002. She writes a blog, *Mulier Fortis*.

Dora Nash

Dora Nash hails from recusant Lancashire and is a graduate of Cambridge University. She is married with four grown-up children and teaches at The Oratory School near Reading where she is Head of Sixth Form. She has contributed to the Maryvale PGCE course and is the author of two successful sacramental preparation books: *Confirmed in the faith* and *Jesus comes to me*.

Fiorella Nash

Fiorella Nash studied English at Cambridge University (New Hall) specializing in recusant literature including the works of Robert Southwell. She has written a booklet about Southwell (CTS 2003) and two novels. She is married with two small children and writes a regular blog, *Monstrous women*.

Josephine Robinson

Josephine Robinson was educated at St Antony's Convent,

Sherborne, and St Hilda's College, Oxford and has an MA from the Maryvale Institute. She has worked as a volunteer for Pro-Life and is Chairman of the Association of Catholic Women. Her books include *The Inner Goddess, Feminist Theology in the Light of Catholic Teaching*; *Marriage and Gift, a Catholic Perspective* and a short biography of Blessed John XXIII. She is married with three grown-up children.

Sr Penny Roker, RSM
Sr Penny Roker taught history for over twenty years, latterly at Our Lady's
    Convent School in Abingdon. Inspired by the pioneering work of the early Sisters of Mercy she left teaching to enter religious life herself as a Sister of Mercy, and has worked with offenders in prison. Her book on Julian of Norwich, *Homely Love* (Canterbury Press) was published in 2006.

Dr Tracey Rowland
Tracey Rowland is a graduate of Cambridge University and the Dean and Associate Professor of Political Philosophy and Continental Theology at the John Paul II Institute in Melbourne, Australia. She is a member of the editorial board of the English language edition of *Communio: International Catholic Review* and the author of *Culture and the Thomist Tradition: after Vatican II* (Routledge, 2003) and *Ratzinger's Faith: the Theology of Pope Benedict XVI* (Oxford University Press, 2008).

Sr Pauline Joan Shaw, MFIC
Pauline Joan Shaw is a Missionary Franciscan of the Immaculate Conception. She has spent years in teaching, educational administration, on pastoral school boards for Queensland Catholic Education and as consultant for Brisbane Catholic Education. Her research on Elizabeth Hayes adds a new dimension to the history of Christian development in the nineteenth century, and her book *Elizabeth Hayes Pioneer Franciscan Journalist* is also published by Gracewing.

Sr Gemma Simmonds, CJ

Gemma Simmonds is a Sister of the Congregation of Jesus. She has worked in secondary education and as assistant at the university chaplaincies in Cambridge and London. She is a chaplaincy volunteer in Holloway Prison and lectures in pastoral theology at Heythrop College, University of London, where she is convenor of the Religious Life Institute.

John Skinner

John Skinner trained for thirteen years as a Jesuit. He then joined *The Times*, and, after a short career on Fleet Street, started The Red House with Judith, his wife. He was a children's bookseller for the next twenty years, and in 1990 he became a full-time writer with a special interest in the English mystics. His first book *Hear Our Silence*, a portrait of the Carthusians which has led to an ongoing relationship with the Order, as well as his two books of silent prayer: *Sounding the Silence* and *Echoing the Silence*, and his translation into modern English of Julian of Norwich's *Revelation of Love* are all also published by Gracewing.

Fr Mark Turnham Elvins, OFMCap

Fr Mark Turnham Elvins is Guardian of Greyfriars Friary, Oxford and was the last Warden of the previous University Hall. He studied at Oxford, Rome and London acquiring an MA and a graduate diploma. He has written several books on topics including heraldry, liturgy and Catholic history.

Lucy Underwood

Lucy Underwood read history and English (Joint Honours) at Corpus Christi College, Oxford, graduating in 2005. Having completed her M.Phil. at Cambridge University, she is now studying for a Ph.D. in Early Modern history at Magdalene College, Cambridge.